Where Have All the Heroes Gone?

A Pilgrimage Through the Bible,
the Battlefield, and Back Home Again

Jeff Tiegs

To my wife, Julianne, who is far more precious than jewels, and to my sons Aaron and Jonah, whom I love; with whom I am well pleased.

Contents

INTRODUCTION

I. Easter Eggs

"That's him, I'm sure of it. Let's go get him." the commander announced to everyone in the Tactical Operations Center (TOC). Assaulters poured out of the TOC, the chow hall, their hooches, or the gym, and converged on the kit room.

The ritual of putting on body armor, checking gear, conducting commo checks, double checking ammo loads, and heading out to the helos was a transformative process. The man entering the kit room was not the same man exiting the kit room. With every layer of equipment he strapped to his body, he changed a little more. Weapon in hand, locked and loaded, he became part man and part machine.

Deadly and determined.
Ready to kill or be killed.

At my core, I am a soldier. Less than a month after graduating from high school, I was in basic training, seventeen years old, trying to find my role in this world. I never imagined the life that would follow—a life of war, love, loss, leadership, friendship, and fatherhood, all lived under the ever-present shadow of conflict and combat. I started my journey as a Private in the 1st Ranger Battalion and finished my career as a Lieutenant Colonel in the unit commonly referred to as Delta Force.

I will never forget a lesson I learned from a seasoned Special Forces commander on my first trip overseas. I had broken my leg in the training course and I was waiting for the next class so I could start over. Still in a plastic "boot" as my leg healed, I went downrange to work in the Operations Center (OPCEN). I didn't really have a defined role. I tried to add as much value as I could, but it was mostly an opportunity for me to watch and learn. My role was largely as an observer.

The operational tempo was dizzying. The intelligence and operations symbiosis was magical. The number of aircraft, drones, linguists, and other technical support was staggering. I watched targets develop and get racked and stacked in a prioritized list. I watched each target get wiped off the board.

There were at least a dozen monitors in the OPCEN that displayed the feeds from each drone that was flying high, meticulously hunting. Sometimes the target was obvious – the drone caught men burying Improvised Explosive Devices (IEDs) or moving with weapons. Sometimes we knew exactly who the targets were- terrorist cell leaders, bomb makers, financiers, media emirs, suicide bombers.

But many times, things were not so black and white. They were gray. Flat gray. We, as leaders, needed to decide what we were seeing and what we were going to do about it.

One evening I left the OPCEN and went down to the Tactical Operations Center (TOC) to observe a team in action. It was a short walk across the airfield where helicopters sat in the sticky heat waiting for a target to reach the "trigger" that would launch the force. Assaulters and analysts were glued to the real-time drone footage, meticulously taking notes, and searching for patterns and clues that might lead to another successful raid.

The Assault Commander, Doug, sat down next to me, stared up at the screens, and got an update from his Team Leaders. He absorbed it all seemingly effortlessly and began to communicate with each drone giving them a direct tasking and repositioning them according to his hunches. I asked Doug what he was looking for. He said, "I'm not sure, but I'll know it when I see it."

He continued, "I call it the Easter egg approach. When you go on an Easter egg hunt, you don't know exactly what you are looking for, but you have a general idea of what the Easter egg should look like. But more importantly, you are looking for what is out of place. It doesn't really matter what color the Easter egg is, even if it is painted with camouflage and blends in with its surroundings, it just doesn't fit. You start by eliminating places that the egg will most likely not be and then shift your focus to where it most likely will be. And when you see it, you know it."

My role as an observer, even with a broken leg, began to transition to that of a hunter. I've hunted men this way ever since. And I even read my Bible this way. I hunt for "Easter eggs" in the Bible. And I know it when I find one. Thanks, Doug.

The Time is Now

With a broken leg still healing, this was not my time. Frustrated, I had to settle on just watching and learning. I knew my time would come later.

I found comfort in the words of Solomon:

> There's an opportune time to do things, a right time for everything on the earth: A right time for birth and another for death, A right time to plant and another to reap, A right time to kill and another to heal, A right time to destroy and another to construct, A right time to cry and another to laugh, A right time to lament and another to cheer, A right time to make love and another to abstain, A right time to embrace and another to part, A right time to search and another to count your losses, A right

> *time to hold on and another to let go, A right*
> *time to rip out and another to mend, A right*
> *time to shut up and another to speak up, A*
> *right time to love and another to hate, A right*
> *time to wage war and another to make peace.*[1]
> *(Ecclesiastes 3:1-8, MSG)*

One of the main things that kept me grounded all these years was my faith in the ancient stories found in the Bible. Our individual stories are unique but many elements of them have been played out before, years ago, in lands far away.

The Bible is not merely a collection of stories to me; it is a guidebook. It helps me find my way and when I stray, it beckons me back on track. The Bible stories and the characters bring me comfort. I find strength in them, and they have taught me to cope with the life of war that I chose.

The Bible is where I met my first heroes and the Bible is where I faithfully return to find more.
I want to share these ancient stories that are so dear to me.
These stories helped me survive; they've kept me alive.

---

[1] Eccles. 3:1–8 (The Message).

They can help you too.

Have you ever felt as if you are part of a bigger story? That's because you are.

You are the hero, the lead character in your own adventure that is interwoven with everyone else's. There have been times in my life when people deemed my actions heroic, but I felt I was just doing my job. Other times people thought me villainous, but I was just lonely, hurt, confused, angry, or overwhelmed.

My journey in faith has been similar. There have been times when I felt I was being faithful or diligent and other times when I felt rebellious or apathetic. I always looked for inspiration and understanding by digging deeper into the stories of the Bible and other ancient texts.

The Bible tells us that before we even left the womb, God knew us, wove us together, and created us in His image.[2]

God knows every single one of us by name. He wrote a part in this world specifically for each one of us. It is a role only you can fill; you are the star. Nobody else can play it.

---

[2] Jer. 1:5–8; Ps. 139:13–18.

A Soldier's Perspective

While serving in the military, I was fortunate enough to be assigned to Jerusalem for a few years. There I felt like I had been given access to truths that had been locked away in a vault, long forgotten. Seeing the actual terrain, rereading old Bible stories, and praying with intention seemed to open more and more sections of this vault to me.

My sense of adventure drove me to dig into the ancient stories as I had the opportunity to walk, hike, climb, bushwhack, swim, and crawl in the steps of these amazing characters. What I discovered was that we have lost many of the important details over time. The stories in the Bible are way more beautiful, layered, detailed, and deeper than you can grasp in a single reading. The stories must be examined over and over again. They change over time as you mature and experience the highs and lows that life inevitably brings with it.

One day, I found myself sitting on a mountain ridge near Jericho, looking down upon the Jordan River and all the way up the ridgeline toward the crest of Mount Nebo. I was praying, and a clear image entered my mind. I could clearly see some of the events that happened here: Joshua crossing the Jordan, Elijah preparing for his chariot ride, Jesus emerging from the river as His Father smiled down on him. It was suddenly clear to me that all three of these events, though separated by thousands of years, happened in the same location right before me.

This was not an accident.
This was a pattern.

My military mind is trained to detect patterns, and this was clearly an intentional pattern. Other overwhelming thoughts filled my mind, and at the time I didn't understand that this would become the origin of this book, but that is where it all began.

An Inclusive Perspective

While this book digs into my personal faith tradition, it is not meant to be exclusionary. I have great respect for the faith traditions across this incredible world. These are just my thoughts and discoveries.

I am not a theologian. I am not a pastor, priest, scholar, or even an academic. I am just a soldier who sees the world in a particular way. I look for patterns. I look for links and clues. I search for intent. I hunt for ways to anchor events into terrain and purpose. This is how I see the world. This is what I look for when I read and hear Bible stories. I will do my best to credit those who have gone before me and those who have spoken or written about these same stories with the same or similar intent of drawing out their richness.

Do the Work, Decide for Yourself

This book is my pilgrimage through the Bible, the battlefield, and back home again. I want to invite you to come with me on this journey, get a taste of different battlefields, dig deeper into some ancient bible stories, learn from my mistakes, meet some of my heroes, and return home with a renewed passion and purpose in your own life.

I am as confident about these stories I will share with you as I have ever been when deciding to commit men to combat.

I am also confident that if you study with an open mind, pray, and ask for revelation, you will see these stories in a new light.

I want you to decide for yourself what you see, and hear, and feel.

How to Use this Book

Each entry is designed to be read in one sitting. You can jump around however you like. This story is not linear, and neither is yours. The twists and turns of our lives are unpredictable. Sometimes we are even forced to backtrack and start some parts of our lives over again.

In each of these stories, I ask you to imagine yourself at its center. You'll see there is the account of each story, straightforward and factual. Then there is more to the story, the hidden meanings and lost traditions that add so much.

As you read this book, ask yourself questions like:

- How did it feel to be a young Jewish shepherd facing a giant, with only your sling?
- Or an Army Ranger parachuting into an already raging firefight below?
- Or a Roman legionnaire observing the sky darken and the earth shake as a man slowly succumbed to the tortures of crucifixion?
- Or a teenage virgin being told by an angel that she was pregnant with the Messiah?

- Or a Delta Force Troop Commander, pinned down by enemy gunfire, watching another American soldier bleeding to death?

I want you to enjoy each story as it stands alone on its own merits and I want to invite you to dig just a little bit deeper. There is a section at the end of the book called the Chavruta Complement, that can help you go as deep as you want to. Be bold, stretch yourself.

Reflect on how you feel after reading each chapter. What is stirred in you?

What do these stories drudge up in your life? When you finish this book, you should be different.

You should be prepared to look for deeper meaning in your own life.

You should be looking for more heroes to hang around with.
You should be looking for the hero in the mirror staring back at you each morning when you brush your teeth.

II. Easter Eggs

I've watched men die. Some of them were by my hand, many more of them were by my command. Every man dies differently. Some go quietly and some thrash about, refusing to surrender until death finally demands their last breath.

I've cut many evil men's lives short. Some of them were surprised to see us. Others seemed relieved to see us, almost as if they expected us, welcomed us. They knew their story was ending, they could feel it.

There were times I felt like the grim reaper, or more like the commander of a troop of grim reapers.

It was a role I relished.
I was good at it and I dedicated my life to it.

Life as a soldier comes at a cost. Many parts of my body are broken and I have lost many friends. I grew distant from my parents and barely stayed connected with my brother and sister. My wife was forced to raise our sons mostly on her own. She protected them from the reality of the ever-present threat of death that hung over their dad. Both of us did our best to seamlessly flip between the many complicated roles we were expected to play and so far, we've survived. We've made it to the other side. Battered and bruised, but mostly intact.

ARE YOU READY?

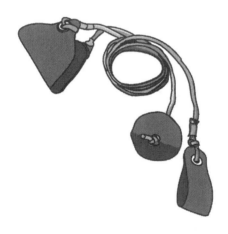

DAVID THE SNIPER:
ALWAYS READY

CHAPTER 1

I. Are You Ready?

Praise be to the Lord my Rock, who trains my hands for war, my fingers for battle. (Psalm 144:1, NIV)

"Shoot around the kids. I repeat, shoot around the kids." I hung my upper body out of the helicopter, left hand clutching the airframe and my right arm extended, pointing directly at the target below us. "I gave the order to engage".

The sniper in the door raised his weapon and placed the driver squarely into the reticle of his rifle scope.

"God be with us," I said to myself. If I was Catholic, this was where I would have made the sign of the cross on my body. But I was raised Lutheran so we are a little less flamboyant.

We were hunting an Al Qaeda military emir who was responsible for thousands of deaths in Iraq. We watched him on the Intelligence, Surveillance, and Reconnaissance (ISR) air platforms for hours before we made the decision to go get him.

When I launched the assault force it was just him in a white sedan heading south on Highway 1 out of Mosul. When we were twenty minutes out from the assault, he stopped on the side of the road and picked up a man and two kids, a young boy and a small girl. We suspected the man who got picked up was an Al Qaeda bomb maker and assumed the kids were his. He was in play, his kids were not.

For many commanders, this would have constituted an "abort" call. We had zero tolerance for killing women and children. I had zero tolerance for killing women and children.

But, I did not call abort. I waited and let things play out instead.

We continued to close on the target. I was hoping that the Al Qaeda military emir would drop the kids off somewhere and we could continue with our plan. Unfortunately, he did not drop off the kids but he did head out into the vast empty western desert of Iraq making it easier for us to track him. He was ours for the taking. He had nowhere to escape.

We had him dead to rights, things were going exactly as planned except for one thing– well, two things–the kids were still in the back seat of the car. Two innocent kids not in play.

This Al Qaeda emir was a monster and I am a monster hunter. My entire team had already been in combat for years and had perfected the art of killing monsters.

Unquestionably, he needed to die.

As we sped toward the target, I watched the ISR feeds intently.

"Please drop off the kids," I whispered under my breath.

I started running different scenarios in my head. When we catch up to him and he realizes that he is trapped, he might surrender- all good. Kids will be safe.

But I knew better. He would never let us take him alive.

I knew that as soon as he saw us he would make a run for it. He had nowhere to go but he'd still try to escape. Monsters don't die easily.

I knew we would have to kill him and the bomb maker with nearly impossible precision.

As a young corporal in the Rangers, I had been trained as a sniper. This was not a shot I could have taken back then. But the operators sitting next to me, within arms reach, were mature seasoned professionals. Many of them had also started out as young Rangers but through tireless work, fearless risk, a healthy dose of self-confidence, and a little bit of luck, moved through the ranks of US Special Operations. They became Operators where they were freed up, encouraged—no, EXPECTED—to perfect their killing skills.

This team was well known for their audacity, fearlessness, and never-quit attitude. We never backed down. Ever.

Coming in as their commander was one of the greatest honors of my life and one of the heaviest responsibilities I've ever carried. My job was to create space back home where they could prepare for any fight that would come our way. Then it was my job to lead them into that fight, step back as they prosecuted the target, and get them home safely again.

After giving the command to engage, a calm came over me. Yes, the call was audacious. Yes, it could result in disaster. But I knew we were ready. We had been preparing for this. I had been preparing for this.

Nevertheless, I said to myself one more time, "God be with us, steady our hands. Guide our bullets to hit their marks."

I depressed the button of my assault radio and calmly said into my headset, "Shoot around the kids. I repeat, shoot around the kids."

A lowly shepherd boy, destined for greatness, overlooked by most but eventually recognized as the heir to a throne is one heck of a plotline. It has been done a million times in stories, books, and movies, but it captures our imagination every time. Why? Could it be because it's a part of our own story?

David has always been one of my favorite characters in the Bible. David the giant killer. The young sniper. The small unit leader. The restless king. His courage, cunning, faithfulness, leadership, and humility are all traits I aspire to, benchmarks for me to work toward. Even his faults, his mistakes, and his sins give me hope that I am worthy to be "a man after God's own heart."[3]

Many of the details of David's life are well known, but truly understanding David as an archetype of Jesus, a foreshadowing of what was to come, is a plotline that takes some time to absorb. We often

---

[3] 1 Sam. 13:14; Acts 13:22 (New International Version).

think of David's great triumphs and his absolute failures, but what about the in-between moments? That is where we live most of the time. The highs are great, the lows suck—but how do we describe the in-between times? In between is a place where I really try to find God.

If I take the time to look for Him.

The in-between is where we sometimes sit engulfed by a shadow or a heaviness that makes us feel like we are unworthy of the good in our life and don't deserve peace. Not only do we feel that we are unworthy and cannot be forgiven, we certainly do not deserve a close relationship with our creator. Examining David's life should reassure all of us that not only are we forgiven, we can walk with the Lord and have a relationship that is close, intimate, and edifying.

My walk with God is all of the above. Some moments I feel so close to Him that I feel like I am floating. Other times He feels so distant from me that it physically hurts. Combat was the same. Sometimes I felt safe in His hands and other times I felt like He was busy attending to something else.

One thing I knew was that I did not want to have the blood of kids on my hands. Innocents deserve to be innocent. But that is not how war works.

Innocent people, including kids, die. That is part of it.

Innocent blood stains my hands and that is something I live with. It is a burden I carry, for God created me as a soldier and that's what soldiers do. We carry the blood and pain of war so our families and communities don't have to.

Some men do not bear this burden well. God created me in a way to be able to shoulder this burden. It's not light, don't get me wrong, but it's not too heavy, either. It's just something I carry. I'm used to it.

God prepared me for war and He gave me a wife who could carry some of the burden for me. He gave me two sons who grew up with a father that spent half of their youth overseas in weirdly named countries fighting unwinnable wars. Nothing felt heroic about any of it.

My boys don't see me as a hero. I don't see myself as a hero. My wife certainly doesn't see me as a hero. Heroes are complicated. Doing something heroic usually involves split-second decision-making, the results of which the hero may regret forever. Sometimes doing something heroic thrusts the "hero" into a spotlight that he is not ready to face. Heroes very often melt in the spotlight of praise and attention they receive.

I never wanted to be a hero.

David the Sniper: Always Ready[4]

David, one of my heroes, is a perfect example of this. He kills a giant, becomes a king, and still melts under the spotlight of praise and attention. But his story begins as a young shepherd boy, a mundane and monotonous job sometimes interrupted with real danger and risk.

War broke out in Israel again and David, too young to be a soldier, was sent by his father, Jesse, to bring

---

[4] https://en.wikipedia.org/wiki/Always_Ready,_Always_There-
"Always Ready, Always There!" refers to the official organizational march of the United States National Guard and the National Guard Bureau.
Lyrics

some fresh food to his older brothers. None of them were full-time soldiers. The Israelite army consisted of some full-time soldiers, but the rest were more like the Army Reserves or the National Guard, called upon when needed. David's brothers were encamped with King Saul and the Israelite army about seven miles away from Bethlehem, at a place called the Valley of Elah, also called Ephes Dammim (the Boundary of Blood). Some say the name comes from the dry, rocky cliffs surrounding the lush valley. These cliffs have distinct reddish-tinted bands throughout the rock that can appear to be boundary lines. Others say the name comes from the many battles fought and the blood shed on that terrain throughout the years.[5]

Either way, this relatively small plot of land has borne witness to much death.

Here is the story as the prophet Samuel records it:

> *The Philistines drew up their troops for battle. They deployed them at Socoh in Judah and set up camp between Socoh and Azekah at Ephes Dammim. Saul and the Israelites came together, camped at Oak Valley, and spread*

---

[5] https://bibleatlas.org/ephes-dammim.htm

out their troops in battle readiness for the Philistines. The Philistines were on one hill, the Israelites on the opposing hill, with the valley between them.

A giant nearly ten feet tall stepped out from the Philistine line into the open, Goliath from Gath. He had a bronze helmet on his head and was dressed in armor—126 pounds of it! He wore bronze shin guards and carried a bronze sword. His spear was like a fence rail—the spear tip alone weighed over fifteen pounds. His shield-bearer walked ahead of him.

Goliath stood there and called out to the Israelite troops, "Why bother using your whole army? Am I not Philistine enough for you? And you're all committed to Saul, aren't you? So pick your best fighter and pit him against me. If he gets the upper hand and kills me, the Philistines will all become your slaves. But if I get the upper hand and kill him, you'll all become our slaves and serve us. I challenge the troops of Israel this day. Give me a man. Let us fight it out together!"

When Saul and his troops heard the Philistine's challenge, they were terrified and lost all hope.

Enter David. He was the son of Jesse the Ephrathite from Bethlehem in Judah. Jesse, the father of eight sons, was himself too old to join Saul's army. Jesse's three oldest sons had followed Saul to war... While his three oldest brothers went to war with Saul, David went back and forth from attending to his brothers to tending his father's sheep in Bethlehem.

Each morning and evening for forty days, Goliath took his stand and made his speech.

One day, Jesse told David his son, "Take this sack of cracked wheat and these ten loaves of bread and run them down to your brothers in the camp. And take these ten wedges of cheese to the captain of their division. Check in on your brothers to see whether they are getting along all right and let me know how they're doing—Saul and your brothers, and all the Israelites in their war with the Philistines in the Oak Valley."

David was up at the crack of dawn and, having arranged for someone to tend his flock, took the food and was on his way just as Jesse had directed him. He arrived at the camp just as the army was moving into battle formation, shouting the war cry. Israel and the Philistines moved into position, facing each other, battle-ready. David left his bundles of food in the care of a sentry, ran to the troops who were deployed, and greeted his brothers. While they were talking together, the Philistine champion, Goliath of Gath, stepped out from the front lines of the Philistines and gave his usual challenge. David heard him.

The Israelites, to a man, fell back the moment they saw the giant—totally frightened. The talk among the troops was, "Have you ever seen anything like this, this man openly and defiantly challenging Israel? The man who kills the giant will have it made. The king will give him a huge reward, offer his daughter as a bride, and give his entire family a free ride."

David, who was talking to the men standing around him, asked, "What's in it for the man who kills that Philistine and gets rid of this ugly blot on Israel's honor? Who does he think he is, anyway, this uncircumcised Philistine, taunting the armies of God-Alive?"

They told him what everyone was saying about what the king would do for the man who killed the Philistine.

Eliab, his older brother, heard David fraternizing with the men and lost his temper: "What are you doing here! Why aren't you minding your own business, tending that scrawny flock of sheep? I know what you're up to. You've come down here to see the sights, hoping for a ringside seat at a bloody battle!"

"What is it with you?" replied David. "All I did was ask a question." Ignoring his brother, he turned to someone else, asked the same question, and got the same answer as before.

The things David was saying were picked up and reported to Saul. Saul sent for him.

"Master," said David, "don't give up hope. I'm ready to go and fight this Philistine."

Saul answered David, "You can't go and fight this Philistine. You're too young and inexperienced—and he's been at this fighting business since before you were born."

David said, "I've been a shepherd, tending sheep for my father. Whenever a lion or bear came and took a lamb from the flock, I'd go after it, knock it down, and rescue the lamb. If it turned on me, I'd grab it by the throat, wring its neck, and kill it. Lion or bear, it made no difference—I killed it. And I'll do the same to this Philistine pig that is taunting the troops of God-Alive. God, who delivered me from the teeth of the lion and the claws of the bear, will deliver me from this Philistine."

Saul said, "Go. And God help you!"

Then Saul outfitted David as a soldier in armor. He put his bronze helmet on his head and belted his sword on him over the armor. David tried to walk but he could hardly budge.

David told Saul, "I can't even move with all this stuff on me. I'm not used to this." And he took it all off.

Then David took his shepherd's staff, selected five smooth stones from the brook, and put them in the pocket of his shepherd's pack, and with his sling in his hand approached Goliath. As the Philistine paced back and forth, his shield-bearer in front of him, he noticed David. He took one look down on him and sneered—a mere youngster, apple-cheeked and peach-fuzzed.

The Philistine ridiculed David. "Am I a dog that you come after me with a stick?" And he cursed him by his gods.

"Come on," said the Philistine. "I'll make roadkill of you for the buzzards. I'll turn you into a tasty morsel for the field mice."

David answered, "You come at me with sword and spear and battle-ax. I come at you in the name of God-of-the-Angel-Armies, the God of Israel's troops, whom you curse and mock. This very day God is handing you over to me. I'm about to kill you, cut off your head, and serve up your body and the bodies of your Philistine buddies to the crows and coyotes. The whole earth will know that there's an extraordinary God in Israel. And everyone gathered here will learn that God doesn't save by means of sword or spear. The battle belongs to God—he's handing you to us on a platter!"

That roused the Philistine, and he started toward David. David took off from the front line, running toward the Philistine. David reached into his pocket for a stone, slung it, and hit the Philistine hard in the forehead, embedding the stone deeply. The Philistine crashed, face down in the dirt.

That's how David beat the Philistine—with a sling and a stone. He hit him and killed him. No sword for David!

Then David ran up to the Philistine and stood over him, pulled the giant's sword from its sheath, and finished the job by cutting off his head. When the Philistines saw that their great champion was dead, they scattered, running for their lives.[6]

1 Samuel 17: 1-51 (MSG)

---

[6] 1 Sam. 17:1–51 (The Message).

More to the Story

What a story. A young man kills a giant and becomes a hero, a legend.

Most people have heard it before. It is one of the best-known accounts from the ancient Hebrew Scriptures. There is plenty to unpack from this story, a young boy too small to wear the combat gear of a king, steps up to literally face a giant that had been taunting the Israelites for forty days. There are some interesting details to unpack from this story. Any good story has many layers and this one doesn't disappoint.

When Bible writers include specific numbers, we should pause and try to figure out what is being expressed. Oftentimes numbers in the bible are like a combination to a lock on a door that is waiting to be opened. With a little patience and persistence, we can open the lock and see what's inside. Sometimes the number combination will open a lock that leads to multiple doors for us to explore.

Do we have the patience to examine the combination?

Do we have the courage to enter the doors it may open?

This story highlights two simple numbers: forty and five.

Let's start with the number forty.

For forty days, Goliath challenged, berated, and denigrated the Israelites. Boldly he stood, gaining more confidence and arrogance each day.

It is commonly accepted by biblical scholars that the number forty generally symbolizes a period of testing, trial, or probation.[7] When we read the account of David and Goliath, it doesn't really matter if it was actually forty days of taunting or not. The writer of the story was relaying a more important concept for us. I personally believe it was an actual forty days that encompassed this larger meaning of testing and trial, but this could also be symbolism intended to communicate something deeper and richer.

---

[7] "The Meaning of Numbers: The Number 40," Unique Studies, Bible Study, accessed March 17, 2023, https://www.biblestudy.org/bibleref/meaning-of-numbers-in-bible/40.html.

For forty days, the Israelite Army was tested. For forty days, King Saul was tested. For forty days, the Israelites retreated to their camp, humbled and fearful. The deeper meaning is clear.

It took a young shepherd's trust and confidence in his God to confront this giant. Against all reason and against all odds, he emerged the victor. A new hero.

Now, let's look at the number five.

Through other texts in the Hebrew Scriptures, there is reason to believe Goliath had four brothers.[8] As was the custom in tribal cultures, Goliath's brothers would be expected to avenge the death of one of their kin.[9] It wasn't doubt that drove David to choose the five smooth stones from the river, rather it was confidence he would need them, one at a time, to defeat the rest of Goliath's family.

---

[8] "Did David Fight Goliath's Brothers?,"Questions, Bible Study, accessed March 17, 2023, https://www.biblestudy.org/question/did-david-fight-goliath-and-his-four-brothers.html. The deduction that Goliath had four other huge brothers comes from other accounts of the Israelites facing giants in battle (2 Sam. 21:16–22; 1 Chron. 20:5).
[9] This tradition continues in some tribal cultures to this day. While working in Iraq and Afghanistan, I saw this firsthand.

David picked up each stone, examined it quickly for defects, predicting how it would fly through the air. He rubbed each stone, squeezed it, felt its density, and tried to predict how it would react on impact. David did not choose five stones in case he missed his mark; David chose five stones to strike each mark with one shot.

One shot, one kill.
Repeated five times.

David was a sniper.
He needed some high-quality sniper ammo.

When he was ready, he fired a shot, reloaded another round, and was ready to keep slinging stones until all the threats were eliminated or until he ran out of ammo.

Imagine yourself as a soldier in this story. You need to wake up, put away your sleeping gear, make breakfast, tighten up your uniform, inspect your buddy, double-check your weapons, assemble, march into position, face the unknown, and then head back up to your high ground position, sit around the rest of the day and repeat everything again the next morning. Like any military event, it was "hurry up and wait." Hours of complete and utter boredom exist mere seconds away from potential chaos, violence, death, victory, or defeat. This went on for nearly a month and a half.

Depending on the time of year, both sides were either suffering through the Israeli sun beating down on this mostly shadeless area or bearing the damp cold of the valley in the winter seasons. Either way, this was not a pleasant event. It would've sucked.

The human element of this story is fascinating. The Bible is very descriptive of where it takes place and with a little bit of research, patience, and exploration, you can stand within a couple of football fields' distance of where this encounter happened about three thousand years ago.

When you stand in this spot and ponder the story, it is incredibly dramatic. As tranquil as it is in modern times, it's difficult to envision how much blood was shed on this ground over the years.

The Philistine troops were securely positioned on one side of the valley, maintaining one side of the high ground, while the Israelite army encamped on the high ground opposite them. The battlefield waited in the valley floor between them.

Each morning, the opposing troops would descend to the field and form their battle lines. And as was the case sometimes, instead of armies clashing and losing hundreds and thousands of lives, they would send two champions to face off with a winner-take-all challenge. The residents of Socoh and Azekah would have been acutely interested in this standoff as their own lives hung in the balance.

Each morning the armies would assemble their battle lines. Each morning a champion would emerge from the Philistines. He would stand between the battle lines, alone but for his shield-bearer, and he would berate the Israelites. It is unlikely that you could hear Goliath's taunts in the two cities, but King Saul could certainly hear it from atop the ridgeline where he sat in his command post.

That fateful morning began like the previous forty mornings, with battle lines assembled and Goliath's taunting and gesticulating visible from the king's perch and the surrounding villages. But something was different on this day.

A boy, likely a speck from the villagers' vantage point, burst from the streambed and ran toward Goliath. Who was he? He wore no uniform. What was he doing?

What happened next was shocking. The giant fell face down. The boy approached the giant and stood over his motionless body. The boy bent down and seemingly struggled to pick up Goliath's sword. He raised it as high as he could and when he let it fall, the giant's head rolled away from his body. The battle lines erupted, and the Israelites routed the Philistines for miles until they reached exhaustion.

Cheers mixed with relief must have swept the towns as the clash became a running battle through the valleys and woods, all the way back to the Philistine strongholds of Gath and Ekron.

II. Are You Ready?

As the snipers took aim, I really didn't want to kill any kids but I trusted my men. They could make the shot, even if I couldn't. I was not ready to take that shot, but I was ready to make the call and order the shot taken. I wasn't a Ranger sniper anymore. I was an Assault Force Commander now.

My pilgrimage from a Private in the 1st Ranger Battalion to a Lieutenant Colonel in the 1st Special Forces Operational Detachment Delta spanned twenty-five years. For more than half of that time, America was at war; my family was at war. I was at war.

I went to sniper school in 1989 as a Corporal when my job was a Ranger Assault Team Leader. I was expected to carry all the standard issue gear, a basic load of ammunition and my share of mortars and explosives.

It was heavy.

As a sniper, I jumped into Panama with my accurized M16A2 and got my M24 sniper rifle once other elements landed on the airfield we seized. I carried the Team Leader Basic Load of 210 rounds of full metal jacket, "green tip" ammo, and 100 rounds of special load sniper ammo.

It was heavy.

At the last minute, I was also tasked with being the Platoon Demolitions Lead. The logic was simple. I carried a small calculator in my kit to calculate winds and holds for any sniper shots. Seeing that I already carried a calculator, it stood to reason by my platoon leadership that I should also be the demo guy.

Because of this palm size calculator, I also carried the combat load for the Demolitions Lead that consisted of C4 explosives, TNT, det cord, time fuse, blasting caps, electric and non-electric igniters, crimpers, non-sparking knife, and plenty of tape.

I was ready for any role I was expected to play. I felt ready. I had trained for each role, but this was going to be real combat. Against an armed enemy.
My M16A2 carried a magazine with thirty rounds in it. We would usually only load 28-29 rounds in each mag to relieve some of the tension on the springs inside that, when pressured, could lead to double feeds. Once you fired a round, the weapon would extract the casing and automatically load another one.

The M24 was much more intimate. Once you fired a single round, you would need to disengage the bolt, draw it to the rear, and extract the spent cartridge calmly and cooly. The bolt would catch another round, place it in position, and you would manually push the bolt forward carefully, smoothly seating the round into the chamber for your next shot.

All the while you are doing this, you need to keep your eye in the scope to observe your target with your cheek melded to the buttstock, until all the threats are eliminated or you run out of ammo.

I was ready for whatever I needed to face. I tucked the explosives into my demolition bag and loaded magazines.

Coincidentally, like David's five smooth stones that he loaded into his ammo bag, the M24 sniper rifle magazine holds five rounds.

Returning home after Panama, we were not welcomed as heroes. We just quietly melted back into the fabric of America. I didn't feel like a hero but I felt like I did my job and did it well.

I felt ready for whatever was next.

I killed men and accepted that weight. It was part of who I was now.

At the time, I never dreamed that I would become a Delta Force Operator or a man who spent half of his children's lives in combat.

Before David killed Goliath, he had been tested with confronting a lion and bear. A giant seemed the next logical test.

Like David, my tests have come over time, and I've met them head-on, with the confidence that God had prepared me sufficiently. Lion or bear, it made no difference—I killed it.

But unlike David, I want to finish strong and when I am no longer expected to hunt monsters, I pray that God will continue to help me tame the monsters that still wander around inside me.

2

FIRST BLOOD

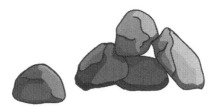

DAVID THE SNIPER:
NEVER RETREAT

CHAPTER 2

I. First Blood

You have shed much blood and have fought many wars. You are not to build a house for my Name, because you have shed much blood on the earth in my sight. But you will have a son who will be a man of peace and rest. (1 Chronicles 22:8-9, NIV)

The man in the center of my sniper scope crosshairs looked over in the direction of the assault element. I think he heard the platoon moving into position.

He stood up.

He looked at his rifle that was propped against the wall next to him. I could see that the rifle was loaded with a thirty-round magazine sticking out of the magazine well.

I said to myself in a quiet whisper. "Don't do it."

After I went to Sniper School, precision marksmanship became an additional duty for me, a skill that I was expected to keep up. Whenever the mission required a sniper or counter-sniper, I had to be ready. My everyday rifle was an accurized M16A2 with a fiberglass inlay keeping the upper and lower receivers tight. It had a 7x power scope and a buttstock with an extension for a solid cheek weld. I carried accurized ammunition for it but saved those rounds in a special pouch in case I needed to take a precision shot. Usually, I just used the green tip full metal jacket standard Army issue. I was formally trained on the new M24 sniper system and it was left up to me to remain proficient on this platform. If and when the mission depended on it, I had better be ready.

The first time I was called upon to take a sniper shot, I was ready.

Killing has some common elements but it can also be very unique. Killing a man by dropping a bomb on his head is very impersonal. Shooting him can be from a distance or up close. Killing a man with your hands, either with a blade or tomahawk, would seem incredibly personal and intimate but the adrenaline skyrockets and the actual physical effort needed masks the intimacy. Killing a man with a sniper rifle is very personal and intimate; it requires complete calm and a calculation that is cerebral.

Even though you can be hundreds of meters away, the scope amplification makes it feel like your target is right in front of you. When you take the shot, their face and head often fill your entire field of view and you are focusing on a tiny part of their body or face as your precise aim point. When you squeeze the trigger, it takes a moment for the bullet to leave your rifle and find the target. In this moment, you observe everything as if in slow motion and look for the red mist that lets you know immediately that you have scored a direct hit.

The target I had been observing seemed innocuous and unimportant. The target was about three hundred and fifty meters away, across a deep jungle ravine, sitting on his front porch. He looked to be in his mid to late thirties. He was dressed in a pair of loose, dark pants, a button-down shirt that was unbuttoned revealing his paunchy belly. He wore a pair of flip-flops and was alternating between sitting on his porch, feeding his chickens and going inside his modest hacienda where I could not observe him. He had an M16-style rifle leaning against the house, next to the chair he would sit in.

I reported all of this to my platoon and company chain of command and continued to observe him.

I could barely identify the rest of the platoon moving into position. The jungle was thick. I could only see them because I knew where to look and had a scope that magnified the rustling leaves to reveal Rangers stealthily moving into their assault positions.

My job was to ensure that the Rangers got into position without being surprised by the target individual or anything else in and around the target that we did not know about.

If the target went for his rifle and threatened the Rangers at any time, I was supposed to eliminate him. If he was holding his rifle when the assault was supposed to commence, I was supposed to initiate the assault by killing him.

After hours of watching this man, I really hoped that I did not have to kill him. I hoped and prayed that he would realize that he did not have a chance and needed to surrender.

The support by fire was in position. The assault element was in position. I waited.

The target sat on his porch.

My crosshairs were on his chest but I was watching his face, his expression. My spotter was observing the assault element as they quietly closed on the target building.

"They are at the LCC", he said. The LCC is the Last Covered and Concealed position. After the LCC, the target would be able to see them.

The man looked over in the direction of the assault element. I think he heard them.

He stood up.

He looked at his rifle.

Twice I said to myself in a quiet whisper. "Don't do it."

"Don't do it."

He stepped off of the porch.

Without the rifle.

Faced the direction of the assault element and put his hands up.

Thank you, Lord.

He chose correctly. Little did he know that this split-second decision would be a heroic one for his children. He would live to see them again.

I packed up my sniper gear and we moved through the jungle to link back up with our platoon.

David the Sniper: Never Retreat

David stood over Goliath's body and held the giant's head up so all could see it. As he tossed the head aside to double-check the second stone in his sling, making sure it was still seated correctly, the emboldened Israelites attacked the Philistines with a ferocious surge. Half in shock from Goliath's death and half in shock from the Israelite hordes rushing towards them, the Philistines broke ranks and retreated. They fled all the way back home leaving their dead and wounded behind.

> *The men of Israel and Judah were up on their feet, shouting! They chased the Philistines all the way to the outskirts of Gath and the gates of Ekron. Wounded Philistines were strewn along the Shaaraim road all the way to Gath and Ekron. After chasing the Philistines, the*

Israelites came back and looted their camp. David took the Philistine's head and brought it to Jerusalem. But the giant's weapons he placed in his own tent.

When Saul saw David go out to meet the Philistine, he said to Abner, commander of the army, "Tell me about this young man's family."

Abner said, "For the life of me, O King, I don't know."[10] 1 Samuel 17: 51-55 (MSG)

More to the Story

It wouldn't take long for Abner and Saul to get to know the details about David and his family. David was the new champion of Israel. After this triumph, all of King Saul's court celebrated this victory over the Philistines, but the celebration would not last long. It soon gave way to greed and jealousy.

Saul and David would soon become bitter enemies with plenty of intrigue, death, betrayal, murder and redemption mixed into the storyline.

---

[10] 1 Sam. 17:51–55 (The Message).

Standing in the very spot where David killed Goliath, I surveyed the battlefield and envisioned what it might have been like over three thousand years ago.

In fact, one of the major inspirations to begin this book started twelve years ago in this very field. I stood with an Israeli tour guide who oriented me to the battlefield from the floor of Elah Valley.

He pointed to one side and then the other, describing where the Israelites and Philistines were and where they drew up their battle lines.

But something didn't add up. He was pointing out the high ground where the Israelites would have been encamped, and the opposite ridgeline where the Philistines would have been camped. But he had it backward.

Military forces don't retreat through their opponents' lines. They retreat away from their opponents' lines. The Bible clearly states that the Philistines retreated to Gath and Ekron. This means that as the Philistines assembled each morning, the Israelite warriors were to their front, and their families and homes in Gath and Ekron were behind them.

How could this tour guide have the details backward? When I searched Google, at the time, even Google had it wrong.

I couldn't shake the thought of what else I had been taught that just simply wasn't right. This started the search that prompted this book.

My searching continues to this day.

I am still on this pilgrimage.

II. First Blood

Before 9/11, the day war came directly to America, crashing into two skyscrapers in New York City, war was only a distant dream. As young Rangers, we yearned for it. As a young Army Ranger in the late 1980s, I prepared for war and trained for it tirelessly. We literally prayed for war. We wanted to be tested.

Be careful what you pray for.

On a cold, rainy day in December of 1989, we were tested. Some of us passed the test and some of us failed. I guess it really depends on how you look at it. Some men are satisfied with simply surviving combat. That was never my goal. I wanted to be the best. I wanted to master warfare. In many ways, I did master warfare but as a young man, you never know how to measure the costs. This pursuit to be the best nearly cost me my life. My wife. And my kids.

War demands everything from you and gives you nothing in return.

I'm ok with all of it.

I wouldn't change a thing.

It hurt.
It still hurts.
But it is a pain I resolved to carry a long time ago.

Knowing what it is like to take another life is something a combat soldier comes to terms with eventually. The first man I killed in Panama felt just like training. No emotion at all.

In fact, I felt a little sorry for him. He never had a chance.

After all of these years, I am stained. I have shed much blood on the earth and have fought many wars. I have two sons now and I pray that they will have lives of peace and rest.

3

UNIFORMS MATTER

DAVID THE SPY:
DUPLICITY AND DECEPTION

CHAPTER 3

I. Uniforms Matter

We have devised a perfect plan! Surely the human mind and heart are cunning. (Psalm 64:6, NIV)

"Clearly this was a set-up." I said to Bill.

"Yup," he answered.

"Any idea what's going on?" I asked.

"Nope." Bill answered.

"This is gonna be a bloodbath getting outta here." I stated.

"Yup." Bill repeated. He was not a man of many words.

I've literally worn different hats as a soldier.
I think the beret is one of the most ridiculous hats ever invented. Any hat that takes two hands to put on is just too damn complicated.
However, the berets I've earned over the years are very dear to me. Smoothing that silly hat so it canted just right and fell slightly over my left ear became a motion that transformed me into something else.

An Airborne Trooper.
A Ranger.
A Special Forces Green Beret.
A Delta Force Operator.

Good military organizations have assessment and selection programs where each person is tested and trained. Each group is looking for something and someone different. I seemed to gravitate to the units that valued daring and cunning and then gave you a hat as a reward.

At the completion of selection and training, there is a bond that is difficult to break. Shared suffering and pain are powerful tools for producing trust, cooperation, and teamwork. As old as I am now, my identity is still intricately tied to the US Army Rangers, Special Forces, and Delta Force.

The risk we shared, putting our lives in each other's hands, and simply enduring whatever war threw at us, created a bond that is stronger than anything else I have ever experienced. Marriage and fatherhood can be similarly understood, but brothers in arms still hold their own in a distinct category of bonding.

This bond is powerful and is rarely understood by wives, sons, daughters, and family. This bond can feel like abandonment to your family, putting them second. In all practicality, it is putting your family second. I always bristled when commanders would say that their priorities were God, family and then the unit they were leading. That briefs well but just isn't fully honest.

Your belief and trust in God should guide your decision-making and everything we do is for our families but it is service to the military, the specific unit we are part of, that gets priority. Every time. The sooner we become honest about this, the sooner we can attempt to balance it better. My job was taking men and women into combat and getting them back home to their families. The stakes were literally life and death. Missing one of my boys' soccer games, or birthdays, just couldn't trump these high stakes. It doesn't feel good to admit and it still hurts my wife and sons, but it is just the simple truth.

The best I could do was to pray to God each day. No, I literally begged God to let me live so I could make it up to them over time. He let me live and now I am trying to keep up my end of the bargain.

In both Iraq and Afghanistan, but especially in Iraq, I often bonded with our indigenous partner forces. We did our best to assess, select and train them, but our bonding was always solidified under fire. We were prepared to die for them, and they were prepared to die for us.

When someone in this very small circle betrays you, your life is changed forever. Betrayal feels like a dagger to your heart. The hurt eventually fades, but it never fully leaves you.

Back in 2004, we were fighting for our lives in Samarra, Iraq. Our Iraqi partners were with us day in and day out, bearing the brunt of the losses. One day, one of our trusted sources contacted us about an insurgent meeting about an hour's drive from our compound. Our source was an Iraqi patriot who had been fighting with us for months. He was a trusted NCO in the New Iraqi Army and had come across some valuable information about a high-ranking terrorist who was planning a meeting in the small town north of us called Ad Dwar. This is where Saddam Hussein was pulled out of his underground bunker and captured about ten months earlier. It was a dangerous place. Full of monsters.

The actual location of the meeting was an apartment complex that resembled a maze that had only one way in and one way out.

But we had an ace up our sleeve. We had an agent on the inside who could guide us directly to the meeting location.

My detachment teamed up with another detachment to double our combat power. My best friend Bill was the other Detachment Commander, and we knew that this night would be significant. It could change the outcome of the war. Missions like this don't often fall in your lap. I was shocked that our higher command even approved it.

I don't think they really understood the potential repercussions of us killing this high level Shiite cleric.

The complex was split down the middle by a two-lane road that ended in a circle at the heart of the complex. We split the objective in half. Bill and his team would take the west side and my team would take the east side. We'd clear our sides independently, and if anything went wrong, we would fight our way to each other, consolidate our forces, and keep on fighting.

Simple plan.

As soon as we hit the first target, something didn't feel right. We hit a second target. It was another dry hole; no one was there. Bill was experiencing the same thing on his side.

Something was wrong.

Prior to us hitting the target, we positioned an AC130 Spectre gunship overhead that was acting as reconnaissance and overwatch for us. It had thermal imagery as well as other night vision that gave us a bird's-eye view of the entire complex.

Over the radio, the gunship reported that there were people blocking the exit, barricading it. We were confused. Who were they? Who was blocking us in? Soon we could see the flames from the tires they had set on fire right at the exit we were counting on for our departure.

Something was seriously wrong. Our guide was missing, too.

It was then that I finally realized we were in a trap.

David the Spy: Duplicity and Deception

 Killing a giant with a sniper shot is just the beginning of David's story. There would come much more intrigue and adventure throughout his life. David was destined to become a king that ruled a powerful kingdom but before he ascended to the throne, he had to suffer a bit more.

After killing the giant, David became a folk hero in Israel. They literally sang songs about him. At first, King Saul celebrated the incredible victory along with everyone else. He invited David into his private circle, gave him a coveted seat in the palace, and even promised David his beautiful daughter in marriage.

Unfortunately, Saul's enthusiasm and gratitude didn't last long. He grew jealous of David's popularity and turned on him like a rabid dog. Saul soon became absolutely obsessed with killing David.

After attempting to murder him many different times, David went on the run but found it was not easy to hide from a king.

Saul hunted David relentlessly. After running out of places to hide, David eventually decided to align himself with the Philistines and try to survive under their banner.

David thought to himself, "Sooner or later, Saul's going to get me. The best thing I can do is escape to Philistine country. Saul will count me a lost cause and quit hunting me down in every nook and cranny of Israel. I'll be out of his reach for good."

So David left; he and his six hundred men went to Achish son of Maoch, king of Gath. They moved in and settled down in Gath, with Achish. Each man brought his household; David brought his two wives, Ahinoam of Jezreel and Abigail, widow of Nabal of Carmel. When Saul was told that David had escaped to Gath, he called off the hunt.[11] (1 Samuel 27:1-4, MSG)

This is a part of David's story that has always perplexed me. Saul was hunting David like an animal; I understand that he was desperate and was left with some very poor options, but the Philistines? They were the archenemy of Israel. David had no other options?

---

[11] 1 Sam. 27:1–4 (The Message).

There had to be more to it. What was I missing? I started looking for the "Easter egg."

The story continues:

> *David lived in Philistine country a year and four months.*
>
> *From time to time David and his men raided the Geshurites, the Girzites, and the Amalekites—these people were longtime inhabitants of the land stretching toward Shur and on to Egypt. When David raided an area he left no one alive, neither man nor woman, but took everything else: sheep, cattle, donkeys, camels, clothing—the works. Then he'd return to Achish. Achish would ask, "And whom did you raid today?"*
>
> *David would tell him, "Oh, the Negev of Judah," or "The Negev of Jerahmeel," or "The Negev of the Kenites." He never left a single person alive lest one show up in Gath and report what David had really been doing. This is the way David operated all the time he lived in Philistine country.*

Achish came to trust David completely. He thought, "He's made himself so repugnant to his people that he'll be in my camp forever."(1 Samuel 27:7-12, MSG)[12]

We can see from the text above that David was not really aligned with the Philistines; he was double-crossing them every chance he got. He might have worn the uniform of a Philistine warlord but he was surely not one.

He raided Israel's enemies, he utterly destroyed them, he stole everything from them. All the while he was doing this, the Philistines grew to trust him more and more.

He had a plan, but he was definitely playing with fire.

How long could he keep playing this dangerous game?

Saul betrayed David but David refused to betray Saul.

---

[12] 1 Sam. 27:7–12 (The Message).

What would the Philistines do when they found out David was betraying them? Philistine justice was harsh and swift.

More to the Story

The Philistines were advanced seafaring people who came from the Aegean, most likely the island of Crete. They had been in the land of Israel even before it was called Israel for many years. They slowly moved inland from their settlements and cities that were historically along the Mediterranean coast. They quickly became the archenemy of Israel, with separate and diametrically opposed gods and values that clashed with the strict Hebrew adherence to Mosaic laws. What also made the Philistines so powerful was their mastery of casting iron, while the Israelites were still reliant on bronze.

Imagine taking weapons made of iron (steel) into combat against weapons made of bronze. Imagine tools and chariots equipped with iron parts versus bronze ones. This technology was so groundbreaking that it ushered in a whole new age. They didn't know it at the time, but the Bronze Age was soon giving way to the Iron Age.

David and his soldiers knew that with this technology, they could change the world. With the formula for iron, David could defeat the Philistines and any of his other enemies. David still believed God's promise to him that he would become the King of Israel someday. When that day came, with iron weapons and chariots, David was confident that he could expand Israel into a formidable kingdom.

He needed to understand the secret of smelting iron even if he had to steal it.

Acquiring the secret of smelting and tempering iron was worth the risk to David. Wily as a fox, he played the Philistines until he got what he wanted. He knew exactly what he was doing. With this innovative technology, he would create an Israelite dynasty. His son Solomon would expand on this technology, making thousands of chariots with iron wheels and further establish the Kingdom of Israel, expanding it to its greatest extent in history.

We know this now in hindsight, but at the time, David's life was desperate, difficult, and disappointing. He and his men suffered greatly, but they did it together, they suffered for each other.

They were committed to each other and trusted each other without hesitation.

I feel like God uses me in ways that can sometimes be miraculous, but most of the time I only experience the mundane repetition of daily life. Then there are those times when I feel persecuted or abandoned. Regardless of how things appear on the surface, I need to continue to trust God. I may never know the full extent of the role God wants me to play in this world. There can be great highs and great lows, but most of the time, I simply exist day-to-day. Heroism and betrayal are interesting plot points, but they are not the norm.

We have many examples in the Bible that should help us find some comfort in our own struggles, in our own doubts. Moses was granted the power to perform incredible miracles in rescuing the Israelites from their captivity in Egypt and then he was forced to wander around in the desert for forty years.

Forty years.

David was ordained to be the king of Israel, and then skittered around the wilderness with his band of loyal followers, hiding in caves and marauding to stay alive for years.

Like David, I feel the closeness of God at times, but also His distance. I've surrounded myself with loyal and committed men, creating a band of brothers where I felt safe. Especially in war.

Saul betrayed David and leveraged the whole of his army against him. David eventually accepted the betrayal and relied on the men he knew he could trust. He endured, and survived.

II. Uniforms Matter

Nothing was going as planned. There was no question that we were in a trap. Both detachments started taking intermittent gunfire from seemingly random places in the apartment complex, so we "circled the wagons" and met in the center of the complex. We were not sure what was happening. Our Iraqi partners were just as flummoxed as we were.

One thing we all agreed on is that this night looked like a setup, and we had better not try to exit the way we had come in. The exit route was blocked and now vehicles were lit on fire, further blocking our exfil, our extraction route. The entire complex was fenced in, and we were not sure how to get out cleanly.

Bill and I met face-to-face and it felt good. He was one of my best friends, an incredibly fierce and focused warrior. We hugged, slapped each other on the back, our gear keeping us an awkward distance from each other, rifles, magazines, radios, and knives all clanging together.

All hell was breaking loose around us but Bill was as calm as I was. Together, we would get out of this. Or die trying.

We came up with a quick plan. I would send my team around on foot to try to find another exit route, while Bill and his team would start assembling the vehicles for exfil.

Before we parted, we slapped hands and said at the same time "Good luck."

We nodded at each other and smiled. "Love ya, man," I said to Bill.

Bill smiled again and nodded, "See you on the other side."

"See you on the other side," I repeated.

The complex was surrounded by an irrigation system that was, for all intents and purposes, a moat. Luckily, the exfil team found a bridge across the moat and began cutting through the fence to create a route for our escape.

We still weren't sure who was attempting to block us in, but we didn't care to find out. It was time to go home.

Spectre came up on the radio net again and reported that they could see an assault force setting up an ambush line on our new exit route.[13] The ambush line included machine guns, RPGs, rockets, and a couple dozen men. Who in the hell were these guys?

Spectre could not make out uniforms or anything definitive to identify this force, but they were

---

[13] https://en.wikipedia.org/wiki/Lockheed_AC-130

establishing a textbook ambush line. They were waiting for us. Their trap was set.

Whoever they were, they did not understand the technology we had in Spectre. They did not comprehend that she could see them. And they surely did not understand that she could kill them.

Spectre was not only our overwatch and reconnaissance; she was also our fire support, armed to the gills. Just some of the armament on a Spectre gunship includes 20mm Vulcan cannons, a Bofors 40mm cannon, and a 105mm cannon. That's a lot of firepower to rain down on an unsuspecting enemy.

We authorized Spectre to unleash hell on the ambush line, ceasing fire only as we were ready to flank them. Spectre erupted with all her guns blazing. The sky lit up with fire, seemingly out of nowhere.

I can only imagine what the men in the ambush line thought as they looked up to see a fiery hell descending upon them. It lasted about half a minute. The ambush line was decimated. None of them survived.

We still didn't know who they were. They were dressed in an odd mix of uniforms, civilian clothes, and even police uniforms, but we didn't stick around for long. We crossed the moat and slipped through the fence.

Home was still at least an hour away, so we stopped at a US military compound nearby to try to figure out what had happened. We soon found out that we had been double-crossed. The ace up our sleeve turned out to be a double agent. His name was Mazin. He was part of our team. He was trusted. He was a brother to us. This was difficult to swallow.

We sat down with him in a quiet room, and he explained everything. The terrorists had kidnapped his sister and forced him to lure us into a trap. He was genuinely remorseful for his double-cross. He tried to explain to us that he led us into the trap and not a regular Army unit because he knew us. He knew we would succeed. He knew we would survive.

He said he knew we would figure it out. He knew we could handle it. He was sorry. I felt his remorse. It was genuine. I could feel his shame. It was heavy. There was nothing he could do. He loved his sister.

He knew we would come out with a victory. He had no choice.

Mazin wore the uniform of our ally but underneath that, he was also a big brother to a beautiful younger sister. The uniform of a big brother was one he would die for.

Mazin would betray us but he would not betray his sister.

One of the dry holes we hit was where his sister was being held. He had rescued her. She was safe.

He was forced to betray us, and he understood it would cost him his life. But his sister would live.

I thanked him for his honesty, shook his hand, and told him that I hoped he would find peace with all of it before his death. I never saw Mazin again.

Iraqi justice can be harsh and swift.

In the midst of hardship and betrayal, I try to remind myself that God is like an AC 130 Spectre gunship, flying above us watching out for us, protecting us. I just need to call on Him.

He is stronger than our enemies. He is stronger than our fears. He can survive our betrayals. Even if we can't see Him, hear Him, or even sense His presence, He is there watching over us.

We just need to call on Him.

I called on Him that night to protect us.

I still call on Him and ask Him to show Mazin mercy.

Mazin betrayed us, that is for sure. But he did it to save his sister.

From her perspective, her big brother is a hero.

As time has gone by, I also began to view Mazin as a hero. It's complicated.

What else is complicated is how God throws us curve balls. No, not curve balls– sometimes He punches us in the gut.

My friend Bill fought for many years after that night. We went to Delta selection together and served in the Unit together. We were best friends. He was a remarkable Special Operations Officer.

He retired to be with his wife and two small daughters. He took off the uniform and wanted nothing more than to be a husband and a dad.

But God took him. Bill died on a mountain, crushed by a freak rockfall, just as he was beginning his next chapter. My heart aches as I write this. Bill was truly a special man.

He was a man after God's own heart. I can barely face his wife and children. It hurts so bad.

I don't fully understand why God took Bill before he could live out more of his days as a husband and dad.

Sometimes I feel mad about it but most of the time I trust God has a good reason.

And more importantly, I know Bill isn't gone. He's just somewhere else now.

I can feel Bill. Even as I write this, I can feel his presence. Sense his smile.

Bill, thank you for being such a good friend.

I am looking forward to seeing you again on the other side.

4

FIND YOUR MIGHTY MEN
BETTER YET, BECOME ONE

DAVID'S A-TEAM:
FORTITUDE AND FAILURE

CHAPTER 4

I. Find Your Mighty Men, Better Yet, Become One

> *Greater love has no one than this: to lay down one's life for one's friends. (John 15:13, NIV)*

"I cannot get to you!" I yelled over the gunfire, "You've got to crawl to me."

"I can't move my legs." He said. "They don't work."

I yelled at him again, "You better figure it out, I can't get to you. You're gonna die right there if you don't move now."

He put his head back, looked up at the night sky, and just laid there. I didn't know if he really couldn't move or if he was paralyzed with fear.

There was no way I could get to him without getting myself shot or killed.

Servant leadership is how David started. This is what I try to emulate. We know that good leaders need to surround themselves with good people. Sometimes we are the leader and sometimes we are the follower. Leadership is a blend of both.

There are times as a leader when I wonder if I am living up to the expectations of the people I lead. There have been a few times in my life when I asked myself, "Am I living up to them?" And God was gracious enough to show me, "Yes, you are living up to them. You are right where I want you to be right now."

Other times, as I've said before, God appears to be silent and I'm left to continue moving forward in humility and trust that He will show Himself to me again and guide my decisions.

Leadership is an incredible honor, and it is also a heavy responsibility. Leading men in combat is an honor and responsibility all its own.

The base element of a Special Forces Unit is the Operational Detachment Alpha, called the A-Team for short. It is a twelve-man team.

As the war in Iraq went on, we would split up our teams and work to be force multipliers for the conventional troops on the ground. We would send a handful of men to be the lead element for other units.

During one trip, we were scattered around northern Iraq, working hard to keep the pressure on the remnants of Al Qaeda and ISIS radicals that refused to quit.

An assault team and some leadership, including the Sergeant Major and me, led an Army Infantry company to a target deep in the heart of the Sunni Triangle. We pinpointed the target house and handed the objective over to the Company Commander, an Infantry Captain, to lead his men in the assault.

The lead platoon did not do what we were expecting them to do, and we entered the enemy compound with no covering support. Two machine guns from the target building erupted and seven US soldiers immediately fell under the withering fire. A soldier collapsed to my left front, and I presumed he was dead. I had seen him get hit with a couple of bursts from the machine gun. He was lying still.

I positioned myself to engage the target building, trying to skip some rounds through the open doorway and windows into the enemy position deeper inside the building.
The two terrorists were bunkered in, and our small arms fire was not affecting them.

The downed soldier diagonal from me began to move a little. Apparently he wasn't dead. The ISIS terrorists also noticed he was moving, and fired another machine gun burst into him. I yelled at him to lie still and when ready to crawl to me. He said he could not move; his legs were paralyzed. He asked me to come get him.

He was straight in the line of fire of both machine guns, with nothing for me to hide behind. I looked around and all my men were fully occupied with either returning fire, carrying casualties, or climbing onto the roof of the target building with the intent of chopping a hole and dropping a satchel charge explosive to end this fight.

I knew I would get shot running out there, and I accepted that. I just didn't want to let my guys down. If I got shot, they would never let me hear the end of it. I could picture myself lying in a bed in a hospital and them all showing up and giving me smack for trying to be a hero.

"Hey hero," I could hear them taunting me, "Who do you think you are, John Wayne?"

Strangely enough, this is what occupied my mind. I didn't want to do something stupid. And secondly, I thought, if that kid can walk, and isn't hurt badly, and I have to go out there and get him, only to find out he was overwhelmed with fear, I will shoot him myself.

I certainly wasn't feeling heroic or even gracious at that point. I wanted to do my job but I wasn't exactly sure what my job was at that exact moment. My job was usually to manage the fight up and off the target. As officers, we were specifically taught not to get sucked into the close fight. That was NCO business.

Running into the line of fire and rescuing soldiers is definitely NCO business. I say this partly in jest, but it is actually what I thought. My duty is this entire mission, getting everyone home, not just this one guy lying in a heap. He was still alive, but I didn't know for how much longer.

I looked around again.
Everyone was doing their job.
There was no one else.

Grabbing this young man became my responsibility.

I said a quick prayer to God to please just cover my balls. I didn't really care about getting shot, I just didn't want to get shot in the balls.

David's A-Team: Fortitude and Failure

David was a remarkable combat leader. He thrived on danger and excelled in life-and-death conflicts. He led by example and suffered the same hardships as his men. They trusted him completely. War and conflict were where he felt the most comfortable. When peace broke out, David, like many successful men, faltered. He didn't know how to live without death at his doorstep.

Hardships create bonds and forge character. The men David surrounded himself with were dedicated and fearless followers. Some of David's men were endowed not only with loyal hearts but also with seemingly superhuman skills.

These men in David's loyal band of followers were called his Mighty Men. They were a group of between thirty and forty of David's best warriors, his crack troops, his Green Berets.[14] He also had a leadership cadre of chiefs who stood out among the rest. Many of them are listed by name in 1 Chronicles and 2 Samuel, with some of their personal exploits highlighted.

> *Josheb-Basshebeth, once killed eight hundred men at one time, using only his spear.*[15]

---

[14] 2 Sam. 23:24–39 (New International Version).
[15] 2 Sam. 23:8 (NIV).

Jashobeam, Chief of the Thirty, single-handedly killed three hundred men.[16]

Similarly, Abishai became famous for single-handedly killing another three hundred men with a spear.[17]

Benaiah, was a Mighty Man with many exploits to his credit: he killed two famous Moabite giants, a giant Egyptian, and he climbed down into a pit and killed a lion on a snowy day. He was ultimately put in charge of David's personal bodyguard.[18]

I'm not sure if you just cruised past one of these last lines, but it is one of my favorite comments in the entire Bible.

Benaiah *"climbed down into a pit and killed a lion on a snowy day."*[19]

That is all the Bible says about that. That is all that needs to be said. These were brave warriors, ready

---

[16] 1 Chron. 11:11 (NIV).
[17] 1 Chron. 11:20–21 (NIV).
[18] 1 Chron. 11:22–25 (NIV).
[19] 1 Chron. 11:22 (NIV).

for battle, adept with shields and spears, armed with bows, and able to shoot arrows or sling stones right-handed or left-handed. "*Their faces were the faces of lions, and they were as swift as gazelles in the mountains.*"[20]

These were David's loyal men, his faithful few—his Special Forces Operators. They would do anything for him, and David learned that he needed to be careful with this loyalty. He could not take it for granted and certainly could never abuse it.

On one occasion, David casually remarked that he was thirsting for some water from his favorite well where he grew up. The well was not too far off, and the nostalgia was aching in him. Samuel records it:

> *While David was holed up in the Cave, the Philistines had their base camp in Bethlehem. David had a sudden craving and said, "Would I ever like a drink of water from the well at the gate of Bethlehem!" So the Three penetrated the Philistine lines, drew water from the well at the gate of Bethlehem, and brought it back to David. But David wouldn't drink it; he*

---

[20] 1 Chron. 12:8 (NIV).

> *poured it out as an offering to God, saying,*
> *"There is no way, God, that I'll drink this!*
> *This isn't mere water, it's their life-blood—*
> *they risked their very lives to bring it!" So*
> *David refused to drink it.*[21] *(2 Samuel 23: 14-*
> *17, MSG)*

David understood the sway and influence he had with his men. He loved them and cared about them, and he led them with honor, courage, and nobility.

Until he didn't.

With leadership, failure is always lurking. Pride and arrogance are the precursors to failure. Every time.

In Special Forces, we would warn every man to beware of the 3 B's. Booze, Bucks, and Broads. Men in general, but warriors specifically, too often fall into the trap of one of these three categories.

They turn to alcohol or drugs to quiet the incessant cacophony of long-ago battles in their heads. They become careless with money and abuse the trust granted them to be forthright, honest, and

---

[21] 2 Sam. 23:14–17 (The Message).

accountable with the treasure they are entrusted with.

And women. So complicated.

With no battlefield to conquer, no enemy to pursue, too many men chase women instead. They pursue them because the hunt is exhilarating. They sleep with them to find solace from the demons in their heads. Nothing soothes a soldier's wounds like the touch of a woman. If only for a few minutes.

David was no different. The season for warfighting came and David decided to stay home.

He got restless. He wandered about and fell right into a trap. He saw a beautiful woman and wanted her.

> *In the spring, at the time when kings go off to war, David sent Joab out with the king's men and the whole Israelite army. They destroyed the Ammonites and besieged Rabbah. But David remained in Jerusalem.*
>
> *One evening David got up from his bed and walked around on the roof of the palace. From the roof he saw a woman bathing. The woman*

was very beautiful, and David sent someone to find out about her. The man said, "She is Bathsheba, the daughter of Eliam and the wife of Uriah the Hittite." Then David sent messengers to get her. She came to him, and he slept with her. (Now she was purifying herself from her monthly uncleanness.) Then she went back home. The woman conceived and sent word to David, saying, "I am pregnant."

So David sent this word to Joab: "Send me Uriah the Hittite." And Joab sent him to David. When Uriah came to him, David asked him how Joab was, how the soldiers were and how the war was going. Then David said to Uriah, "Go down to your house and wash your feet." So Uriah left the palace, and a gift from the king was sent after him. But Uriah slept at the entrance to the palace with all his master's servants and did not go down to his house.

David was told, "Uriah did not go home." So he asked Uriah, "Haven't you just come from a military campaign? Why didn't you go home?"

Uriah said to David, "The ark and Israel and Judah are staying in tents, and my commander Joab and my lord's men are camped in the open country. How could I go to my house to eat and drink and make love to my wife? As surely as you live, I will not do such a thing!"

Then David said to him, "Stay here one more day, and tomorrow I will send you back." So Uriah remained in Jerusalem that day and the next. At David's invitation, he ate and drank with him, and David made him drunk. But in the evening Uriah went out to sleep on his mat among his master's servants; he did not go home.

In the morning David wrote a letter to Joab and sent it with Uriah. In it he wrote, "Put Uriah out in front where the fighting is fiercest. Then withdraw from him so he will be struck down and die."

So while Joab had the city under siege, he put Uriah at a place where he knew the strongest defenders were. When the men of the city came out and fought against Joab, some of the men

*in David's army fell; moreover, Uriah the
Hittite died.*

*Joab sent David a full account of the battle. He
instructed the messenger: "When you have
finished giving the king this account of the
battle, the king's anger may flare up, and he
may ask you, 'Why did you get so close to the
city to fight? Didn't you know they would shoot
arrows from the wall? Who killed Abimelek son
of Jerub-Besheth? Didn't a woman drop an
upper millstone on him from the wall, so that
he died in Thebez? Why did you get so close to
the wall?' If he asks you this, then say to him,
'moreover, your servant Uriah the Hittite is
dead.'"*

*The messenger set out, and when he arrived he
told David everything Joab had sent him to
say. The messenger said to David, "The men
overpowered us and came out against us in the
open, but we drove them back to the entrance
of the city gate. Then the archers shot arrows at
your servants from the wall, and some of the
king's men died. Moreover, your servant Uriah
the Hittite is dead."*

David told the messenger, "Say this to Joab: 'Don't let this upset you; the sword devours one as well as another. Press the attack against the city and destroy it.' Say this to encourage Joab."

When Uriah's wife heard that her husband was dead, she mourned for him. After the time of mourning was over, David had her brought to his house, and she became his wife and bore him a son.

But the thing David had done displeased the Lord.[22] *(2 Samuel 11: 1-27, NIV)*

More to the Story

David should have been at war with his men.
He should not have been wandering around the palace roof alone.
He should have looked the other way when he saw Bathsheba bathing.
He should never have thought he could have her.
When he found out she was Uriah's wife, he should have turned around and went back to his room.

---

[22] 2 Sam. 11:1–27 (New International Version).

I have mixed feelings with this story. On one level, I am shocked and disgusted at the betrayal of a friend, the incredible abuse of power by a King, and David's escalation of terrible choices. But on the other hand, this story gives me some comfort. I am a sinner. I make mistakes every day. I fall short repeatedly. But I never had an adulterous affair with the wife of one of my soldiers, got her pregnant and then set her husband up to be killed in combat.

David is referred to as a "man after God's own heart."[23] I want to be a "man after God's own heart," and when I feel that I am not worthy of this title, I sometimes think of David, and it makes me feel a little bit better about myself.

How did David fall this far? How did he go from the honorable warrior leader to this? Unfortunately, this is a story that repeats itself time and again, right up to the present day. Many men do not finish well. We strive in our youth to be respected. Our ambition is unbridled. We want to make a difference. And when we achieve our dreams, we too often lose our way.

---

[23] 1 Sam. 13:14; Acts 13:22.

David made a series of poor decisions that led him into a predicament that he made even worse by trying to cover it up. It ended in murder. Look at Samuel's account above again. Do you see each mistake? How many can you identify?

Winter ends and the spring war campaigns begin. David chooses to stay behind in his palace.

That is his first mistake. But it can be excused away. Maybe he was injured, or simply tired of war. He had done his share of fighting. Maybe he was confident in his men.

Some of these excuses may be true. Regardless, he was home in his palace getting bored as his men were fighting 50 miles away in Rabbah, otherwise known as Rabbat Ammon. This is the modern city of Amman, Jordan's capital. The people of this kingdom were called "Children of Ammon" or "Ammonites."[24] The Israelites and the Ammonites were bitter rivals. For some reason, David did not feel like he needed to be in Amman for this campaign.

---

[24] https://en.wikipedia.org/wiki/Ammon

The next thing I notice is he is waking up from a late afternoon early evening nap. (It's good to be the king.)[25]

David goes for a stroll on his palace roof and sees a woman bathing. Mistake number two: he lingers. He gazes at her long enough to become aroused.

Mistake number three: he sends a servant to go fetch her. (It's good to be the king.)

David sleeps with the woman, the wife of one of his Mighty Men. The mistakes are getting worse.

She gets pregnant and David panics. He plots a cover-up—mistake number five.

He recalls Uriah, the husband, from the battlefront, but his plan doesn't work. He digs in deeper, getting Uriah drunk. But Uriah is honorable, and David's cover-up fails.

---

[25] Mel Brooks has a hilarious song from History of the World that is called "It's Good to Be the King." I can't think of David in this situation and not hear this song in my head.

I've lost track of David's mistakes already. He sits and drinks with his friend knowing he slept with his wife, knowing she is pregnant.

Despicable.

David's next decision is murderous. He orders his most trusted commander Joab to ensure that Uriah is killed. This plan succeeds. Uriah the Hittite, one of David's Mighty Men is killed in Ammon.[26] Uriah was one of David's most trusted commandos and he sacrificed him to hide his own shame.

Disgusting.

And then, David plays the role of the good guy. He takes in the widow Bathsheba into his own house. Unaware of his treachery, everyone else sees him as a "man after God's own heart."
Unforgivable?

David appears to get away with his sin until God sends a prophet to confront him.[27] David repents and is truly remorseful.[28] He is forgiven. Fully.

---

[26] 2 Sam. 23:39.
[27] 2 Sam. 12:1–25.
[28] Ps. 51.

When you feel like you are falling short, when you feel like you are not worthy of God's love or His forgiveness, let this story bring you comfort.

Did you ever murder one of your best friends to cover up your adulterous affair with his wife?

It's unlikely. Even if you did, no sin is too big for God to forgive. He sent His son to cover our debt.[29] We serve a good King.

II. Find Your Mighty Men, Better Yet, Become One

After praying one more time for my balls, I ran to the wounded soldier in a weird sideways skipping kind of way, thinking that I would present my body armor and get hit there instead of a death shot near my armpit that avoided my body armor. Of course, this approach left my balls facing the enemy. Hence the prayer.

---

[29] Rom. 5:5–9; 1 John 2:12; Isa. 1:18; 1 Pet. 2:22–25; Eph. 2:1–9; John 3:16.

I reached the soldier, whose name I found out later was Anthony, and grabbed the handle on his body armor. It broke off in my hand and I fell flat on my butt. A burst of machine-gun fire strafed above my head, hitting the wall above me right where I was previously standing.

I gave a quick nod to God and said "thanks," counting at least six holes in the wall above my head.

I was able to drag Anthony behind some cover, and our EOD Sergeant, Scott, and I went to work plugging the holes in his body and trying to stop the bleeding. I felt bad for doubting Anthony. I felt bad for leaving him out there so long, alone. He had six to eight holes in him. Both of his femurs were shot through and both of his brachial arteries under his armpits were severed. As soon as I moved him, I was showered with blood spraying from his armpits. He also had a sucking chest wound. He was so torn up, I wasn't even sure where to start. We did our best. And that was enough.

Anthony lived that day.

One of the medics on the MEDEVAC bird turned out to be a tattoo artist. Before I left Iraq that trip, I paid him a visit and had him tattoo the Apostle's Cross on my back in memory of this event. The Apostle's Cross is a standard Latin Cross with three buds on the ends of each cross arm. These buds represent the twelve disciples. I don't think about this tattoo very often. It is hard for me to even see it, especially as I get older and my neck doesn't work like it used to. The cross is just there. If I think about it or not, it's just there, a reminder of that day.

On this target there were seven soldiers wounded. All of them lived. Thanks to twelve Special Forces Operators.

I love those guys. They were my Mighty Men. I think of them often. There were times when I failed them. I made mistakes, and I carry that burden. While I carry that burden, it is not too heavy. I truly did my best. I never skipped a campaign. I didn't nap when my men were fighting. I never slept with their wives.

But I am not letting down my guard.

I am growing old, and my life is getting comfortable.

I want to finish strong.

VALUE WHAT IS TRULY IMPORTANT

MARY THE PREGNANT VIRGIN:
THIS WOMAN'S WORK

CHAPTER 5

I. Value What is Truly Important

A wife of noble character who can find? She is worth far more than rubies...Charm is deceptive, and beauty is fleeting; but a woman who fears the Lord is to be praised. (Proverbs 31: 10,30, NIV)

We were running from cover to cover trying to avoid any direct fire when the man behind me said, "You're hit."

I turned to look at him. "What?"

"You're hit," he repeated, and then he announced it on the radio: "Tiegs is hit, moving to exfil. Doc, meet us at the vehicles–he will need your attention."

I kept running to the armored personnel carrier, confused. How did I get hit? Where? I didn't feel a thing! We got to the vehicles, and Doc was already there.

"Where are you hit?" he asked.

"I don't know," I answered as I looked down at my chest, inspected both of my arms, and scanned the front of my legs. Doc was behind me doing the same when he said, "Lotta blood. You're hit in the leg. Lie down, I'll pack it."

Around the third or fourth night of one of my rotations in Iraq, we hit a tough target. It was in bad guy country, downtown Baghdad. We knew it was going to be dicey and it did not disappoint. Before we even exited the vehicles, we were under fire, rounds impacting the sides of our armored personnel carriers as we dismounted straight into a gunfight.

We fought our way to the objective building, did what we get paid to do, captured our primary target, secured him, and moved to exfil. Things had gotten quiet when we were inside the target building but as soon as we got about a hundred meters from the vehicles again, the insurgent fighters went all out. Rocket Propelled Grenades (RPGs) flew past us, and small arms fire plunged into our position from multiple angles. There really was nobody to shoot back at– they were hidden well and just harassing us as we left their neighborhood.

This was when the man behind me said, "You're hit."

As Doc was cutting my pants trying to access my wound, I looked down at my left leg. My hammy. Now I knew what had happened. In the scuffle, running back to the exfil point, my stitches must have burst, and my playground splinter wound was bleeding profusely.

I looked like I had been shot in the leg.

"It's ok. It's just a splinter." I tried to explain.

Doc was pushing me down on my belly in the back of the vehicle as we started rolling.

"It's a splinter," I said again.

Doc began to apply pressure to the bleeding gash.

"It's a splinter. I got it a few days ago on the playground. It's fine. The stitches must have burst."

Doc didn't care if it was an AK47 round, or a piece of shrapnel from an RPG, or a splinter from a playground back in Southern Pines, North Carolina. His job was to stop the bleeding.

I gave up and lay there on the hard metal floor of the armored personnel carrier with rounds slamming into the hull, and just let Doc do his thing.

I lay there and thought about my sons.

It had only been a few days but it already felt like I hadn't seen them in years.

Doc's bedside manner, digging deeply into the back of my leg brought on sharp, stabbing pain, but the aching in my heart for my two little boys was way worse.

I thanked God for their mom.

Mary the Pregnant Virgin: This Woman's Work[30]

What do you really know about Mary?

---

[30] The song "This Woman's Work" by Kate Bush moves me deeply, every time I hear it.

How often do you think about her?

How often do you think about your own mother
and the sacrifices she made to raise you?

Mary was Jesus's mom, plain and simple. Of all the
women ever born, Mary was chosen to be the
mother of the Messiah. She carried him in her
womb, fed him from her body, and raised him to
become strong, wise, and filled with God's grace.[31]

Throughout the accounts of Jesus's life in the Bible,
she quietly enters and exits the stage at various
points throughout his life. She always seems to be
present when he needs her.

Mary was magnificent.

Take a few moments to consider this woman, her
story, and her son. Luke tells it this way.

---

https://www.google.com/search?q=a+womans+work+kate+bush&oq=
a+womans+work+kate+bush&aqs=chrome..69i57j0i10l3j0i22j30l6.1
1016j0j4&sourceid=chrome&ie=UTF-
8#wptab=s:H4sIAAAAAAAAAONgVuLRT9c3LDYwrUyvLMh-
xGjOLfDyxz1hKb1Ja05eY9Tg4grOyC93zSvJLKkUkuJig7IEpPi4U
DTy7GLSS0lNSyzNKYkvSUyyyk620s8tLc5M1i9KTc4vSsnMS49Pz
iktLkktssqpLMpMLl7EKl6SkVmsUJ6fm5gHooqyFSAyABKEi1yVA
AAA

[31] Luke 2:40.

*God sent the angel Gabriel to Nazareth, a
town in Galilee, to a virgin pledged to be
married to a man named Joseph, a descendant
of David. The virgin's name was Mary. The
angel went to her and said, "Greetings, you
who are highly favored! The Lord is with you."*

*Mary was greatly troubled at his words and
wondered what kind of greeting this might be.
But the angel said to her, "Do not be afraid,
Mary; you have found favor with God. You
will conceive and give birth to a son, and you
are to call him Jesus. He will be great and will
be called the Son of the Most High. The Lord
God will give him the throne of his father
David, and he will reign over Jacob's
descendants forever; his kingdom will never
end."*

*"How will this be," Mary asked the angel,
"since I am a virgin?"*

*The angel answered, "The Holy Spirit will
come on you, and the power of the Most High
will overshadow you. So the holy one to be born
will be called the Son of God. Even Elizabeth,
your relative is going to have a child in her old*

age, and she who was said to be unable to conceive is in her sixth month. For no word from God will ever fail."

"I am the Lord's servant," Mary answered. "May your word to me be fulfilled." Then the angel left her.[32] *(Luke 1:26-38, NIV)*

Then the angel left her. That's quite an abrupt exit. Imagine it. A young girl, still only a teenager, a virgin, being told she is pregnant. But Mary doesn't flinch. She ponders it for a moment and then accepts it. And then she is left alone.

Her work had just begun.

More to the Story

The Bible tells us very little of Mary's personal history. We are told she was part of the tribe of Judah and was a direct descendant of King David through David's son Nathan. (Psalm 132:11; Luke 1:32). Joseph, her husband, was a direct descendant from King David through his son Solomon who inherited his throne.

---

[32] Luke 1:26–38 (New International Version).

Mary's name in the original manuscripts of the New Covenant was based on her Aramaic name Maryam or Mariam- מרים. [33] The meaning is not known for certain, however, it was most likely originally an Egyptian name that meant "beloved," "loved," or "the exalted one." In Hebrew, Miriam means both "rebellion" and "exalted one."[34] While at first glance these meanings may seem quite separate, if we join all of them together, we have "Beloved, Exalted One Who Brings Rebellion Into the World."

This truly was Mary.

Jesus was not only born into this world to bring peace, He also brought rebellion. He directly confronted Satan, knocked him down a few pegs, and banished many of his minions back to hell. Jesus would usher in a new order and empower His followers to do miraculous things. He was the Messiah that Israel had been waiting for.

When Jesus was forty days old, Jewish tradition required Mary and Joseph to bring him to the temple. This was to purify Mary after childbirth and to perform the redemption ritual on Jesus, the

---

[33] https://en.wikipedia.org/wiki/Mary,_mother_of_Jesus
[34] https://en.wikipedia.org/wiki/Miriam_(given_name)

firstborn son.[35] Waiting for them at the temple was a prophet who told Mary and Joseph,

> *This child is destined to cause the falling and rising of many in Israel, and to be a sign that will be spoken against, so that the thoughts of many hearts will be revealed. And a sword will pierce your own soul too. (Luke 2: 35, NIV)*

Being the mother of Jesus would ultimately include a broken heart and a pierced soul.
Mary never forgot these words that would haunt her years later.

How we revere and respect Mary is one of those viewpoints that we have allowed to divide the church. In the Protestant tradition, Mary is not treated with the same reverence as in the Catholic tradition. In an effort to separate from the Catholic veneration of Mary, some of the incredibly beautiful and fascinating details that go along with her story have been discarded. Mary is relegated to the supporting cast, which ultimately does a disservice to her and to us

---

35 https://en.wikipedia.org/wiki/Presentation_of_Jesus_at_the_Temple

Mary was not a supporting actor, but a lead protagonist, a bonafide hero, in this incredible story. What is amazing and somewhat forgotten now is that the people of her day knew it. Everyone knew that Mary was special. Years before she became pregnant, years before she became a disgrace to her community, Mary was a celebrity.

Mary's father, Joachim, was in the direct lineage of David, and her mother, Anna, was a direct descendant of the Levites.[36] The Levites were the priestly tribe from the line of Aaron, the brother of Moses. Joachim and Anna had the credentials to bear some special children, but they were barren.[37] This common plotline throughout the Bible befell Mary's mom and dad.

After praying diligently and promising to commit any child to the service of the temple, Joachim and Anna were visited by an angel and told that they would be blessed with a special child who would alter the course of the world.[38] Mary arrived and when she was born, as promised, she was dedicated

---

[36] https://en.wikipedia.org/wiki/Joachim

[37] The Gospel of James, also known as the Infancy Gospel of James or the Protoevangelium of James, is an apocryphal Gospel written about 150 C.E.

[38] Ibid

to the temple. At three years old, Mary was presented to the priest Zechariah (likely her uncle), moved onto the temple grounds, and settled in for a life of service.[39] The girls and women dedicated to the temple had many different duties, including cleaning the priestly garments that would continually get stained from the blood of sacrificed animals. When the garments were too stained or worn out, they were cut into strips and repurposed for different special purposes. Some of the worn-out priestly garments would be used to swaddle the specially selected sacrificial lambs as they were inspected for any blemishes.[40]

The temple servants cleaned, cooked, comforted the poor, and most importantly maintained a steady flow of prayer and praise throughout the temple. Another duty they were proud of was to clean and maintain the temple curtain that separated the holy of holies from the court of the priests.[41] No one was allowed behind this curtain but the High Priest once

---

[39] Ibid

[40] Deb Cool, "5 Things About Jesus' Birth that You May Not Have Known," The Connection, December 22, 2021, https://www.connectingwomenwithgod.com/blog/5-things-about-jesus-birth-that-you-may-not-have-known--170.

[41] The Gospel of James, also known as the Infancy Gospel of James or the Protoevangelium of James.

a year. The design of the curtain was very specific and strictly adhered to the details that God Himself laid out fourteen hundred years before.[42] This curtain separated the Shekinah, the divine presence of God, from the rest of the earth. This very specific spot on the planet was regarded as the place where God, in His glory, actually resided and was where He pierced through the universe to share himself with mankind.

Needless to say, this was a special place, this curtain was an important part of the temple, and the care of this curtain was one of the most highly regarded duties of the women dedicated to the temple. When time, wear, and tear took its toll, and the temple curtain needed to be replaced, this was not taken lightly. Very specific instructions were laid out for recreating the curtain, and only a few were given the honor of weaving the new sections.

Seven girls were selected to spin different colors for the sections of the curtain. The highest honor would go to whoever was chosen to spin the purple that ran down the center of the curtain and joined it into one

---

[42] Exod. 26.

continuous piece. As a young teenager, Mary was selected for this honor.[43]

Artists have been representing this detail in their paintings for centuries, and if you look closely, you will see it.[44] Many old paintings that depict the angel appearing before Mary to tell her that she will be the mother of the Messiah also show Mary weaving or spinning the thread for the curtain.[45]

When the angel visited Mary, the Weaver was spinning a child inside her, planting the Messiah at the center of her womb. The Messiah that would mend the tear that originated in the garden and separated mankind from His eternal love and peace.

For centuries this was the story. For centuries we shared this detail and found comfort, satisfaction, and closure with it. Now it is largely forgotten. Lost to time, hurriedness, busyness, distraction, and the desire for divisiveness.

---

[43] "The Gospel of James," also known as the "Infancy Gospel of James" or the "Protoevangelium of James."
[44] https://painting-planet.com/madonna-with-spinning-wheel-leonardo-da-vinci/
[45] Maria gravida, or Mary at the Spinning Wheel

I invite you to ponder the details of these events and feel comfort, satisfaction, and closure to an already immaculate story.

II. Value What is Truly Important

Every time I left for war, it felt like I was walking to the gallows. Death was not certain, but neither was life. Panama and Desert Storm were different because I was so young and did not have kids. The initial invasion of Iraq was also different because there was so much unknown, but leaving for every rotation after the first one was difficult. Painful. Agonizing. Most every day before I left, I would play with my sons and hang out with my wife. We would go to the park and play tag, play soccer, or some other games and just be together. Those days were incredible, but they were extremely painful, too. I hid it well, but my gut was churning and my heart was aching. I didn't want to leave my wife and feared that I would not live to see my sons grow up.

I don't want to exaggerate the danger or the risk of death. The odds were in my favor, but what odds do you need before taking something deadly seriously?

One day before I left, we were at the park playing ball tag. It was a favorite of ours. We would start a ball tag game and many of the kids at the park would join in. We'd sometimes have ten to twenty kids playing, often with their dads joining in. The park was awesome. It had these structures that were half fort and half obstacle course made of wood, tires and other composite playground equipment.

Bill was there with us. He and I were in different squadrons so when I deployed, he was home and vice versa. We had an unwritten code that he would look after my family when I was gone and I would do the same for him. At this time, Bill was still single, but he was already committed to looking after my family.

We had a raucous game of ball tag going, and as I was evading one of the local kids with a ball, I vaulted over a wooden fence and caught it just right with the bottom of my hamstring. A wood splinter about three inches long embedded itself deep into my hammy. I had to call a timeout and walk over to the car. Bill followed me over and looked it over. He didn't think I was going to die but he acknowledged that it was deep. He recommended a quick stop at the emergency room, but we didn't have time. We were supposed to finish up this game, go home and eat dinner, hang out a bit, and put the boys to bed. After they fell asleep, I was supposed to slip out quietly like I almost always did, except once.

Bill and I concluded that with the Leatherman tool in the back of my SUV, he could use the blade to cut some of the skin away and the pliers to pull out the splinter.

Sounded good to me. And that's what we did.

When we got home, we put the boys in the tubby, and my wife cleaned my ball tag wound, wrapping it in gauze and an ace bandage.

The time was moving agonizingly slowly but in a haze that always felt weird. I was there, in my home, with my family, but I was already gone too.

When the time came, I slipped away and drove myself to the compound. I had the medic look at my wound when I got to work; he put a few stitches in it and wrapped it back up.

Good as new.

Until the stitches tore open in the middle of a gunfight.

Women create life. Women create a life worth living. We fight for the feminine ideal. Any man of honor would lay down his life to protect women and children.

In combat, we think about the people we love. But mostly, we think about our girlfriends and our wives. We want to get home to them and disappear into the safety, warmth, and security of their embrace. We crave the curves of their bodies as a place where we can rest and heal. It is a strange phenomenon that few people talk about. But God knows; He created us this way. His masterpiece was the woman named Eve.

The name Eve means living or enlivening. How fitting. My wife not only brought my sons into this world, she also nurtured them, raised them, and helped them develop into incredible young men.

Before each deployment, I would slip away from my home at night when the boys were sleeping. We would finish our day together; my wife and I would tuck them into bed, and then sometime in the still of the night, I would head to work.

One time we did it differently. I don't remember why. We spent the day together, but then sometime before dinner, we all drove to the compound, about twenty-five miles away. It took about half an hour to make the drive.

The boys were in their car seats in the back, and they began to realize what was happening: I was leaving again. Remembering their tears makes my heart ache now. It was terrible. I felt terrible. I couldn't wait to get out of there and escape this flood of emotion. I was sick. That ride seemed to last forever, but eventually we got to the compound. Both boys clung to my legs and begged me to stay. I pried their tiny fingers off my legs and walked away.
I left.
And didn't look back.

My sons continued to whimper and sob quietly. I think it would have been easier if they would have wailed. Even as young boys, they were trying to act like men, stoic and enduring, but their little hearts ached.
My heart exploded.

We never did that again. Or rather, I never did that again. The fact is that my wife faced this every time I left. At some point, the boys would come to realize I was gone. At war again. It fell to my wife to wipe

their tears, hug them, comfort and console them—
as well as deal with her own sadness and fears. She
carried this burden for me. And I don't think I have
ever thanked her for it.

For too long, I dismissed Mary. The Lutheran
tradition I grew up in de-emphasized her
importance. But I am a man now. A man who
stayed alive simply so I could get back to my wife.
She waited patiently, raised our sons, and healed me
each time I returned home just a little more bruised
and broken.

Mary is the person who was always there for Jesus.
She wiped his tears, hugged him, comforted and
consoled him.

I am going to do something right now that I have
never done before. I am going to pray the Catholic
"Hail Mary" prayer, not that I believe Mary was
holy, but because I am sorry that I have shown her
such little respect.

Mary was chosen as the mother of our savior. She is
one of my heroes. She deserves my utmost respect.

Hail Mary, full of grace, the Lord is with thee. Blessed art thou among women, and blessed is the fruit of thy womb, Jesus. Holy Mary, Mother of God, pray for us sinners, now and at the hour of our death. Amen.

6

DEFEND THE WEAK

MARY THE DISGRACED:
PERSECUTED BUT NOT ABANDONED

CHAPTER 6

I. Defend the Weak

Husbands, love your wives, just as Christ loved the church and gave himself up for her. (Ephesians 5:25, NIV)

"Rami?" I said again.

The woman in front of me slowly turned, and I looked up at her bearded face. It was Rami.

He took one step toward me as I raised my rifle. The baby was cradled in one arm and he held a long curved knife to its throat.

"Let me walk out of here, or I kill this child." Rami said. My interpreter relayed the message.

The mother of the baby shrieked behind him, and the other women closed around her as if to shield her from what may come next.

I looked at the baby and then back up at Rami's face.

"I mean it. I will cut this child's throat. Right here. Right now," He snarled.

This was a huge operation, an entire Infantry battalion and three Special Forces ODAs went all in on this one. The intel came from my ODA, the plan was built by my ODA, and I was the Assault Commander.

Most everything had gone as planned. We got everyone in safely, secured the village and captured five of the six terrorists we were going after, including Sami, one of the cell leaders. But his brother Rami was still out there. Was he hiding? Was I wrong about the intel? Had we left a gap for him to escape?

Where the hell was he?

How did we miss him?

The assault force was going house to house, room to room, back-clearing everything. I wandered around on the objective, ducking into different buildings and rooms to see the progress and encourage the soldiers that were getting frustrated. We could not find one of the main targets.

I slipped into a small building with my Radio Telephone Operator (RTO), a Medic, and an interpreter to look around. There was a group of about five women huddled in a corner, some seated and some standing. Three of the women were facing the door, two of them had small babies in their arms. The other two women had their backs to us, one of them sat on a bed. All of their faces were covered with hijabs. The Medic noticed the women were shivering and through the interpreter suggested that they go into the adjacent room that had a space heater and more blankets.

None of them moved.

The interpreter repeated the suggestion.

No one moved.

The three women facing me looked down at the woman that was seated on a rickety bed that had a very thin mattress on it. She wore a flowery robe and I noticed she had peculiarly wide shoulders. They were murmuring to each other but we couldn't make out what they were saying.

They looked pensively at the woman on the bed and then back at me.

Something felt strange.

The interpreter was no longer asking or suggesting, this time he ordered the women to move into the next room. I could feel the tension growing.

What was happening?

The woman sitting on the bed with her back to us reached her arms up and one of the women with a baby gingerly handed her baby to the woman on the bed. The woman on the bed clutched the baby to her chest as the baby's mother inhaled deeply and her eyes widened abnormally.

"You," the interpreter barked "Stand up." He pointed at the woman on the bed, with her back to us, clutching the baby.

The woman stood up, still with her back to us, and now I finally began to see what was before me.

She was tall. Really tall. Over six feet tall. That's tall for an Iraqi let alone an Iraqi woman. I looked down at her feet, her long robe was not long enough to cover her boots.

They were men's boots and her feet were big.

"Rami?" I asked.

Mary the Disgraced: Persecuted but not Abandoned[46]

To call the birth of Jesus a scandal is an understatement.

At about age fourteen, the temple girls were usually released from their duties and prepared to marry and start families. When this time came for Mary, she stood firm with the vow her parents had made and opted to remain as a servant in the temple. She was already well known in Jerusalem for her devotion and purity, and this decision endeared her even further with the community.[47] So, when the word got out that Mary was pregnant, it was absolutely shocking. She was just a kid.

Who got her pregnant?

The only men she was ever around were the priests?

Here is the story according to Matthew, the tax collector.

---

[46] 2 Cor. 4:9.

[47] "The Gospel of James," also known as the Infancy Gospel of James or the Protoevangelium of James

The birth of Jesus took place like this. His mother, Mary, was engaged to be married to Joseph. Before they came to the marriage bed, Joseph discovered she was pregnant. (It was by the Holy Spirit, but he didn't know that.) Joseph, chagrined but noble, determined to take care of things quietly so Mary would not be disgraced.

While he was trying to figure a way out, he had a dream. God's angel spoke in the dream: "Joseph, son of David, don't hesitate to get married. Mary's pregnancy is Spirit-conceived. God's Holy Spirit has made her pregnant. She will bring a son to birth, and when she does, you, Joseph, will name him Jesus— 'God saves'—because he will save his people from their sins." This would bring the prophet's embryonic sermon to full term: Watch for this—a virgin will get pregnant and bear a son; They will name him Immanuel (Hebrew for "God is with us").

Then Joseph woke up.

He did exactly what God's angel commanded in the dream: He married Mary. But he did not consummate the marriage until she had the baby.

He named the baby Yeshua.[48] *(Matthew 1: 18-25, MSG)*

More to the Story

The person we commonly call Jesus was really named Yeshua: ישוע

The name Jesus is the Greek form of the common Hebrew and Aramaic name Yeshua.[49]

There are several meanings attributed to the name Yeshua that can be found in Hebrew and Aramaic biblical texts: "to deliver, save, or rescue." So, simply because it is his actual name, we will refer to Jesus as Yeshua from here on out in the rest of this book.

ישוע.

---

[48] Matt. 1:18–25 (The Message). Mary and Joseph did not choose their son's name. They were specifically instructed to name Him Yeshua. During the 1st Century, even though Greek and Aramaic were common languages, it was important for a Jewish child to have a Hebrew name because it was considered the language of the "celestial court" and at the end of the whole story, the Messiah would use Hebrew names when calling the dead to rise.

[49] Doug Hershey, "Yeshua: The Meaning of the Hebrew Name of Jesus," Learning Center, Fellowship of Israel Related Ministries, December 22, 2015, https://firmisrael.org/learn/who-is-yeshua-meaning-of-hebrew-name-jesus/.

With His name already chosen, he still needed to be born. We forget about the period in which this story took place and the culture and laws that governed it. Mary was not simply facing judgment and disgrace, she was facing death. Getting pregnant out of wedlock was a capital offense. The punishment for it was death.[50]

Death by stoning. For her and her unborn child.

Mary knew it. Joseph knew it. Everyone knew it. Imagine this heavy burden on young Mary.

If we do some simple math, Mary was pregnant at around fourteen and gave birth to Jesus around the age of fifteen. When we read that she pondered the events happening around her, I stand in awe and reverence of her. Almost like a bystander she was swept up in the story, watching it all unfold. As a teenager, she was still figuring out who she was as a person while simultaneously coming to terms with the true identity of the child she was about to bring into the world.

On top of this, she was facing a possible death penalty.

---

[50] Deut. 22.

It is hard for us to accept the brutality of this sentence, but there is some sense to it. If you look at ancient Israel, the punishment for premarital sex seems to be more appropriate for rape, but keep in mind that girls of that era were usually betrothed at thirteen and married by fourteen, which does not leave much time for premarital sex.

 Nevertheless, death by stoning is brutal. This is what Mary was facing the day she found out she was pregnant.

To many in her town, to many in her family, Mary had become a pariah and a disgrace. How do you think that felt to a fourteen-year-old girl?

II. Defend the Weak

Rami held the baby out in front of him. He clutched the baby's swaddling clothes in his left hand while pressing the knife blade closer to the baby's neck with his right hand.

"I don't know that baby." I said. "I came here for you. Kill the kid, what do I care?"

As my interpreter repeated my words, the mother of the baby appeared to pass out in the arms of the women comforting her.

Rami looked at me. I could see the black evil in his eyes but I could also see the doubt on his face.

"I came to arrest you. Drop the kid or I'll shoot you in your fuckin' face," I said. I knew Rami understood English well enough but he still waited for the interpreter to repeat my words.

His face tightened. I raised my rifle a little bit higher and switched the selector lever from safe to fire and applied pressure to the trigger.

"Do what you're gonna do," I said as I braced myself for the horror of seeing a baby get his throat cut.

It was a lethal game of chicken. Who was going to flinch first?

Rami looked into my eyes trying to read them.

I tried to appear totally apathetic, cold, and heartless.

The seconds slowed as time seemed to abandon me.

Finally, Rami relented.

He threw the baby on the bed, dropped the knife, and raised his hands to surrender.

The women threw themselves on the baby and it was only then that the baby began to cry.

Rami put his hands on his head as my interpreter put flex cuffs on him. My medic rushed to the child to ensure he was all right.

Not a scratch.

"Jackpot," I said over the radio. "We have Rami in cuffs. Prepare to exfil."

I reached down, picked up the knife and stuck it in my gear.

I looked at the women. They glared at me like I was a monster. They had heard my words to Rami and hated me. Even today, I can still feel their disgust and hate. It's like a smell or a taste that won't go away.

They didn't know that I was bluffing.

I was bluffing, right?

I'm not sure that I was.

Wars are mostly fought by men, but the women and children really end up suffering at least as much, often more. While women and children are sometimes purposely targeted, this is usually done for shock value. In modern warfare, in any civilized culture, women and children are safeguarded as much as possible. International Humanitarian Law and the Laws of Land Warfare are intended to protect women and children.[51] This is why cowardly dictators and

---

[51] Office of General Counsel of the Department of Defense, *Department of Defense Law of War Manual* (Washington, DC: General Counsel of the Department of Defense, 2015), https://dod.defense.gov/Portals/1/Documents/pubs/DoD%20Law%20of%20War%20Manual%20-%20June%202015%20Updated%20Dec%202016.pdf?ver=2016-12-13-172036-190.

oppressors hide behind human shields composed of the innocent. They feel safe. And for good reason. A society that does not value its women and children is doomed to failure.

I spent over five years of my life on the ground fighting in Iraq. I was involved in over a thousand hits, many of which I cannot remember. But I can vividly recall every single target where a woman or child was injured. It was very rare. We protected them with great care. We were only coming for the men.

There was a strange phenomenon with the wives and families of Al Qaeda and ISIS. When we killed their husbands, the wives did not mourn. I am not sure if this is part of their fatalistic acceptance that men who "live by the sword will die by the sword" or if these evil men were abusers and would never be mourned.

I think it was a combination of their fatalism and fundamentalist belief that "whatever happens is God's will."

On the rare target where the wife became upset, it would force us to double-check everything to make sure we had the right guy.

Out of roughly a thousand targets where men were captured or killed, I can recall fewer than five where the wife or kids were visibly upset that their husband or father was killed.

The Middle East culture is much more fatalistic than the West. In ancient warfare, women and children were taken as slaves. They were part of the spoils of victory. ISIS reinstated this practice when they gained power in Iraq and Syria. The conquered men in a village were murdered and the women were taken as sex slaves. The children were often left behind to fend for themselves.

ISIS is largely defeated now, but not fully, and most of these sex slaves are free. Sort of. Many of these women cannot return home because their tribes will not accept them with their children. The children are products of rape and will not be accepted back into the tribe. The women must make a choice. Do they abandon their children so they can return home? Or do they live with their children in exile? They have no home. They are disgraced.

I'm pretty sure that Sami and Rami survived the war. They've continued on with their lives. How come they are not disgraced? When men abuse women and children, why is it that much of the stain is on the victim and not the monster?

This scenario of ISIS sex slaves and their forbidden children is not a perfect analogy to Mary's tenuous situation but it's similar to when she found herself pregnant out of wedlock.

She was a woman in exile. She had no home. She was a disgrace. She could have been stoned to death. Her son was a bastard and would not be accepted.[52]

He should not be accepted.

And yet he was. He became the King of all who breathe. He became the Redeemer for all who are lost and rejected. He is my King and I believe that one day Rami and Sami will stand before Him and answer for their actions.

But so will I.

When my King asks me if I was bluffing that night I will answer Him honestly.

---

[52] Isa. 53.

FINDING YOUR TRIBE

MARY THE PREGNANT FIANCÉE:
FROM THE HOUSE OF DAVID

CHAPTER 7

I. Finding Your Tribe

> *In Christ's family there can be no division into Jew and non-Jew, slave and free, male and female. Among us you are all equal. That is, we are all in a common relationship with Jesus Christ. (Galatians 3:28, MSG)*

When I went to basic and advanced training to become an Infantryman, they stripped us down, broke down our individual identities and rebuilt us into a new identity. We were soldiers, we were Infantry, the Queen of Battle[53] We served her proudly.

---

[53] https://en.wikipedia.org/wiki/Infantry_Branch_(United_States)

Then I went to Airborne school and learned how to jump out of airplanes. Actually there's not much to learn in the jumping part, it's the landing part that counts the most. After Airborne school, I was awarded a maroon beret to distinguish myself from non- jump qualified soldiers, aka "legs." I learned to look down on "legs." They disgusted me. I was Airborne. They were not.

Then I went to the Ranger Indoctrination Program (RIP) to pass a series of grueling tests to gain entry into the Ranger regiment. When I successfully graduated from RIP, I was awarded a black beret. Now I looked down on the soldiers that were simply Airborne. They disgusted me. I was a Ranger. They were not.

I am glad to say that I grew out of this ridiculousness and by the time I got my green beret for qualifying in Special Forces or got my designation as a Delta Force Operator, I didn't look down on anyone.

I was honored. I felt lucky. I felt the weight of the responsibility that came with these designations and the responsibility to represent these units the best I could.

I am sorry to say that my life as a Christian has been similar. When I was young, I looked down on people who believed differently than I. I was even disgusted with some of them.

Well, I am older now. I've made all the mistakes. I've sinned all the sins. I've failed over and over, fallen short repeatedly. Now I feel honored to be called a Christian, a follower of Yeshua. I feel lucky that my parents exposed me to this faith so long ago. I am thankful that God is so faithful to me. And, I feel the weight of responsibility to represent Him as best I can.

Mary the Pregnant Fiancée: From the House of David

The only reason Mary was not put to death is that Joseph stepped in to redeem her. He was an honorable man, another character in the "greatest story ever told"[54] that goes largely unnoticed.

He was the stepfather of Yeshua. He was selected out of every man who ever walked or will walk on earth to show Yeshua what it meant to be a man.

Joseph took care of Mary throughout her pregnancy and set off on a journey when she was nine months pregnant to comply with the new

---

[54] https://en.wikipedia.org/wiki/The_Greatest_Story_Ever_Told

Roman decree that demanded every Jew return to his tribal hometown for a census.

Here is the story as told by the physician Luke:

> *About that time Caesar Augustus ordered a census to be taken throughout the Empire. This was the first census when Quirinius was governor of Syria.*
>
> *Everyone had to travel to his own ancestral hometown to be accounted for. So Joseph went from the Galilean town of Nazareth up to Bethlehem in Judah, David's town, for the census. As a descendant of David, he had to go there. He went with Mary, his fiancée, who was pregnant.*[55] *(Luke 2: 1-5 MSG)*

When Joseph and Mary got to Bethlehem, they were relegated to lodging with animals in a stable. No one would take them in. *There was no guest room available for them.*[56]

---

[55] Luke 2:1–5 (The Message).
[56] Luke 2:7.

More to the Story

Was there no guest room for Mary and Joseph because all the inns were full or because the innkeepers would not, could not, offer her and Joseph a place to stay that night?

Mary was a teenager carrying a child who was about to be born. It didn't matter that they were traveling from Nazareth to Bethlehem, at least a ninety-mile journey through challenging terrain.

Her son was conceived out of wedlock. The only reason he wasn't born a bastard is that Joseph stepped in to wed young Mary. Many doubted the child was even his.

I am sure the innkeeper took pity on her but he didn't want to get involved. He likely knew Mary and Joseph, or even was a distant cousin, and was caught between his human sympathies, tribal loyalties, and the Jewish law. This was a national scandal that he wanted no part of.

Joseph was from the tribe of Judah, same as David, and was a direct descendant of the great King of Israel. Many years before, David had been promised that the Messiah would come from his line.[57] This promise made his family an important one, well known, a family to watch, a family that needed to avoid scandals.

The tribe of Judah was a big one. Joseph's family members were all in Bethlehem, and family was everything. Family and tribe were absolutely paramount to the identity of people in ancient Israel. It is still that way throughout Israel and much of the Arab world as well. Even today, an Arab or Jewish child's name reflects the family, tribe, and region they come from. Even the parents' names change as soon as they have a child. With a child, the parents' identity is altered to reflect their offspring.

In the Jewish tradition, a young man is referred to as the son of his father. For example, Jonah Ben-Jeffrey means Jonah the son of Jeffrey. And in Arabic culture, it gets flipped around– Jeffrey would be called Abu Jonah, Father of Jonah. These familial and tribal connections, even today, are much more important than nationalism and other loyalties. The

---

[57] 2 Sam. 7:8–16; Ps. 89:3–4.

first loyalty is to family, and then to your tribe. Everything else is a distant consideration.

Religion permeates all of this, but even the religions of Islam and Judaism emphasized family and tribal commitments as only a short step below commitment to the Almighty. Islam and Judaism are fundamentally built on the family and protecting the tribe.

While Mary and Joseph were a disgrace to many of their relatives, don't you think someone in the family would take pity on them? Would you have shown them hospitality? Would you have shown them grace? Would someone, say a close relative who manages an inn, give them a place to shelter for the night?

I think so.

In tribal and nomadic cultures such as Islam and Judaism, welcoming someone in need and showing them hospitality is a requirement built into the religion, tradition, and culture.

According to the Old Covenant laws, you could not turn away any stranger or traveler who sought comfort.[58]

Pretend that you are the innkeeper on this cold evening and before you is a young woman in labor, grimacing in pain, convulsing with birth pangs, drenched in sweat and breathing erratically. A desperate husband stands beside her. Her protector.

What does the law tell you to do? What does tradition tell you to do? What does your heart tell you to do?

Perhaps, as that innkeeper, you could cover all your bases with a compromise. You could refuse formal shelter to the disgraced couple, thereby showing your commitment to the law, but also give them a little food and informal shelter, thereby demonstrating your adherence to another law.

Don't think this is a complicated way of thinking. This is the way it was done and is still done throughout the Middle East. This line of thinking, reasoning, consideration, and balance with your

[58] Lev. 19; Exod. 23; Deut. 10; Mal. 3; Exod. 12; Jer. 22; Isa. 58; Prov. 19 (and more).

faith tradition is entwined with every decision made throughout the day.

I lament the fact that we have separated ourselves from this way of thinking. Western Christians have gone out of our way, at our own expense, to separate our faith life from our daily life. The two are not intricately intertwined as with other faith traditions. In fact, we pride ourselves on being able to separate the two. Throughout history, we have separated ourselves from these other traditions, and in our haste to identify our uniqueness, we have lost so many of the stories and truths that are meaningful.

Western Christians have deliberately and with calculation buried the fact that our faith roots are in Judaism. We occasionally give it lip service, but if we truly honored this fact, we would work harder to uncover the stories of old that still have meaning for us today.

Many Protestants distance themselves too far from the Jewish traditions and have gone out of their way to distance themselves from the Greek Orthodox and Catholic Churches, as well. While the Protestant faith tradition does not hold Mary to be perfect and holy, it sure hasn't given her the respect or reverence she deserves as Yeshua's mother.

I invite you to take a pause and ponder this in your heart for a few minutes.

This young girl brought the Savior of the world into existence, grew him inside her body, nursed him, raised him, struggled to understand the enormity of it all, and eventually watched him beaten, abused, and murdered on a cross.

Mary's story is incredible while also mundane. Like every mother's story.

This story concludes with a young man rising from the grave and visiting his mother again, complete with stigmata, to bring her comfort and closure to the drama into which she was thrust into many years before.

II. Finding Your Tribe

America is the world's salad bowl. This is a beautiful thing. We are all Americans. But what does it mean to be an American? It means many different things to many different people.

We are no longer tribal in the ancient sense. So we create our own tribes. Unfortunately, most of the tribes we create are superficial and nonsensical and lack the unifying and protective aspect that make tribes valuable.

- Democrat
- Republican
- Libertarian
- Packers fan
- Bears fan
- Black
- White
- Gay
- Straight

Instead of our new modern tribes being vehicles for unity and purpose, they are used to divide and pit us against each other.

As a soldier, I was prepared to give up my life for every one of these tribes. In the military, to build a cohesive fighting force, we first orient each recruit and integrate them into a tribe.

Tribe matters. My first tribe was the Rangers. Our tribal motto was "Rangers Lead the Way." My second tribe was the Special Forces with the motto "De Oppresso Liber" ("Free the Oppressed"). My third tribe was Delta Force. Our tribal motto was "Oppressors Beware." I paid dearly to join these tribes. We protected each other.

I will die as a member of these tribes.

I am also a member of the tribe led by the Lion of Judah. Our tribal motto is all of the above: Yeshua Leads the Way. He Frees the Oppressed, and Oppressors Should Beware of Him.

Family still matters as much as ever. I am proud to be called Abu Jonah. I am proud to be called Abu Aaron. These are my sons, whom I love, and with whom I am well pleased.

8

SEIZE THE HIGH GROUND

SPECIAL FORCES SHEPHERDS:
HOLDING THE HIGH GROUND

CHAPTER 8

I. Seize the High Ground

Now it's up to you. Be on your toes—both for yourselves and your congregation of sheep. The Holy Spirit has put you in charge of these people— God's people they are—to guard and protect them. God himself thought they were worth dying for. (Acts 20:28, MSG)

"Is this the guy?" I asked.

"We're not sure. It looks like him. Hard to tell," the Team Leader, replied.

We hovered over the sleeping man, trying to figure out if this was the Al Qaeda terrorist we came for. There were about five men sleeping on the roof, about a half dozen women, and a few kids too.

It was a kill mission, but we didn't want to kill the wrong guy.

Mark, the Sergeant Major, came over and said, "That's not him. Look at his mustache. Too small."

"Any other distinguishing features we looking for?" I asked.

Mark shook his head. "Don't think so."

Two teams moved off the roof and began clearing the structure. Another team continued to examine each man sleeping on the roof trying to narrow it down. Andy reached under the main suspect's pillow and pulled out a pistol and a cell phone. That was another strike against this guy. They flipped the phone open and handed it to our commo guy. If the phone belonged to the man we were looking for, it was a death sentence. It would take a few minutes to figure it out.

Was this our guy or not?

Special Forces Shepherds: Holding the High Ground

Sitting in my house one quiet Christmas morning, drinking my first cup of coffee of the day, I thought again about Mary, the journey she had to endure, and the shepherds who were in the fields that frigid night. We sing about these shepherds, and we marvel at the revelation of the angels to this lowly group of men. We are comforted by the fact these simple men were included in the Christmas story and invited to be the first to visit and witness the Messiah.

My first year living in Israel, I remember kind of praying, kind of thinking, kind of listening, but definitely asking some questions:

Why these shepherds?
Why this location?
How did they know where specifically to find the baby?

For those of you who are not familiar with the story, I will let Luke tell it:

> *And there were shepherds living out in the fields nearby, keeping watch over their flocks at night. An angel of the Lord appeared to them, and the glory of the Lord shone around them, and they were terrified. But the angel said to them, "Do not be afraid. I bring you good news that will cause great joy for all the people.*

Today in the town of David a Savior has been born to you; he is the Messiah, the Lord. This will be a sign to you: You will find a baby wrapped in cloths and lying in a manger." Suddenly a great company of the heavenly host appeared with the angel, praising God and saying, "Glory to God in the highest heaven, and on earth peace to those on whom his favor rests."

When the angels had left them and gone into heaven, the shepherds said to one another, "Let's go to Bethlehem and see this thing that has happened, which the Lord has told us about." So they hurried off and found Mary and Joseph, and the baby, who was lying in the manger.

When they had seen him, they spread the word concerning what had been told them about this child, and all who heard it were amazed at what the shepherds said to them. But Mary treasured up all these things and pondered them in her heart. The shepherds returned, glorifying and praising God for all the things they had heard and seen, which were just as they had been told.[59] (Luke 2: 8-20) NIV

More to the Story

How many times have you heard this story? Even if this is your first time, did you wonder why the angel chose these specific shepherds to speak with? What was so important about *these* particular men and *these* specific fields they tended with their sheep?

As a child, I was taught that there was no great significance to the shepherds chosen to be the first to see Yeshua the day he entered this world. Like what I was taught about Mary, I was told these shepherds were men of low stature, unimportant, and that being chosen with this incredible honor was representative of how God is calling all of us. He wants even the least of us to feel important to Him.

It feels good to say that, but I have to say that answer is bullshit. These shepherds were special, and the location was specific, precise. People who lived during those times would have recognized the seemingly odd little details of this story.

---

[59] Luke 2:8–20 (New International Version).

These were not random men the angel happened upon; they were not simple, lowly shepherds. These were specially selected and specially trained temple shepherds, known as the Levitical Shepherds, who were watching for the unblemished sacrificial Passover lamb.[60]

These were Special Forces shepherds.

The Shepherd's Fields on the outskirts of Bethlehem are the same fields that King David watched over as a young man. These were the fields where he practiced his sniper sling. These are the fields where he killed a lion and a bear. These were the fields he departed from to bring his brother's food in Elah Valley before he confronted Goliath. These were the fields that David was expected to return to but found himself in the king's court instead. These specially designated fields were where the Passover lamb and the other special sacrificial animals were born and raised.

The shepherds there were the best of the best.

These shepherds were selected for their boldness, discipline and attention to detail. They were tasked

---

[60] Alfred Edersheim, *The Life and Times of Jesus the Messiah* (London: Longmans, Green, 1886).

with identifying and protecting the lambs worthy to be brought to the temple for inspection and ultimately sacrificed to atone for the people. They took exceptional care of each birth, bringing the pregnant ewes to a special place. The shepherds would immediately inspect the newborn lamb for any blemishes or imperfections and then wrap the lamb in swaddling clothes and lay it in a manger for safekeeping.[61]

I want to say this again, the unblemished lambs were wrapped in *swaddling clothes* and *laid in a manger*.

These *perfect* lambs were wrapped in swaddling clothes so that they would not thrash around and injure themselves or suffer any injury or broken bones. The swaddling clothes were used to quiet and comfort the lamb after it was inspected. These were the same swaddling clothes that Mary made from the worn-out priestly garments.

For generations, these special temple shepherds were keeping watch for the Paschal lamb: inspecting it, selecting it, and raising it in purity until the time of sacrifice would draw near. When the time came for

---

[61] Alfred Edersheim, *Sketches of Jewish Social Life in the Days of Christ* (New York: James Pott & Co., 1876).

that lamb to be slain, the shepherds would bring it to Jerusalem where the elders and high priests would inspect it. By law, it would undergo three examinations, and if still found without blemish, only then would it be assigned as the ultimate sacrifice for the people of Israel.

The angels announced to the shepherds that the baby could be found wrapped in cloths or swaddling clothes and lying in a manger.

Have you ever wondered how the shepherds knew where to go? How many mangers do you think there were in Bethlehem? What if there is the slightest oversight in the translation that has slipped through over the years?

What if verse 12 reads,

> *This will be a sign to you: You will find a baby wrapped in cloths and lying in* **THE** *Manger.*

There were many plain and simple mangers throughout Bethlehem and in Israel, but was there one manger that was special, known as The Manger?

This special manger was at a place called Migdal Eder. Translated into English, Migdal Eder means the Tower of the Flock. It was built to overwatch the temple fields. Inside the tower was a birthing place known as The Manger. This was a renowned and revered spot, a place that the shepherds would definitely recognize. It was the place where the ewes were brought to give birth and where the pure lambs were wrapped in swaddling clothes to be laid in The Manger.[62]

At first the angels did not say where the child was, but later they gave very specific directions: he is in the town of David (Bethlehem) lying in The Manger (at Migdal Eder).
While researching this book, I imagined myself standing upon Migdal Eder. I thought about what it would be like, how the terrain would appear.

Designed to watch over the Temple Fields, the Tower of the Flock would be at the highest point of the terrain. Towers are not built on the low ground or even on the second-highest point in a region. If they

---

[62] "Migdal Eder and the Birth of Christ," Bible Things in Bible Ways, May 21, 2020, https://biblethingsinbibleways.wordpress.com/2020/05/21/migdal-eder-and-the-birth-of-christ/.

are designed to be watchtowers, then they are built where they have the greatest field of view.

They are built so no lion, bear, or thief can sneak up on an unsuspecting flock of sheep.
The shepherd stood watch, ready to battle any threat. At all times, a shepherd sniper would be in the tower keeping watch, weapon at hand.
The Church of the Nativity is historically acknowledged to lie in the exact spot where Yeshua was born and therefore must have been built over Migdal Eder.[63]

One night, from my home in the US, I woke up from a sound sleep with a thought that I could not shake. If the Church of the Nativity is where Yeshua was born, and Yeshua was born at Migdal Eder, then this would be an easy test.

Is the Church of the Nativity the high ground in Bethlehem or not? I remembered going up to the church, but I did not remember if it was the actual high ground.

---

[63] "Birthplace of Jesus: Church of the Nativity and the Pilgrimage Route," UNESCO, accessed March 20, 2023, https://whc.unesco.org/en/list/1433/.

There was a pit in my stomach. My gut was telling me that this story was true, but it was testable. If the church ended up not to be the high point, what else was I getting wrong?

I got up, booted up my computer and searched some topographical maps that included elevation markers. I was relieved to see that the church appeared to be the high point. I was temporarily satisfied.

With a return visit to Israel planned, I added this reconnaissance to my list of important things to check out.

Months later, I returned to Bethlehem to confirm my assumptions and visit the church. The ongoing renovations brought tears to my eyes. The old church from my memories had been dark with centuries of soot built up along the walls and ceiling. Now, the mosaics and paintings looked brand new. The story of this place was fresh and new, ready to be shared with a new generation.

I visited the grotto cave, underneath the Church of the Nativity,[64] built over the very spot where Yeshua was

---

[64] https://en.wikipedia.org/wiki/Church_of_the_Nativity

born. I returned to the Tomb of the Innocents where the babies slaughtered by Herod are commemorated.

Then I climbed the stairs out of the crypt, crossed a courtyard, and began climbing up to the roof of the church. The stairs ended, and all that remained was a ladder, which I also climbed. I was a little nervous as I peeked over the edge. Finally, I was on the rooftop.

The moment of truth.

I looked out across the land as it stretched below me. I stood at the highest point in this region, right where Migdal Eder would have been overlooking the temple's flock. A sense of relief, awe, and inspiration overwhelmed me as I stood in reverence.

All these details are important because they demonstrate a direct fulfillment of old Jewish tradition, prophecy, and expectation. Even early Christian writers like Eusebius wrote of the significance of these details only a few hundred years after Yeshua's life.[65] Scholars, writers, rabbis, and theologians have been discussing these details for a

---

[65] Eusebius Pamphilus, *Eusebius' Ecclesiastical History*, trans. C. F. Cruse (Peabody, MA: Hendrickson Publishers, 1998). , https://en.wikipedia.org/wiki/Church_of_the_Nativity

long time. I suspect that at one time, this was a "no-brainer," as everyone understood the significance of the location of Yeshua's birth and all the specific details included in the story.

Now you know more about the story that you were taught in church. I can't say that it is "the rest of the story" because, most likely, in the future there will be much more revealed to us.

If you read, study, pray, and test out the ideas revealed to you, you will find it is an adventure worth taking.

II. Seize the High Ground

A few blocks away from the target building, we quietly exited the vehicles, unhooked the ladders from the sides of the vehicles, and prepared to climb. We weaved our way through the parked cars until we got to the base of the first building we needed to scale. Gaining the high ground can be difficult in crowded cities like Baghdad, sometimes we had to pull out the ladders.

The first man on the ladder was all alone, facing whatever was in front of him by himself until the rest of the team could scale the building and get into position.

In the summer months, families in Iraq would sleep on their rooftops, trying to take advantage of any cool breeze that may drift by in the night. When we saw people sleeping on the roof, we knew that we could access the main house without having to blow our way in with explosives.

We could climb quietly, gain access to the roof, and simply creep into the target building without making any fuss with a noisy breach. These were some of my favorite raids.

That last step before peeking over the roof ledge always carried some nervous energy for everyone. We would gather on the rooftop in our battle gear, including our helmets, antennas, and night vision goggles, making us look like creatures from outer space. The night vision goggles gave off a faint green glow that simply added to the extraterrestrial appearance.

We would search for the target individual with our infrared flashlights, sometimes standing over him as he slept, comparing him with any photo we had. We would look at him. Then look at the photo. Then look at him again. Get a second opinion. Is it him? I think so. I'm not sure.

If we reached a deadlock, we could always wake up a woman or child nearby and ask them. Once confirmed, we could cuff him in his sleep, walk him downstairs and be on our way. No muss. No fuss.

A successful capture mission without firing a shot was always a good night. But things did not always go as planned. A gunfight could erupt at any time.

"Well, this looks like our man," our commo guy confidently announced.

The man beneath us was likely our target. As we stood over him, a woman sat up and the young boy in her arms was awakened by her sudden movement. She looked at us in the dark, rubbed her eyes, and simply sat there, not sure what we she was seeing. We looked like monsters in the dark, strange silhouettes with green glowing eyes. The boy looked at us wide-eyed and then hid his head in the folds of his mother's dress and blanket. We pointed at the sleeping man that we believed was our target. "Is this Abu Anas?" we asked. The woman shook her head "no" and pointed over her left shoulder.

Andy walked over to where she was pointing and stood over another sleeping Military Aged Male (MAM). He looked very much like the other man. Andy pointed down at the sleeping man as our interpreter said to the woman quietly, "Is that Abu Anas?"

"Are you sure that's him?" I asked again.

She nodded her head and said, "Abu Anas. Very bad. Abu Anas. Al Qaeda. Very bad."

"Thank you," I said. "Go back to sleep."

The woman turned over, repositioned her son, and pulled the blanket over both of their heads.

Andy reached under the pillow but nothing was there. We stared at Abu Anas for a little while longer but finally came to a consensus that this was our guy. We figured he must have forced the other man to sleep with his pistol and cell phone.

Nice try.

Andy put steel handcuffs on the man before he even woke up. He didn't make a sound. We put a blindfold hood over his head and walked him across the other sleeping bodies, through the cupola and down the stairs into the target building. He would be interrogated there.

He was our guy.

We were sure of it.

Seizing the high ground has been a basic military tactic since time began. Make your opponent fight uphill.

From the high ground you can see the battlefield below and you can make better and more informed decisions.

In modern warfare, we work hard to seize the high ground in different ways. The most basic way, and where the United States is unparalleled, is in our ability to control the sky. The only high ground beyond the sky is outer space, and look at the race between nations to have influence there. Just a few years ago, the US created the Space Force. We definitely want to control the high ground.

In more terrestrial terms, combat operations in Iraq and Afghanistan relied heavily on Intelligence, Surveillance, and Reconnaissance (ISR) platforms like Predator drones to be able to see the battlefield. We also relied on helicopters to put us on rooftops so we could fight downhill. Another reason to fight from the roof is to give your adversary an opportunity to evacuate the building. If you fight from the ground up and force your enemy to the top floor, this can cause them to feel trapped and they are more likely to fight to the death, feeling they have no other options.

Whenever possible, we want our side of the gunfight to go from the top down and flush any combatants out into the open where they run into a trap. The trap is designed to force them to surrender, or for them to receive immediate justice.

I am comforted by knowing that Yahweh holds the high ground. He can see the battlefield below. He doesn't want to force us into a situation where we feel desperate and trapped. He always gives us a way out. We can simply drop to our knees and surrender to Him.

Once we surrender to Him, He will not put handcuffs on us and force us to go with Him. He will not throw us in a jail cell and interrogate us. Instead, He will pull us to our feet, dust us off, and invite us to follow Him. He offers us something to eat and to drink. He offers us rest.

He offers us peace.

9

EVIL CANNOT WIN

MURDER OF THE INNOCENTS:
EVIL IS NOT ETERNAL

CHAPTER 9

I. Evil Cannot Win

Don't you see that children are God's best gift? (Psalm 127:3, MSG)

"Sergeant Major Soran's niece and nephew are missing. He thinks they were kidnapped by Al Qaeda and he's asking for our help to find them," Jamey said.

"When did they go missing?" I asked.

"Yesterday. They're his brother's kids, a boy and a girl. He's expecting a ransom call today, no later than tomorrow. Wants to know if we can track the call."

"No problem," I said. "Get him anything he needs."

The kidnappers called and demanded a ransom. The deadline was seventy two hours. If the ransom was not paid, they would kill one of the kids. Twenty-four hours after that and they would either kill both kids or sell them as sex slaves. Both kids were around eleven years old.

Kidnapping for ransom was a common way to raise money for Al Qaeda, but usually they didn't mess with the families of our partner forces. We figured they made a mistake and didn't know the kids were related to Soran. Regardless, they would pay dearly for this mistake.

After the ransom call, we hustled to try to find the kids but when I asked my boss for permission to use some of the sophisticated assets we had at our disposal, I was curtly denied. The commander calmly told me that we were not in Iraq to rescue kids from sex trafficking and our technology and equipment needed to remain focused on counter terrorism instead.

I understood from one perspective, but in another way, I was floored. These were real, live kids. We'd spend millions of dollars and hundreds of man-hours dedicated to finding some dirt farmer that might lead us to another Al Qaeda leader but we wouldn't help save these kids?

Refusing to take no as an answer, I spun the request from a plea to find two kids into a logical explanation of how this would build rapport with our partners. These guys were our partners. They laid their lives on the line for us every night and we did the same for them. Helping them recover these kids would go a long way in demonstrating our commitment to them and they would owe us one. Sergeant Major Soran was a true friend and a brave warrior.

This approach resonated with the commander and he gave us twenty four hours to find the kids. When the clock ran out, wherever we were at in the case, he demanded the assets return to the main mission.

We stopped everything else we were doing and committed ourselves to finding and recovering these two children. They were out there somewhere and we were their only hope.

Time was running out.

Murder of the Innocents: Evil is not Eternal

We don't know very much about Yeshua's infancy or childhood. We know that Herod tried to kill him and that he escaped to Egypt with Mary and Joseph before

Herod's soldiers swept through Bethlehem and murdered all the baby boys under the age of two. This dramatic story is largely underplayed by the gospel writers and leads off with the visit from the Wise Men (Magi).

> *After Jesus was born in Bethlehem in Judea, during the time of King Herod, Magi from the east came to Jerusalem and asked, "Where is the one who has been born king of the Jews? We saw his star when it rose and have come to worship him."*
>
> *When King Herod heard this he was disturbed, and all Jerusalem with him. When he had called together all the people's chief priests and teachers of the law, he asked them where the Messiah was to be born. "In Bethlehem in Judea," they replied, "for this is what the prophet has written:*
>
> *"'But you, Bethlehem, in the land of Judah, are by no means least among the rulers of Judah; for out of you will come a ruler who will shepherd my people Israel.'*
>
> *Then Herod called the Magi secretly and found out from them the exact time the star had*

appeared. He sent them to Bethlehem and said, "Go and search carefully for the child. As soon as you find him, report to me, so that I too may go and worship him."

After they had heard the king, they went on their way, and the star they had seen when it rose went ahead of them until it stopped over the place where the child was. When they saw the star, they were overjoyed. On coming to the house, they saw the child with his mother Mary, and they bowed down and worshiped him. Then they opened their treasures and presented him with gifts of gold, frankincense and myrrh. And having been warned in a dream not to go back to Herod, they returned to their country by another route.

When they had gone, an angel of the Lord appeared to Joseph in a dream. "Get up," he said, "take the child and his mother and escape to Egypt. Stay there until I tell you, for Herod is going to search for the child to kill him."

So he got up, took the child and his mother during the night and left for Egypt, where he stayed until the death of Herod. And so was fulfilled what the

Lord had said through the prophet: "Out of Egypt I called my son."

When Herod realized that he had been outwitted by the Magi, he was furious, and he gave orders to kill all the boys in Bethlehem and its vicinity who were two years old and under, in accordance with the time he had learned from the Magi.[66](Matthew 2: 1-16, NIV)

More to the Story

Some scholars don't believe that this massacre actually occurred, because there aren't any accounts of it outside of the Bible. But if we take into consideration all of Herod's atrocities, it's just a matter of scale.

Killing a few babies just didn't make the cut.

The population of Bethlehem at the time of Jesus's birth is estimated to be between 300-500 people.[67] The

---

[66] Matt. 2:1–16 (New International Version).
[67] Gordon Franz, "The Slaughter of the Innocents: Historical Fact or Legendary Fiction?," Associates for Biblical Research, December 8, 2009, https://biblearchaeology.org/research/chronological-categories/life-and-ministry-of-jesus-and-apostles/2411-the-slaughter-of-the-innocents-historical-fact-or-legendary-fiction; Paul Maier, "Truth or Fiction: Did Herod Really Slaughter Baby Boys in Bethlehem?," December 22, 2015, in *Ask Pastor John*, podcast, 12:46,

number of male children in Bethlehem under two years old would have been about six or seven, with about another dozen or so in the surrounding area. This low number is a likely explanation for why there is no historical evidence of this slaughter occurring.

Simply put, a handful of children killed by Herod, a ruthless ruler, was not noteworthy enough. This gives you a pretty good idea of the value of a life back then, especially a child's life.

II. Evil Cannot Win

We should not feel too sanctimonious about how "advanced" we are today, that nothing like this could ever happen now, and if it did happen, even on a small scale, it would definitely make headline news.

The value a life holds in most of the western world today is not consistent across the globe and it can change depending on circumstances, especially hardship. During war, we witness the worst of

https://www.desiringgod.org/interviews/truth-or-fiction-did-herod-really-slaughter-baby-boys-in-bethlehem.

mankind and sometimes we get to observe the best of mankind.

I have seen men hide behind women and children as they continued to try to shoot us, using their family members as human shields. I'll never forget the first time I told my team over the radio to "shoot around the kids." It was easier to say the second time. By the third time, it became Standard Operating Procedure (SOP): shoot around the kids.

More than once, I have stood before a man as he held an infant in his arms, threatening to bash the child against a wall or onto the hard ground beneath his feet.

I have been confronted by a man with a knife held to the throat of an infant, threatening to cut the child's head off if I did not allow him to escape.

Unfortunately, we bury stories like this and let the atrocities of our enemies slide into oblivion. At the same time, we have a tendency to levy charges against our own people that are not only unfounded, but part of our enemy's plan to bog us down, create infighting, and ultimately claim victory.

On several occasions during the wars in Iraq and Afghanistan, I tried to get the word out about the barbaric, monstrous, and cowardly tactics our enemies used. I could never get any traction to share the stories.

It is my sincere belief that if we had advertised the atrocities, abuses, and sexual deviancy of the Taliban, ISIS, and Al Qaeda, we could have settled those wars a long time ago.

I am now going to share with you a report I wrote about the Taliban. It is written in the military style with no emotion and just the facts. I am redacting a few details but otherwise, it is pretty much how I initially wrote it. This all happened over the course of seven days, one week in Afghanistan.

Using Infants As Human Shields

- In the past week we've seen three separate incidents where Military Aged Males (MAMs) hid behind infants in order to protect themselves. We've seen this before in the past, but the consistency we've seen lately is alarming. This disturbing trend can be used to

highlight the cowardice and
dishonor of the Taliban.

- The primary target exited his
residence with an infant in his arms
and began to walk away from the
entire target complex. He was
surrounded by two women and three
children in addition to the infant he
held in front of him as an apparent
shield. He disregarded instructions
from the interpreter on the bullhorn
and his reaction to warning shots
was to extend the baby in his arms as
a hostage. Ultimately, the assault
force closed on the primary target
and detained him, returning the
infant to its mother.

- Taliban were observing us in the
target area and reporting on our
movement. A military aged male
with an ICOM radio was on a roof
of an adjacent compound building
that was approximately 800 meters
away. Sniper warning shots in his
vicinity convinced him to leave the

roof. Moments later, he returned with the ICOM radio in one hand and holding an infant in the other. He remained on the roof, reporting our movements up until we conducted exfil. The infant never left his side.

- An interdiction was conducted on 2x MAMs just outside of a small structure. The MAMs fled the scene, dumping weapons as they ran and entered the structure. After surrounding the compound, the primary target exited the structure holding an infant in front of him. A red dot laser was on the MAM, and he continued to place the infant so the red dot was on the infant instead of on himself. The women on the target were very upset that this man grabbed one of their children as a human shield.

- Taliban ordered spotters to drive toward the target and report on what we were doing. Numerous motorcycles drove near to us, on two of the motorcycles, the driver was holding an infant in his lap as he approached our position. After a while, different motos could be identified with the same infant. Apparently, they were meeting at a location beyond our field of view and handing off the infant for cover.

- An interdiction was conducted outside of a compound that resulted in 5x enemy killed in action. A MAM from the compound interacted with our target so the compound was contained and surrounded. After being surrounded, the MAM of primary interset exited the structure holding an infant in his arms. He would hold it tight and then extend the infant whenever a weapon was pointed in his direction.

This all happened in the span of one week. I reported this to my chain of command and also to the Public Affairs Officer (PAO).

Nobody was interested. The war marched on.

Shocking stories? I hope so.

It is easy to judge these wicked men overseas, but what about right here in America? What is the value of a child or a young woman?

Since retiring from the military, I have worked tirelessly to free the oppressed. I have helped build organizations to defend women and children and seek justice for evil men.

Right this minute, you can order up a girl on the open Internet and have her delivered to wherever you are, just like you would order a pizza. What type of "toppings" would you like? These girls can be purchased for around $100, even less if you haggle well.

My heart breaks at the thought of a priceless young girl or child for sale. For sale at the cost of a simple meal. One meal.

Most people are completely unaware or don't understand that this is happening at an unimaginable scale, right here in the modern western world. But it begins to make sense when you think about how we have literally put a price on everything. Everything.

If my heart breaks at the thought of this, how do you think our Creator feels about it? He sent His son to purchase all of us back to Him. We are redeemed. At one price. The same price for each one of us.

Yeshua's sacrifice is the once and for all atonement for us. We have been purchased with his blood. Do not lose heart, regardless of the wickedness and evil, apathy and indifference. Evil does not outlive this creation.[68]

Love wins in the end.

I am sure of it.

---

[68] Rev. 11; Rev. 20; Rev. 21; Rom. 8; John 16.

GRIEF. GRATITUDE. RELIEF

CHRIST AS CATECHUMEN:
STUDENT BEFORE TEACHER

CHAPTER 10

I. Grief. Gratitude. Relief.

> *Jesus matured, growing up in both body and spirit, blessed by both God and people. (Luke 2:41-52, MSG).*

I joined the US Army in 1987 and went to Fort Benning, Georgia. The first time I got onto an airplane was to fly south and begin my life as a soldier. I had no idea what to expect.

After a warm welcome, a fresh new haircut, and plenty of "team building," I became Private Tiegs. I would return to Fort Benning many more times throughout the years for Airborne School, Sniper

School, Ranger School, the Officer's Basic Course, the Officer's Advanced Course, Best Ranger Competitions and much more. Each time I was at Fort Benning, I was being molded into something new. I was testing myself, proving to myself and to others that I "had what it takes."

A few years ago I returned to Ft. Benning to speak at the Officer's Advanced Course. I was a retired Lieutenant Colonel who had concluded my service at the legendary Delta Force. I had fought in wars all across the globe. I had literally done everything a soldier can do. And not only had I survived war, I had mastered it.

All of this was something Private Tiegs could never have imagined.

I drove to where I went through Basic Training. It's all gone now. Built over with modern buildings or lost to nature. I stopped at the place where I underwent the grueling Ranger Indoctrination Program (RIP). It's all gone now, too. All that remains are some patches of red Georgia clay where nothing will grow. These patches of clay are poisoned with broken dreams, fear, and failure that overtook many Ranger candidates. This heartbreak seeped out of their bodies into the earth beneath them. killing the grass and staining the red clay even more crimson.

I drove out past Ranger School to some of the training areas where I was taught, trained, and tested. To my surprise, I was overcome with emotion. I literally sat in my car and cried. The emotion was heavy, mixed up, and confusing. I had survived the worst of war. I felt relieved. But the sadness was mixed in, and at times overpoweringly so. I felt deep sadness for dead friends and the lost memories that now lie buried under many layers of the past.

But I felt incredibly grateful, too. I said aloud to no one present, "Thank you." Thank you to that Drill Sergeant, the Airborne Black Hat, the Ranger Cadre, the Sniper stalkers. Thank you for taking the time to prepare me. Test me. You set out to create a soldier who would not only survive in combat, but keep his mates alive. And win.

Grief. Gratitude. Relief.

It was a hard life. Harder than I can even describe or explain. The sacrifice was almost unbearable. Some of the trauma I carry alone.

But some of it still weighs on my wife.

And my two sons.

Christ as Catechumen: Student before Teacher

We don't know what happened to Yeshua when he went to hide in Egypt. We do know that after a few years he eventually returned from Egypt to live in Nazareth. Mary and Joseph did not raise Yeshua in Bethlehem. Perhaps this was because even though Herod the Great was dead, nobody was quite sure how his sons would behave. Herod Archelaus, ruler in the north, seemed to be less volatile and dangerous than his brother Herod Antipas in the south, so it made sense to steer clear of him.[69]

---

[69] Flavius Josephus, *The Antiquities of the Jews*, trans. William Whiston (Blacksburg, VA: Unabridged Books, 2011); Flavius Josephus, *The Jewish War: Revised Edition*, trans. G. A. Williamson (London: Penguin Books, 1959). https://en.wikipedia.org/wiki/Antiquities_of_the_Jews.Antiquities of the Jews is a 20-volume historiographical work, written in Greek, by historian Flavius Josephus. This work, along with Josephus's other major work, The Jewish War (De Bello Iudaico), provides valuable background material for historians wishing to understand 1st-century AD Judaism and the early Christian period.

Like every kid, Yeshua went to school, did chores, and learned a trade. There is only a brief verse in Luke about Yeshua's time as a student:

> *When Joseph and Mary had done everything required by the Law of the Lord, they returned to Galilee to their own town of Nazareth. And the child grew and became strong; he was filled with wisdom, and the grace of God was on him.*[70] *(Luke 2: 39-40,NIV)*

Most of the non-canonical accounts of Yeshua as a child in Nazareth portray him as precocious, even spiteful, as he came to terms with some of his extraordinary gifts.[71] But I find it hard to believe that Yeshua was ever precocious or spiteful. We can only make logical guesses about what life was like for everyone in his family.[72]

---

[70] Luke 2:39–40 (New International Version).
[71] The Infancy Gospel of Thomas.
https://en.wikipedia.org/wiki/Infancy_Gospel_of_Thomas. The Infancy Gospel of Thomas is a biographical gospel about the childhood of Jesus, believed to date at the latest to the second century.
[72] https://en.wikipedia.org/wiki/Christ_the_Lord:_Out_of_Egypt. Anne Rice, *Christ the Lord: Out of Egypt* (New York: Ballantine Books, 2005). Christ the Lord: Out of Egypt (2005) is a book by Anne Rice that depicts the life of Jesus Christ at the age of 7 to 8. Rice wrote the novel after returning to the Catholic Church in 1998.

The only real glimpse we have of Yeshua as a boy in Israel is when his family traveled to Jerusalem for the Passover. Luke records the story this way:

> *Every year Jesus' parents traveled to Jerusalem for the Feast of Passover. When he was twelve years old, they went up as they always did for the Feast. When it was over and they left for home, the child Jesus stayed behind in Jerusalem, but his parents didn't know it. Thinking he was somewhere in the company of pilgrims, they journeyed for a whole day and then began looking for him among relatives and neighbors. When they didn't find him, they went back to Jerusalem looking for him.*
>
> *The next day they found him in the Temple seated among the teachers, listening to them and asking questions. The teachers were all quite taken with him, impressed with the sharpness of his answers. But his parents were not impressed; they were upset and hurt.*
>
> *His mother said, "Young man, why have you done this to us? Your father and I have been half out of our minds looking for you."*

He said, "Why were you looking for me? Didn't you know that I had to be here, dealing with the things of my Father?" But they had no idea what he was talking about.

So he went back to Nazareth with them, and lived obediently with them. His mother held these things dearly, deep within herself. And Jesus matured, growing up in both body and spirit, blessed by both God and people.[73] (Luke 2:41-52, MSG)

More to the Story

We know quite a bit about the way boys were raised in Jewish homes in the first century.[74] In school, Yeshua learned to memorize Scripture and became fluent in Hebrew, Aramaic, and Greek. He even might have sat next to his cousin John.

We don't have any accounts of John the Baptizer and Yeshua meeting before his baptism, but it must have happened, since they were cousins, and their families were close.

---

[73] Luke 2:41–52 (The Message).
[74] See the Bibliography at the end of this book

Did Yeshua's extended family really believe that he was destined to become the deliverer of Israel? How was Yeshua as a student? As a carpenter's apprentice? As a friend?

Yeshua learned how to be a carpenter, or builder, from his dad, and accompanied Joseph on local jobs. Much of the city of Sepphoris was built during this time.[75] From Nazareth, it was a hilly but beautiful five kilometer walk to work for Joseph, Yeshua, his brothers, and any other workers making the commute to Sepphoris on foot.

Work was essential but learning was even more critical to the Jewish culture then.

At different ages in their development, young Jewish boys were required to choose a piece of Scripture that would be "theirs" to act as a guide they could refer to throughout their education.

---

[75] "Sepphoris," BiblePlaces.com, accessed March 20, 2023, https://www.bibleplaces.com/sepphoris/; Paula Fredriksen and Eric Meyers, "The Surprises of Sepphoris," *From Jesus to Christ*, Frontline, accessed March 20, 2023, https://www.pbs.org/wgbh/pages/frontline/shows/religion/jesus/sepphoris.html.

I have heard one tradition that asserts Yeshua chose the Prophet Isaiah:

> *The Spirit of the Sovereign Lord is on me, because the Lord has anointed me to proclaim good news to the poor. He has sent me to bind up the brokenhearted, to proclaim freedom for the captives.*[76] *(Isaiah 61:1, NIV)*

This makes sense because this is the verse we first heard Yeshua recite at the synagogue in Nazareth as he began his public ministry. After stating these lines in the synagogue, he boldly added, *"Today this scripture is fulfilled in your hearing."*[77] *(Luke 4:21) NIV*

This infuriated the people of Nazareth, who wouldn't accept that the boy they watched grow up in their own village could be the promised Messiah foretold by Isaiah. They were so angry that they drove him out of town and attempted to kill him by throwing him off a cliff.[78]

Not a great start to his ministry. But we know how this goes. People who watch us grow up have a hard time

---

[76] Isa. 61:1 (New International Version).
[77] Luke 4:21 (NIV).
[78] Luke 2:28–30.

ever seeing us for more than that child with doubts, failures, and insecurities.

Yeshua as a boy must have experienced all these things too.

He knew his purpose and he knew God was with him. When his parents feared he was lost, left behind in Jerusalem, Yeshua was steadfast in his mission.[79] Sadly for Mary, this would not be the last time Yeshua's mission would break her heart.

There must have been many other people, of whom we have no record, who poured into Yeshua. Teaching him. Training him. Developing him. Loving him.

Being the Christ didn't mean he didn't need help from others.

II. Grief. Gratitude. Relief.

When I think of Yeshua the boy, I think of his innocence. I think of his training and his testing. He was a student before he became a Teacher.

---

[79] Luke 2:41–52.

I feel gratitude for all the men and women who poured into him, shaping him to be the tender warrior he became.

I feel grief, gratitude, and relief that he grew into a man who would sacrifice it all for me. His sacrifice was almost unbearable. But he did it. For us.

Through him, we win.

When I was a newly tabbed young Specialist in the 1st Ranger Battalion, Sergeant First Class (SFC) Harvey Moore took me under his wing and developed me. I don't remember exactly how it started. I'm pretty sure it must have been tied to some sort of grueling competition where I was lucky enough to distinguish myself and he took notice. It was an odd arrangement; he was in Charlie Company and I was in Alpha Company. He was a legendary badass and greatly feared by most everyone. He had a deep scar running down the full length of the left side of his face allegedly due to a bar fight where a broken bottle was dragged across his face. In the Rangers, SFCs didn't pay Specialists any attention but SFC Moore bent the rules for me. He was a coach and mentor to me and he poured his expertise and toughness into me, creating a "hard"

Ranger. He was part of the Best Ranger Competition winning team in 1985 and placed in the top three in other years. He was hard. Being considered "hard" was the ultimate compliment back then. I was tough, but SFC Moore made me hard.

SFC Moore drowned in Antelope Lake, Utah in 1992 trying to save other Rangers when his helicopter crashed in the cold water.[80] He died trying to save others.

I will never forget him.

He shaped me as a man. He validated me as "hard."

This "hard" man is not ashamed to say that my eyes are leaking and my heart is aching as I write this and remember SFC Harvey Moore.

Harvey, I am looking forward to seeing you again some day in the world after this one.

---

[80] "1SG Harvey Moore,"" ARITS, accessed March 20, 2023, https://arits.org/index.php/biographies/80-training-accidents/327-1sg-harvey-moore.

HIDDEN IN PLAIN SIGHT

JOHN THE PROPHET:
SIGNS AND WONDERS

CHAPTER 11

I. Hidden in Plain Sight

This will be a sign to you. (Luke 2:12, NIV)

We didn't realize it right away but rounds were zinging through our aircraft. The thin skin of the C141 did little to slow anti-aircraft rounds from ripping through the fuselage. Nothing really mattered anymore. The jump door was open and the warm Caribbean air was filling the aircraft. We stared at the red light waiting for it to turn green. We just wanted out.

A man fell in front of us. Shot. But we didn't know it at the time. We thought he was being clumsy and tripped as the aircraft jostled left and right, way worse than any turbulence we'd ever experienced before. It wasn't until later that we found out that it was more than turbulence. The jet was dodging bullets and trying to find a straight line approach to the airfield below so it could drop its cargo of US Army Rangers and get the hell outta there.

The light turned green. The jumpmaster yelled, "Go! Go! Go!" Rangers shuffled to the door. I tried to keep it tight. Nut to butt. We stepped over the clumsy Ranger, gripped the door, and tumbled into the wind.

I felt the rush of warm air as I fell out of the aircraft jump door. Seconds later, my leg straps dug into my groin and my head jerked backwards as my parachute filled with air. I peeked up at it and it was open, fully open, everything looked good.

I looked back at the ground below me and didn't recognize a thing.

It was chaos. There were red and green tracers flying around and ricocheting everywhere. I was really confused and had to think hard about which color was ours. If you are wondering, our tracers and our allies' tracers are red while most of our enemies' are green. The Spectre gunship laid a direct line of red tracers right into the direction of our first target building but it was all still so confusing. We had done full-blown rehearsals in Florida just a few days prior on a mock-up site. But the site we rehearsed on was tiny compared to the real objective. For the rehearsal, a small tent depicted an airplane hangar. The actual scale of it all was truly overwhelming.

I was utterly confused.

I did not have much time to break the confusion or even think very much. After orienting myself to the battlefield, the ground rushed up to meet me and I crashed into the earth with a thud and a grunt. I whipped out the knife on my side and quickly cut myself out of the contraints of the parachute harness and hustled to pull my rifle from its case so I was armed. I felt alone and vulnerable and thought that all of Panama was coming after me. The eight foot elephant grass that enveloped me really made me feel isolated. Once I had my rifle in my hands, locked and loaded, I felt better, ready for whatever lay ahead.

Reviewing the aerial snapshot of the airfield that was fresh in my mind, I knew which direction I needed to go, and headed out in that direction, hacking my way through the tall grass.

"Bulldog," I stated.

"Bulldog," I repeated.

I needed my guys to recognize that it was me. No one could see me but you could definitely hear me slashing at the grass, clawing my way forward.

I finally broke out of the grass and began running toward the assembly area. Everytime my left foot hit the ground I said "Bulldog." This was the running password that we used to differentiate ourselves from the bad guys.

It was dark.

It was confusing.

I still felt utterly alone.

Bulldog.

Bulldog.

A firefight broke out on my right side. It was mostly on the way to the assembly area. I had to decide: do I continue directly to the assembly area or go get in a gunfight?

My job at the assembly area was to gather a team and go gain a foothold on the target building that was assigned to me.

I didn't want to get distracted by something small.

I needed to lead my team. They needed me.

I didn't know who was off to my right but I concluded that whoever it was, he needed me more. At least right now. I angled right and headed his way.

"Bulldog. Bulldog." I continued with every step.

I didn't want to get shot by my own guy.

I needed him to recognize that I was there to help.

"Bulldog. Bulldog."

John the Prophet: Signs and Wonders[81]

John the Baptizer was the GOAP.

He was the direct forerunner of Yeshua, preparing the way for him to be received by the world. John rose to prominence by not only harkening back to the prophets of old, but by pointing directly ahead to the coming Messiah. His messages were widely received and, although there are few detailed

---

[81] Heb. 2:4; Matt. 24:24.

accounts of his ministry, Yeshua referred to his cousin as the GOAP: the Greatest Of All Prophets.[82]

The story of a barren couple that ends up getting blessed with a child is one that is often repeated throughout the Old and New Covenants. John's parents, Zachariah and Elizabeth, were unable to conceive and for years prayed for a child. One day, an angel appeared, telling Zachariah that God had found favor in them and would bless them with a son who would one day be a prophet and the forerunner of the Messiah.

At the time, they were unaware that the Messiah would be born less than a year later to Elizabeth's cousin, Mary.

Here is the account about John's father from Luke:

> During the rule of Herod, King of Judea, there was a priest assigned service in the regiment of Abijah. His name was Zachariah. His wife was descended from the daughters of Aaron. Her name was Elizabeth. Together they lived honorably before God, careful in keeping to the

---

*ways of the commandments and enjoying a
clear conscience before God. But they were
childless because Elizabeth could never
conceive, and now they were quite old.*

*It so happened that as Zachariah was carrying
out his priestly duties before God, working the
shift assigned to his regiment, it came his one
turn in life to enter the sanctuary of God and
burn incense. The congregation was gathered
and praying outside the Temple at the hour of
the incense offering. Unannounced, an angel of
God appeared just to the right of the altar of
incense. Zachariah was paralyzed in fear.*

*But the angel reassured him, "Don't fear,
Zachariah. Your prayer has been heard.
Elizabeth, your wife, will bear a son by you.
You are to name him John. You're going to
leap like a gazelle for joy, and not only you—
many will delight in his birth. He'll achieve
great stature with God.*

*"He'll drink neither wine nor beer. He'll be
filled with the Holy Spirit from the moment he
leaves his mother's womb. He will turn many
sons and daughters of Israel back to their God.*

He will herald God's arrival in the style and strength of Elijah, soften the hearts of parents to children, and kindle devout understanding among hardened skeptics—he'll get the people ready for God."

Zachariah said to the angel, "Do you expect me to believe this? I'm an old man and my wife is an old woman."

But the angel said, "I am Gabriel, the sentinel of God, sent especially to bring you this glad news. But because you won't believe me, you'll be unable to say a word until the day of your son's birth. Every word I've spoken to you will come true on time—God's time."

Meanwhile, the congregation waiting for Zachariah was getting restless, wondering what was keeping him so long in the sanctuary. When he came out and couldn't speak, they knew he had seen a vision. He continued speechless and had to use sign language with the people.[83] *(Luke 1:5-22, MSG)*

---

[83] Luke 1:5–22 (The Message).

John's role was to get the people ready for the Messiah. He was the first prophet in over 400 years. For 400 years, God was silent. He did not speak directly to the people of Israel.[84]

John broke that silence.

More to the Story

When we read the Bible stories, we must recognize how much smaller the world was back then. There is plenty of debate over the actual numbers, but as an example of some of the estimates, during Yeshua's time on earth, it is estimated that earth's entire population was about 300 million, which is less than the population of the United States today.[85] The Roman Empire consisted of about 45 million people with approximately 500,000 living in Israel and about 50,000 living in Jerusalem.[86] Present day

---

[84] "400 Years of Silence Ended with John the Baptist," DissectingtheScriptures.com, August 28, 2019, https://dissectingthescriptures.com/tag/400-years-of-silence-ended-with-john-the-baptist/.

[85] https://en.wikipedia.org/wiki/Estimates_of_historical_world_population

[86] "Roman Empire Population," UNRV: Roman History, accessed March 20, 2023, https://www.unrv.com/empire/roman-population.php; Ted Olsen, "The Life & Times of Jesus of Nazareth: Did You Know?," *Christianity Today*, accessed March 20, 2023,

Israel has over eight million people with about 800,000 residents in Jerusalem.[87]

It really was a small world back then. Much of Jewish Israel was related, and Zachariah was very well known. His tribe had been chosen to offer the incense in the innermost sanctuary of the temple, the Holy of Holies, where the Shekinah, God's spirit, resided. Zachariah had been chosen by drawing lots, and felt incredibly honored to perform this duty. A priest could live a lifetime and never get this honor.

Everyone in the community would have known that Zachariah had "won the lottery" and he enjoyed his fifteen minutes of fame the day he entered the temple. But then something happened. Zachariah's special day ended up getting cursed. When he returned from the Holy of Holies, he was changed, mute; he could not speak the Aaronic blessing that everyone was expecting. Something fearful had happened to him.

---

https://www.christianitytoday.com/history/issues/issue-59/life-times-of-jesus-of-nazareth-did-you-know.html.

[87] "Israel Population 2023," World Population Review, accessed March 20, 2023, https://worldpopulationreview.com/countries/israel-population.

Imagine the scene. The priest reappears from inside the Holy of Holies to bless the people and he stands there mute.

He was supposed to raise his hands and say,

> *The Lord bless you and keep you; the Lord make his face shine on you and be gracious to you; the Lord turn his face toward you and give you peace.*[88] *(Numbers 6:24-26, NIV)*

This was what was expected. Being reassured of this blessing is one of the ways the Jews lasted 400 years with relative silence from Yahweh when He did not speak to them.

They wanted this blessing. They needed this blessing.

This wasn't just awkward, it felt like a curse to them.

Hebrew is a difficult language to translate verbatim. The people of the day would have understood the blessing as something more like "YHWH will kneel before you presenting gifts and will guard you with a hedge of protection. YHWH will illuminate the wholeness of His being toward you bringing order

---

[88] Num. 6:24–26 (New International Version).

and He will give you comfort and sustenance. YHWH will lift up His wholeness of being and look upon you and He will set in place all you need to be whole and complete."[89]

The people craved this reassurance.

The spoken blessing was accompanied by a hand gesture. Traditionally, as the priest emerged, he would hold up his hands in the prescribed manner and recite the words of affirmation. The people would cast their gaze down at the ground and humbly accept the blessing.[90]

I wonder at what point did Zachariah realize he could not speak? I suspect he exited the Holy of Holies, went out to meet the people, lifted his hands and…nothing.

---

[89] Jeff A. Benner, "The Aaronic Blessing from a Hebrew Perspective," Ancient Hebrew Research Center, accessed March 20, 2023, https://www.ancient-hebrew.org/studies-interpretation/aaronic-blessing-from-a-hebrew-perspective.htm.
[90] Lorne Rozovsky, "Hand Signs of the Jew," Chabad.org, https://www.chabad.org/library/article_cdo/aid/407512/jewish/Hand-Signs-of-the-Jew.htm.

How awkward. How confusing for the people. This surely would have been interpreted as a sign. A bad sign. A bad omen.

Imagine this happening in front of a giant crowd. The murmuring and whispering, the shuffling about from the other priests, the crowd bewildered. The confusion would have been an epic story that became the gossip shared throughout the land.

Even though Zachariah could not speak, he still held up his hands in the sign of the Aaronic blessing and likely stood there awkwardly. The crowd would have been confused and stunned, staring at his hands.

Do you realize that the hand gesture associated with the Aaronic blessing is one you most likely already know? Picture in your mind Mr. Spock, the Vulcan from *Star Trek*, when he says, "Live long and prosper." With his hand upheld and his fingers spread apart in an odd way.[91]

Remember it? Try it. Are you looking at your hand right now? I'm looking at mine.

---

[91] https://www.atlantajewishtimes.com/leonard-nimoy-mr-spock-and-the-priestly-blessing/

Leonard Nimoy, the man who played Spock, was familiar with this Jewish tradition and offered it to Gene Roddenberry, the creator of *Star Trek*, as an added alien and mysterious gesture that would accompany the Vulcan salute.[92]

This is true. Even though Zachariah could not speak, I can picture him holding up his hands signifying the Aaronic blessing, aka the Vulcan salute, and doing his best to conclude the ritual as the crowd expected.

But the people did not understand. Zachariah knew this lack of assurance would lead them to feel afraid, unsettled. Not a good way to end the day.

All of this was highly illogical.[93]

Zachariah then went home and tried to explain these events to his wife, Elizabeth. She was already 60 years old, long past the age of bearing children. Being barren was a disappointment that she had learned to live with.

Zacahriah wasn't making sense and she didn't want to get her hopes up, yet she trusted God.

---

[92] https://en.wikipedia.org/wiki/Vulcan_salute
[93] https://en.wikipedia.org/wiki/Highly_Illogical

Could it really be true? Was she going to have a son and name him John?

How long did she have to wait, trusting God each day, before she could feel the miracle growing inside her?

In a very natural reaction, Elizabeth barely left her home. She knew full well the difficulties of pregnancy at her age. Zachariah continued to fumble about in silence and then Mary came to visit, bringing the amazing news of her miraculous pregnancy. She too was going to have a son, and his name would be Yeshua.[94]

In our western culture, names do not normally have deep meaning. Sometimes we have a family name that we pass on or have a certain tone and impact we desire with a name, but usually we simply go with what sounds or feels right.

My two sons' first names are after men in the Bible and their middle names come from frontiersmen in American history who helped settle our nation. In

---

[94] Matt. 2:23–25; Luke 1:31–33.

other cultures, and very much so in ancient Hebrew culture, names were layered in meaning and distinctly chosen.

Zachariah means "the Lord (Yahweh) remembers."[95] Elizabeth means "God is my oath."[96] When you pair them as a couple, their names reveal "the Lord remembers His oath."

Don't forget that Yahweh had been silent for 400 years.

The name John (Yochanan or Johanan) means "Yahweh [God] is gracious."[97] Through this family, God was clearly communicating that He had not forgotten His promise and He would fulfill His promise of grace. He was signaling to all of us.

John was very specifically dedicated to being the forerunner of the Messiah. All of this would have elicited great excitement throughout the community. Promises looked like they were being

---

[95] "Zechariah," Behind the Name, last modified November 16, 2019, https://www.behindthename.com/name/zechariah.
[96] "Elizabeth," Behind the Name, last modified December 7, 2022, https://www.behindthename.com/name/elizabeth.
[97] "John," Behind the Name, last modified December 7, 2022, https://www.behindthename.com/name/john.

fulfilled and there was just enough supernatural *weirdness* to lend credibility to the events.

Remember that years earlier, Mary's parents, Joachim and Anne, had been in a situation comparable to that of Zachariah and Elizabeth. They were unable to conceive, and were granted a child who was destined for favor and a significant role in all of mankind's story.

Mary had been regarded as a very special servant of the Lord, and then she was scandalized by a mysterious pregnancy. She isolated herself in Nazareth, avoiding judgment from the people of Jerusalem, and awaited the birth of her son.

In both angelic visitations, the names Johanan and Yeshua were explicitly directed. Both names were common in Israel, but not common to these families. It was a departure from what would have been expected, and all who heard their names would be looking for something special to occur.

The entire nation of Israel was looking for something special to occur, but would they be ready for it when it happened? Would they even recognize it?

II. Hidden in Plain Sight

Before the technology boom of the past few decades, before cell phones and 5G, we communicated very differently.

There are very few differences in how soldiers in the late 1980s and early 1990s communicated compared to ancient days. We both used far and near visual recognition signals. Different colored smoke meant different things. Hand and arm signals were paramount in communicating commands that could mean life or death.

An open hand meant halt. A closed fist meant freeze. Subtle, but very different. Holding the sign for halt or freeze but transitioning your fingers to the shape of a finger gun meant the enemy was nearby.

We never stopped practicing our hand and arm signals. We also had running password combinations designed to quickly identify friend from enemy. Just as when the Israelites used the word *shibboleth* as a challenge and password, ours

were also designed to reveal any foreign accents.[98]
These codes were changed each day.

When trying to get back to safety from behind
enemy lines, a soldier is challenged with a number
combination or a code word that requires a very
specific response. There is no room for error. You
get one chance to get it right. If you hesitate or say
the wrong thing, you run the risk of getting shot
immediately. If you miss the signal, you can die.
Even when we knew the code words, this was always
a tense confrontation. You could never be sure.

As Special Forces operators, we sometimes moved
around the battlefield dressed in local garb,
gathering intelligence, or pinpointing the objective.
We blended in as well as we could. The biggest
threat for us was not Al Qaeda or ISIS catching us,
it was our own military forces mistaking us for
terrorists. American soldiers are expecting to see
other American soldiers in full gear, not operators in
dishdashas with shemaghs covering our faces.

We went to extreme lengths to ensure the local US
forces knew who we were, what we looked like, what

---

[98] Judg. 12:5–6. https://en.wikipedia.org/wiki/Shibboleth

our cars looked like, and what we would be wearing. We would meet with the entire unit dressed in our low visibility local garb, and brief them about what, where, and when we were doing an operation. We would lay everything out clearly so they knew exactly what to look for.

War can be confusing. Life can be confusing. They can both be scary at times. Fear and confusion are powerful inhibitors. They can obscure what is right in front of us. Sometimes people aren't paying attention or they are distracted.

On one mission, as the night was finishing up, an operator emerged from the target building dressed in local garb, and began moving to his vehicle. The shooting had been over for a while. The night was silent.

Up the street from the target building was a US military armored vehicle. The soldiers in that vehicle challenged the operator and yelled for him to halt. The operator stopped in his tracks, faced the vehicle, put his hands up and called out that he was an American. He reached into his gear to pull out a small American flag. This was a universal symbol for near recognition. His actions were misinterpreted.

He was cut down with a machine gun burst before he could even get the flag fully out of his pocket.

This operator lived, but it was an extremely arduous and painful recovery. I remember visiting him at Walter Reed. His entire torso was covered with this strange black goop that looked like tar. Apparently it was some type of covering that kept the wound clean and able to breath. His body looked wrecked, but his humor and positive attitude assured me he would be back. He would fight again.

He told me what happened. "What more could I have done?" he asked. "We showed them exactly what to look for. We showed them how we would be dressed. We told them what we would say. They just didn't recognize me."

We can't let busyness and lack of focus inhibit us from seeing what is right in front of us. We must not let fear and confusion inhibit us from seeing that Yeshua is right in front of us. We can't be so distracted that we miss what God is communicating to us.

The ultimate hand and arm signals from God are the stigmata in Yeshua's hands and the hole in his side. I can make mistakes. I can fail the challenges. But the password is always the same. It is simply saying, I am sorry. I need you. Please help me.

I can be standing, on my knees, or lying down when I say it. In fact, I don't even need to say it aloud. I can whisper it. Or even just say it in my heart. "Yeshua, I need you."

With those three words, I will live. I will be brought back from behind enemy lines. Of this I can be sure.

BAPTISM BY FIRE

JOHN WITH THE CAMEL HAIR COAT:
A NEW BAPTISM

CHAPTER 12

I. Baptism By Fire

> *So what are you waiting for? Get up and get yourself baptized, scrubbed clean of those sins and personally acquainted with God. (Acts 22:16, MSG)*

"I just got bit by a snake," I said to Bill.

He was sitting on the bank leaning against his heavy ruck and sighed.

"What happens now?" I asked him.

"Well," he said with a pause, "maybe now you will die."

"What?" I said, "I'm not gonna die. I'm just not sure what we do next, we are in the middle of nowhere and if we call this in, we will be kicked out of the competition."

Bill was no help. He just sat there.

"Yeah, maybe you won't die. But, you might." is all he added.

Army leadership has what they call a command team. The team consists of an Officer and a Non-Commissioned Officer (NCO). A bad command team can ruin a unit but a good command team is exponentially more effective than any one man can be. It's a bit of a gamble. I've always enjoyed being part of a command team. Sometimes I was the NCO and sometimes I was the Officer. Doing the right thing is the watchword for both positions.

At any position in the military, they emphasize buddy teams. In basic training, you never moved alone; you always had a buddy with you. The same went for Ranger School and many other military courses. If you were caught without your buddy, the penalty was physical. You'd both be punished with push ups, flutter kicks, or some other medieval punishment that the instructor would dream up. The Best Ranger Competition, held annually, is a two-person team, doing everything together, scoring as one. The Best Ranger champion is a two-man team.

One year, my best friend Bill and I had an opportunity to enter the Best Ranger Competition together. We were at the Captain's Career Course at Ft. Benning, Georgia so had time away from leading troops to go to school and focus on our own individual development. We were fit and well trained. The competition takes place on Fort Benning so we had a home course advantage of being able to recce the course and train on the sites where we thought the competition would be held. The exact locations and series of events are kept secret until the competition begins, but there are a few known points that are used each year and there are only so many places where you can conduct the core events.

Bill and I spent hours in the areas where we felt the land navigation course would be held. We got familiar with the terrain and looked for natural crossings over creeks and streams, even creating some just in case we found ourselves there on competition night. Keeping your feet dry is an important part of being able to continue moving long distances under a rucksack.

In the middle of the land navigation challenge, we needed to traverse a creek that was pretty deep. As luck would have it, we knew this area and knew where there was a tree down that spanned the creek. It was nearly directly on the path we needed to take to get to our next point.

We hit the creek, hand-railed it for about a hundred meters and found the downed tree.

So far so good.

Bill did a rucksack flop on the near bank as I stepped out to test the strength of the makeshift bridge. It was one of those big pine trees that sometimes falls over in the shallow sandy soil in Georgia and crashes with its root system tearing out of the ground in a tangled mess.

As I stepped out onto the log bridge and grabbed a root, I felt a sharp sting in one of my fingertips. I pulled it back quickly and shined my flashlight to see what was happening. What stared back at me was a small water moccasin snake, eyes squinty and mouth open wide hissing.

I saw it for less than a second and it slipped off the root and plopped into the water below. I stood there stunned and flabbergasted.

I didn't exactly know what to do and Bill was little help.

We just moved to our next point.

My hand began to throb as we crossed the bridge and hurried to our next point that was still at least an hour away.

My hand began to swell to a ludicrous size. My forearm was literally the size of a football. It hurt like hell.

We werent ready to quit and I tried my best to monitor the poison in my body.

I washed the snake bit area as well as I could but the venom was not on me, it was already in me.

I felt like I might die.

But, at least our feet were dry.

John with the Camel Hair Coat: A New Baptism

Even though John was the GOAP, he was also the weird cousin. We all have at least one. If you don't know who the weird cousin is in your family, it's you.

We are not sure how much time John and Yeshua spent together as cousins but we do know that they both "*grew in wisdom and stature*" as they prepared for their public ministries.[99] They had different missions but they were absolutely interlinked.

As John went to work preparing the way for his cousin, his life was not easy. As the forerunner for Yeshua, he worked incredibly hard preparing the hearts of many stubborn men to be ready to receive Yeshua and his message. Many people found hope and comfort in John's words, but some grew angry, feeling threatened by any change to the status quo. Not everyone was ready to accept John and his strong words.

> *While Jesus was living in the Galilean hills,*
> *John, called "the Baptizer," was preaching in*
> *the desert country of Judea. His message was*
> *simple and austere, like his desert surroundings:*
> *"Change your life. God's kingdom is here."*
> *John and his message were authorized by*
> *Isaiah's prophecy:*
> *Thunder in the desert!*
> *Prepare for God's arrival!*
> *Make the road smooth and straight!*
>
> *John dressed in a camel-hair habit tied at the*
> *waist by a leather strap. He lived on a diet of*

---

[99] Luke 2:52.

locusts and wild field honey. People poured out of Jerusalem, Judea, and the Jordanian countryside to hear and see him in action. There at the Jordan River those who came to confess their sins were baptized into a changed life.

When John realized that a lot of Pharisees and Sadducees were showing up for a baptismal experience because it was becoming the popular thing to do, he exploded: "Brood of snakes! What do you think you're doing slithering down here to the river? Do you think a little water on your snakeskins is going to make any difference? It's your life that must change, not your skin! And don't think you can pull rank by claiming Abraham as father. Being a descendant of Abraham is neither here nor there. Descendants of Abraham are a dime a dozen. What counts is your life. Is it green and flourishing? Because if it's deadwood, it goes on the fire.

"I'm baptizing you here in the river, turning your old life in for a kingdom life. The real action comes next: The main character in this drama—compared to him I'm a mere

stagehand—will ignite the kingdom life within you, a fire within you, the Holy Spirit within you, changing you from the inside out. He's going to clean house—make a clean sweep of your lives. He'll place everything true in its proper place before God; everything false he'll put out with the trash to be burned."[100] *(Matthew 3: 1-12, MSG)*

Baptisms are a common occurrence in the modern church, but when John introduced baptism, it was a revolutionary idea. It was a heretical idea. The era of ritual washing was over; baptism would be a one-time immersion to signify your commitment to God and your newfound purity in Him.

The dramatic events surrounding Yeshua's baptism are loaded with symbolism, meaning, and significance that would have been fully recognized by those standing on the riverbank watching it unfold.

---

[100] Matt. 3:1–12 (The Message).

More to the Story

To fully understand baptism, you must understand the Jewish tradition of ritual washing and the mikvah. A mikvah is a pool of water with some of it from a natural source like a natural spring, or a well of naturally occurring water, like rainwater.[101] An ocean or a lake can be considered a natural mikvah. More commonly, a mikvah is indoors and looks like a walk-in bathtub that can hold about 150 gallons of water. This is the estimated amount of water needed to cover the entire body of an average-sized man.

A mikvah is not used for actual washing, but for spiritual washing. Before immersing yourself in a mikvah, Jewish law required that the participant's body was already thoroughly clean by means of a bath or shower and all other grooming habits attended to, including clipped nails and brushed teeth. This attention to detail ensures that there are no barriers between the person immersing themself and the mikvah water.

The mikvah was the most important part of a person's home. It was so important in Jewish culture

---

[101] https://en.wikipedia.org/wiki/Mikveh

that the Old Covenant commanded that a mikvah was the priority build and should be constructed first, even before building a synagogue, no matter the cost. Great lengths were authorized to fund the construction of a mikvah, even selling Torah scrolls or the land acquired for a synagogue, if necessary.[102]

When you tour Israel and other locations with Jewish influence, you will be awestruck by the prevalence of the mikvah, often with multiple mikva'ot in a single residence. They are so prevalent because there were numerous events and reasons that required full immersion in a mikvah. The Torah required full immersion for a bridegroom on the day of his wedding and cleansing himself in preparation for uniting with his wife. Married Jewish women were required to visit the mikvah once a month, seven days after the end of their menstrual cycle.

A kohen (priest), prior to a religious service, needed to cleanse himself in preparation to represent the community, unite himself with the spirit, and recite the priestly blessing, complete with Spock's hand signal.

---

[102] Ibid.

For everyone else, weekly, before Shabbat, they needed to enter the mikvah to wash off the week's transgressions and prepare to focus on the Torah and the litany of other requirements for remaining pure.

John's baptism turned all of this tradition on its head.

The New Covenant baptism that John introduced signified a single immersion for the washing away of all sins and to be fully reliant on God's grace for becoming and remaining clean. Repentance and baptism with its "once and for all" approach for purity were groundbreaking concepts at the time.

The only preparation needed before being baptized is acknowledging your need for personal salvation, repenting your shortcomings, and accepting Yeshua as the one who will pay our debts in full.

This story of redemption feels too good to be true for many people. The self-righteous and pompous get upset because redemption levels the playing field for all. No one is inherently better than anyone else, and no one is inherently worse than anyone else, either. We all have sinned and fallen short.[103]

This was a difficult truth for the rich, the ruling class, and the Pharisees and Sadducees to accept. It was threatening to their social stranglehold on the masses. This egalitarian teaching from John was intimidating. John was warning them, almost taunting them. Baptism would be an initiation into a new order.

This will not be the last time the Pharisees and Sadducees play a part in this story. In many of the scenes you have read so far, they were already in the background, watching, waiting, and plotting. Before this book ends, they will move to center stage and expose themselves to be the snakes they truly were.

II. Baptism Under Fire.

I love witnessing baptisms. The church I attend in Oregon has a special event each year where baptisms are conducted in the Deschutes River. People line

---

[103] Rom. 3:23.

up on its banks as the elders of the church step into the water, waist deep, and begin the sacred ritual.

Watching the humility of people young and old enter the water inspires me. Seeing them emerge with a new spirit edifies me.

There are a couple of other things that pop into my head when I think about baptism—times when I was really dirty, I mean beyond dirty, and also when I was "baptized under fire" on the battlefield.[104]

We all know how it feels to soak in a steaming hot bath. It is one of life's simple pleasures. There were times as a soldier when I experienced this at an almost indescribable level. The best I can do is describe it as a cleansing—a catharsis.

At some point, you go beyond dirty. You reach a state where your body no longer releases an odor and your filth just becomes a part of you. You stop noticing it in yourself. You stop noticing it in others around you. If all of you are filthy, it becomes the

---

[104] Aaron Bazin, "Baptism by Fire: A Survey of First Combat Experiences," Modern War Institute, May 15, 2018, https://mwi.usma.edu/baptism-fire-survey-first-combat-experiences/. When soldiers have been baptized in the fire of a battlefield, they have all one rank in my eyes- Napoleon Bonaparte

new normal. When someone shows up clean and washed, they notice your stink immediately. It is only then that you realize how bad things have gotten.

There were times when I didn't shower for a few weeks and wore the same uniform through the hot, humid, muddy jungle or the arid, dry, sweltering desert.

In both instances, I no longer felt dirty. I reached a whole new way of living in the situation. I co-existed with being unclean. Sullied. I got used to it.

And then I got the opportunity to wash, to get clean. I scraped off the layers, trying to get down to fresh skin. I scrubbed away the dirt, the grime, and the blood. I let the water wash over me. I bowed my head as the brown stained water mixed with the fresh water.

I submerged myself in the water, holding my breath as I plunged all the way below the surface. Everything became silent except the sound of my heartbeat. I surrendered to the water.

When I emerged from the hot water and inhaled a deep, fresh breath, I felt clean. Whatever happened before this was washed away. When I exited the water and caught a glimpse of myself in the mirror, I could see that I had lost weight. I looked a little bonier. I looked exhausted. My scratches, scabs, and bruises were all still there, but I knew they would fade. I was clean. I was ready to fight another day.

It felt like a type of baptism.

There is a term called "baptism by fire" that is a reference from Matthew 3:11, but it is also used in the military to refer to a soldier's first time in battle.[105]

The story below was not my first time in battle, but it was the first time I was on the receiving end of an artillery barrage and I had no choice but to surrender myself to fate.

The Iraqi forces were dug in before us. Their trench line was immense. The B52 Stratofortress had already gone "Winchester" and dropped all the

---

[105] https://en.wikipedia.org/wiki/Baptism_by_fire

munitions it had on board. The Iraqis were still dug in. They were not ready to give up.

We were mixed in with the Kurdish forces as we advanced from our last covered and concealed position, into the open ground, trying to close the final distance as quickly as we could. And then it happened.

From the backside of the ridgeline behind the Iraqi front lines, artillery boomed and shells rained down behind us. It felt like an earthquake. We hit the ground and tried to melt into it. The feeling was utter hopelessness. It was a dull acceptance that if this was it, then this was it.

Then an artillery sheaf ripped a straight line of steel and fire in front of us. We were being bracketed. It was time to move. The next bracket would likely be our last. We were not ready to give up just yet.

We jumped up and moved as fast as we could through the debris of the last barrage. Thousands of Kurdish Peshmerga troops and a few dozen Green Berets rushed up the ridgeline toward the Iraqi front lines. We were ready for a close fight.

As we maneuvered toward their trench line, there was no resistance. The Iraqis were not shooting at us anymore. The B52 Stratofortress may not have knocked out their artillery pieces, but it knocked the fight out of the Iraqi soldiers.

They did not survive their baptism of fire. They were broken. They had given up. They were ready to surrender.

We, on the other hand, were invigorated. There was still a ridge to climb and some enemy forces to contain, but we had survived our baptism by fire. There was no going back. Things were different now. We were ready for whatever lay ahead.

That is baptism.

13

FAIL WHILE DARING GREATLY

YESHUA ENTERS THE ARENA:
FACE MARRED BY DUST AND SWEAT

CHAPTER 13

I. Fail While Daring Greatly

This is my Son, chosen and marked by my love, delight of my life. (Matthew 3:17, MSG)

One of my favorite quotes of all time comes from President Teddy Roosevelt. "Citizenship in a Republic" is a speech he gave at the Sorbonne in Paris, France, over one hundred years ago. A notable section of this speech has become known as "The Man in the Arena."

> *It is not the critic who counts; not the man who points out how the strong man stumbles, or where the doer of deeds could have done them better.*

The credit belongs to the man who is actually in the arena, whose face is marred by dust and sweat and blood; who strives valiantly; who errs, who comes short again and again, because there is no effort without error and shortcoming; but who does actually strive to do the deeds; who knows great enthusiasms, the great devotions; who spends himself in a worthy cause; who at the best knows in the end the triumph of high achievement, and who at the worst, if he fails, at least fails while daring greatly, so that his place shall never be with those cold and timid souls who neither know victory nor defeat.[106]

I recited "The Man in the Arena" at my retirement ceremony when I left the military. I think it was the last time that I read it aloud, but it was not the last time I pondered it.

I have stumbled. I could have done better. But I entered the arena and I am proud of the dust, sweat, and blood that marred my face. I erred and came up short, again and again. But I strove valiantly. And knew great enthusiasms and great devotions.

---

[106] Theodore Roosevelt, "Address at the Sorbonne in Paris, France: 'Citizenship in a Republic,'" The American Presidency Project, accessed March 20, 2023, .
https://en.wikipedia.org/wiki/Citizenship_in_a_Republic

I have spent my life in a worthy cause. I have known triumph and high achievement. And I have failed. But I failed while daring greatly. My soul is not cold nor is it timid. I know that victory lies in Yeshua—the man who entered the arena for all of us.

Yeshua Enters the Arena: Face Marred by Dust and Sweat

Yeshua's baptism was also his supernatural entrance into public ministry. It was when he boldly stepped into the arena. He didn't stop until he tasted victory.

The timing of Yeshua's baptism was designed for a seamless transition from John's ministry, the forerunner of the Messiah, to the Messiah himself. The place of Yeshua's baptism was also a precise, purposeful, and significant location. His baptism was the completion of a string of extraordinary events that preceded him by nearly 1,300 years.[107]

---

[107] "Joshua (1355-1245 BCE)," Chabad.org, accessed March 20, 2023, https://www.chabad.org/library/article_cdo/aid/129625/jewish/Joshua.htm. https://en.wikipedia.org/wiki/Elijah

Yeshua's baptism was not random. He was baptized with water and the Spirit. Things would never be the same again.

Let's look at the story of Yeshua's baptism from the Book of Matthew.

> *Then Jesus came from Galilee to the Jordan to be baptized by John. But John tried to deter him, saying, "I need to be baptized by you, and do you come to me?"*
>
> *Jesus replied, "Let it be so now; it is proper for us to do this to fulfill all righteousness." Then John consented. As soon as Jesus was baptized, he went up out of the water. At that moment heaven was opened, and he saw the Spirit of God descending like a dove and alighting on him. And a voice from heaven said, "This is my Son, whom I love; with him I am well pleased."[108] (Matthew 3: 13-16, NIV)*

More to the Story

John was baptizing people in the Jordan River when Yeshua visited him and insisted that John baptize him

---

[108] Matt. 3:13–16 (New International Version).

as well. The precise location of this event is important because it signifies the completion of something special. It signifies the fulfillment of a promise that had been foreshadowed centuries earlier.

Some people still want to debate where this event occurred, but with careful reading, prayer, and examining the archaeological evidence, the location reveals itself.

The Great Storyteller does not disappoint. Patiently, He had been setting the scene for this once in an eternity event. Yeshua's baptism was the third time something miraculous had occurred at this very specific place. This was the third time God demonstrated His faithfulness, His power, and His grace and prepared His people to look for the "rest of the story."

The first significant event at this special location occurred with Yeshua's namesake Joshua the warrior. A century and a half before Yeshua was born, giants had inhabited the land of Israel. These giants were the ancient ancestors of Goliath and his brothers.

Joshua had been one of the members of the twelve-man "A-Team" that Moses selected to patrol deep behind enemy lines, reconnoiter all of Israel and bring back a report.[109] Their mission lasted 40 days.

Years later, when it came time for Moses to retire, Joshua became the leader of the Israelites. Joshua was the chosen successor to Moses for many different reasons. He had prepared himself for this responsibility by serving under Moses for 40 years as the Israelites wandered the desert, forbidden to enter the Promised Land.

Finally, Yahweh relented and allowed the Israelites to enter the Promised Land and dictated that Joshua would be the one to lead them. After Joshua was ready and Moses' work was complete, Moses passed the role of leader, warrior, and lawmaker to Joshua.

The day that Joshua took charge, he was told by God, *"Today I will begin to exalt you in the eyes of all Israel, so they may know that I am with you as I was with Moses."*[110]

And then a miracle happened. When the Levites, carrying the Ark of the Covenant, touched the water of the Jordan River, the water "piled up" and all the people crossed over on dry land. Other than Joshua

---

[109] Num. 13.
[110] Josh. 3:7.

and the spies, it was the first time Israelites had set foot in the promised land.

To commemorate this event, God instructed them to build a monument of twelve stones, one for each tribe of Israel. He added, *"In the future when your descendants ask their parents, 'What do these stones mean?' tell them, 'Israel crossed the Jordan on dry ground.' For the Lord your God dried up the Jordan before you until you had crossed over. The Lord your God did to the Jordan what he had done to the Red Sea when he dried it up before us until we had crossed over. He did this so that all the peoples of the earth might know that the hand of the Lord is powerful and so that you might always fear the Lord your God."*[111]

Joshua was exalted that day. He was the worthy successor of Moses and Israel stood in awe of him.[112] Joshua led all of Israel back into the Promised Land. He took them from their years of wandering and ushered in a new era with a new kingdom.

The second time Yahweh commemorated this place as a special location was when the prophet Elijah handed

---

[111] Josh. 4:21–24.
[112] Josh. 4:14.

his leadership role to Elisha.[113] Elijah was a powerful prophet who had tirelessly called Israel to repent and turn toward their Lord.[114]

Few listened to him.

Elisha was a faithful servant to Elijah.[115] He spent a life of duty in preparation for picking up where Elijah left off. Elisha was a man of the people who did miraculous things to bolster their belief in the messages he brought from God.

The story in the Book of Kings explains how Elijah was ready to hand off his responsibilities to Elisha. They walked along the Jordan near Jericho. Elijah struck the water with his cloak and the water divided. Elijah and Elisha crossed to the other side.[116]

Then another miracle happened. Elijah was taken up to heaven in a chariot of fire inside a whirlwind.[117] While this was happening, Elijah's cloak fell off and landed near Elisha.[118] Elisha watched it all happen and picked up Elijah's cloak, dusted it off and returned to

---

[113] 2 Kings 2:6–14.
[114] https://en.wikipedia.org/wiki/Elijah
[115] https://en.wikipedia.org/wiki/Elisha
[116] 2 Kings 2:8.
[117] 2 Kings 2:11.
[118] 2 Kings 2:13.

the Jordan's edge. Not sure how to cross the river again, Elisha took the cloak and struck the water with it. The water divided, and Elisha crossed on dry land.[119]

It was clear to everyone nearby that Elisha had assumed the spirit, role, and authority of Elijah.[120] Clearly, the Lord's favor was with Elisha, and He reinforced Elisha's confidence that He would be with him and grant him powers at least equal to Elijah's.

Around 500 years had passed between Joshua parting the waters of the Jordan and Elisha repeating the act. Rivers change their course over time, but this spot would be marked for all time. A monument of twelve stones was built to mark the spot. This was a special place, and all of Israel in Yeshua's time honored it.

The third act ties it all together. Moses handed off his warrior leadership to Joshua, Elijah handed off his priestly leadership to Elisha, and John handed off his prophetic leadership to Yeshua. This simple act of baptism at this specific place was much more than most people appreciate today.

---

[119] 2 Kings 2:13–14.
[120] 2 Kings 2:15.

The number three is widely used in the Bible. It is used to illustrate harmony, perfection, and completion.[121] It gives power, significance, and meaning to actions.

You see this pattern many times throughout the Bible stories. Yeshua's baptism and entry into his public ministry were no different. The events followed a pattern that was easily recognized by the Jews of the day for its symbolism and meaning and for its connection to a precise place where significant events happened in the past.

Yeshua's entrance into the arena, his baptism, deserved something special. This event needed to unify different eras, fulfill promises from ages past, and set the tone for the rest of human existence.

The stones Joshua used to build the monument to commemorate the river parting are no longer present in our day, but it is very likely that the stones would have been visible for many years, perhaps even when John was baptizing people there. Even if the twelve stones were lost to the river and time, the Jews would

---

[121] "Biblical Numerology: 3," Numerology.Center, accessed March 20, 2023,
http://numerology.center/biblical_numbers_number_3.php.

have known that spot. It was a place of honor, of a promise kept, a people restored. It certainly was venerated and would have been a tourist destination, just a short walk from the ruins of Jericho. Through time, people remember their precious places.

There is one final thing I want to highlight about this story that is easy to overlook. Let's examine these words. Read them carefully.

> As soon as the priests who carried the ark reached the Jordan and their feet touched the water's edge, the water from upstream stopped flowing. **It piled up in a heap a great distance away, at a town called Adam in the vicinity of Zarethan**, while the water flowing down to the Sea of the Arabah (that is, the Dead Sea) was completely cut off. So the people crossed over opposite Jericho. **The priests who carried the ark of the covenant of the Lord stopped in the middle of the Jordan and stood on dry ground**, while all Israel passed by until the whole nation had completed the crossing on dry ground.[122] (Joshua 3:15-17, NIV)

---

[122] Josh. 3:15–17 (New International Version).

When the priests touched the water's edge, the water piled up at a town called Adam.[123] This town was approximately 20 miles upstream from where the Israelites crossed the Jordan River to attack Jericho.[124]

The water stopped 20 miles upstream. This means that the priests stopped in the middle of the Jordan River as it was still flowing and stood in the middle of the river until it dried up around them. It would take about ten minutes for the water piling up at Adam to stop flowing downstream to where the Israelites stood.

They stood there as the water rushed past them for at least ten minutes. What were they thinking? What was Joshua thinking? Do you think maybe a little bit of doubt had crept in?

This miracle didn't happen immediately. It required an incredible amount of trust.

---

[123] https://en.wikipedia.org/wiki/City_of_Adam

[124] "Crossing the Jordan," in *The Storyteller's Companion to the Bible*, vol. 2, ed. Michael E. Williams (Nashville: Abingdon Press, 1992), 173–77, https://www.ministrymatters.com/all/entry/1901/crossing-the-jordan.

Nothing has changed. Many of God's miracles require trust and faith.[125]

God is faithful. At Yeshua's baptism, the third important event to occur here, He was reminding the Jews that He had delivered them in the past and He was sending a new leader to complete the mission. His son. The warrior. The priest. The prophet.

Joshua was preparing to go to war and retake all of the Promised Land. Elijah was swept up in a whirlwind and a fiery chariot. But Yeshua, even though he was here to go to war with evil, did not part the Jordan. He immersed himself into it.

There was no whirlwind but a solemn voice. There was no fiery chariot but the Spirit of God appearing like a dove. He was blessed by a bird.

Just as Elisha needed a boost of confidence to stop the Jordan's water, Yeshua, the man, needed a boost of confidence. He knew that he was entering his public ministry, that he would be surrounded by spiritual warfare that would ultimately end in torture and a brutal death.

---

[125] David writes about this in one of his poems, "*Commit your way to the Lord; trust in him, and he will act.*" Ps. 37:5.

His Father reassured Him that He was proud of him.[126]

How much confidence and pride do the words of a father instill in a child? What child would not be filled with confidence if their father gave them this praise: "This is my daughter, whom I love; with whom I am well pleased." How endearing and sweet are those words?

When we think of Yeshua as both God and man, it is difficult to separate them. However, we need to understand and be confident that he suffered the same doubts, fears, and temptations that we do. If he didn't, why would his life be special? What would it truly fulfill?

This revolutionary act of one baptism for the remission of our sins was an inflection point for all of mankind. Yeshua was reinforced and filled with confidence as he emerged from the banks of the Jordan at that historic site and saw the dove.

Then he walked into the wilderness for forty days.

---

[126] Matt. 3:17.

II. Fail While Daring Greatly

I wrote earlier about returning to places at Fort
Benning, Georgia, where I was taught to be a soldier.
Whenever I go there, the feeling of nostalgia is heavy. I
think it's because so many of the events there were
proving grounds for me and tests that I needed to pass
in order to fulfill my dream of becoming a Ranger,
then Special Forces, and ultimately Delta Force.

There is another place that weighs heavy on my heart.

My friend Bill, who fought beside me in Ad Dwar and
lacked empathy when I was bit by a snake, died under
a freak rockfall on Mount Rainier in Washington. His
life ended short. He had just retired from Delta Force
and was about to embark on his next great adventure
of being a husband to his wife and daddy to two little
girls. Bill was a bona fide mountain man, strong at
altitude, daring, smart, tireless. He did nothing wrong.
He made no mistakes. He set up the night bivouac in a
safe place.

God decided to take him.

A few times a year I fly in and out of SeaTac Airport
and almost directly over Mount Rainier and the spot
where Bill died. I look down from the plane and my
heart aches.

I love that mountain. I've climbed it many times. I've guided groups up and down it. Mount Rainier used to be a playground for Bill and me. I still love it but now I also hate it. That mountain took Bill from us, from his family, from the world.

I look at Rainier and marvel at its beauty.

I look at Rainier and am in awe of its raw power.

I look at Rainier and can sense that it has no feelings. It does not miss Bill like the rest of us do. This giant block of rock and ice is cold and heartless.

I look at Rainier and I also see God.

I marvel at His beauty.

I am in awe of His raw power.

When I look at Rainier, I can feel God.

God doesn't miss Bill because Bill is standing at His side, a general in the celestial armies.

But God's heart breaks for Bill's wife and little girls that were left behind. God's heart aches for them but He is still with them. He will never leave them. He is with all of us even when we act cold and heartless toward Him.

This is a thought that comforts me.

He is with me when I fail.

He is with me when I prevail.

He is with me in the arena.

BLOOD AND GUTS

YESHUA'S LONG WALK:
FORTY DAYS OF TESTING

CHAPTER 14

I. Blood and Guts

> *Do you not know that in a race all the runners run, but only one gets the prize? Run in such a way as to get the prize. (1 Corinthians, 9:24, NIV)*

Something wasn't right. This was supposed to be the end, the finish. I was exhausted. Throughout the long night and into the early morning, I had paced myself appropriately but as I neared the finish line, I literally sprinted as fast as I could under a ninety-pound ruck, uphill all the way, for the past five kilometers. I had done it. I was about to finish the final physical test to get accepted into a unit I dreamed about when I was a private.

But something was wrong. This point looked like all the other points. It surely didn't look like a finish line.

I knew very little about the Assessment and Selection process. It is supposed to be that way, and in fact I think it's better that way. But I remembered one thing that my friend Brian told me a decade earlier. He said, "When you get to the end of the final trek you will cross some water and be confronted with two options. You can follow the winding road or go straight up the mountain. Straight up the mountain is way shorter, but don't do it. The mountain laurel eats you alive. Take the road."

This was all I remembered. As I neared what I thought was the end of the trek, I crossed some water and had two choices to get to my next point: follow the winding road or go straight up the mountain.

I took the road. I heeded my friend's warning from years ago.

This was the end of the selection. The testing was coming to a close. I was euphoric. I ran up the winding road and dumped all my extra food and water.

I was about to finish the trek with a great time. I literally sprinted to the finish.

Like every other rendezvous point, the cadre met me at the top of the mountain. They instructed me to ground my gear, refill water, and plot my next point. I thought they were joking. Wasn't this the finish? Brian had said this would be the finish. It was not the finish. Dammit Brian.

I plotted my next point and moved down the trail out of sight of the cadre. I was spent, exhausted. I took a knee and refocused myself. My energy was gone, my legs were shot, and my lungs burned. I didn't have anything left. I was going to have to rely on my guts.

Yeshua's Long Walk: Forty Days of Testing

When Yeshua entered the arena, his clock began ticking. From this point on, he needed to balance what he said, where he said it, and how he said it in order to fulfill what his Father expected of him before going to the cross to complete his final task.

Yeshua wasted no time.

When I read the account of him disappearing into the wilderness following his baptism, I wondered, where did he go? We are not certain, but one thing I can tell you, he did not wander. This time was purposeful and intentional.

> *Next Jesus was taken into the wild by the Spirit for the Test. The Devil was ready to give it. Jesus prepared for the Test by fasting forty days and forty nights.*[127] *(Matthew 4:1-3, MSG)*

More to the Story

Immediately following Yeshua's baptism by John the Baptist, he disappeared into the wilderness for forty days of solitude. For forty days he fasted and prayed. This period was the final preparation for his service, his calling, his purpose. After this solitude, he would take the world by storm and usher in a new covenant.

---

[127] Matt. 4:1–3 (The Message).

The Adversary, Satan, met him in the desert, confronted him, tempted him, and attempted to derail the Story.[128] And you better believe Yeshua was tempted.

Forty days–alone in the desert, fasting–is no easy task.

There is only one other account in the Bible of someone undergoing forty days of fasting. It was Moses, the deliverer of Israel, on Mt. Sinai after Yahweh re-consecrated His promise and delivered The Ten Commandments.[129]

I think this is significant. During Yeshua's journey into the wilderness, I believe he traveled to Mt. Sinai and met Yahweh there for His final instructions. Mt. Sinai is located about 400 kilometers (250 miles) from Jericho. A day's journey in that time was between thirty and forty kilometers (twenty to twenty-five miles). Yeshua could have easily walked there in about ten days, spent up to twenty days on the mountain, and returned.

Or perhaps Yahweh moved him miraculously to Mt. Sinai and they spent forty days together before the Tempter showed up.

---

[128] Matt. 4:1–11.
[129] Exod. 34:28.

Where do you think Yeshua went during his forty days?
What do you think was the point of his journey? Think
about it. Pray about it. Maybe you will be given a
revelation that has eluded me.

When we look at the words in the Book of John, it
lends some credibility to the idea that he might have
gone to Mt. Sinai.[130] One thing I am certain of, though,
is that Yeshua did not merely wander or hang out on a
barren mountaintop for forty days. There was a specific
purpose for his journey. A journey to Mt. Sinai and a
direct encounter with Yahweh on His Holy Mountain
would bring some beautiful closure to it all.

While Yeshua was off in the wilderness, the next scene
was being set. While he was away, Herod Antipas
imprisoned John the Baptist in a dungeon at his palace
at Machaerus.[131] [132] The Pharisees, Sadducees, and
Jewish leaders in Jerusalem were becoming sneakier and
wilier.

When Yeshua made the long walk back to Nazareth
and Galilee, he bypassed the contentious areas and soon

---

[130] John 1:17–18.
[131] Mark 6; Luke 3; Matt. 14.
[132] https://en.wikipedia.org/wiki/Machaerus

realized that everything was different now. He was in the arena.[133] His public ministry had begun.

Things would never be the same.
He was emboldened and he began to perform miracles.

Perhaps up until this point, there was a limit to the power that Yahweh had granted Yeshua. Perhaps on Mt. Sinai, the Spirit passed before Yeshua and released some of the gifts and powers that were restrained inside of him.

Either way, after Yeshua returned from his journey, he began selecting his disciples. He began assembling his twelve-man "A-Team."

It was his time to lead.

II. Blood and Guts

Kneeling in the woods, out of sight of the cadre, I had to calm myself down. It couldn't be much further. I could make it. I'd already come this far.

---

[133] Matt. 4:12; Mark 1:14.

I stood up, looked to the sky, and laughed. Apparently I had one more lesson to learn. I set off down the single track trail that was covered in a light snow. The navigation to the next point should be easy, a few kilometers down this trail, a right turn onto another trail and a few more kilometers to some power lines and an opening in the thick woods.

I was too tired to run but I picked up my mantra anyway: "Blessed be the name of the Lord," repeated every time my left foot hit the ground like a cadence. I zoned out and started jogging. I figured it would take me about twenty minutes to hit the trail intersection. I stared at the ground in front of me. There was only one set of boot tracks in the light snow. We start the trek staggered so you never really know who is in front of you or behind you. One thing I was pretty sure about was that they would keep Bill and me separated. Sitting in the covered truck the night before, I thought I heard Bill get called out maybe an hour before me. I was chasing his ghost throughout the night.

The trail was narrow. The one set of boot prints continued in front of me at a very even pace and interval.

I looked at the boot prints.
I stared at the boot prints.
I recognized the boot prints.
They were Bill's.

That's how well I knew Bill. I could recognize his footprints. His stride length, the size of his peculiarly small feet, his heel strike, and how he rolled his foot forward efficiently with each stride.

Bill was in front of me somewhere. That brought me incredible confidence.
I knew that he would know where he was going.
I hit a trail intersection but it was not what I was expecting. I was expecting a four way trail intersection and expected to simply take a right.
There were trails criss-crossing everywhere, it was not a four way intersection but about an eight way intersection with trails seemingly going every which way.
I paused for a second, not knowing which trail to take. I was too far into this and far too tired to make a mistake now.

I looked at Bill's tracks. I decided to follow him.

Throughout the selection course, I enjoyed the anonymity. The burden of leadership was lighter. My responsibility was simply to do my best.

If you are selected, and if you pass the rest of the grueling training, you are expected to lead. That transition can be difficult. You go from being just one of many to being one of one. After you pass the tests, prove yourself worthy, and demonstrate that you should be chosen, you are expected to perform. You can no longer hide in anonymity.

At assessment and selection events, the cadre and commanders are looking at you to see if you have what it takes. But these events are also designed for you to discover for yourself if you have what it takes. The tests are designed to help you become self-aware. You need to find out for yourself what you are lacking. Others may or may not see your struggles and your doubts, but you should know them. You had better know them.

You need to know for yourself if you are ready to lead.

As a commander, you are expected to lead. Immediately. The training and testing are over.

Times like this are both exhilarating and terrifying. You simply accept your fate and lead the best you can. Leaning on God and following where He leads you is always a sound decision.

There are many moments in the life of Yeshua during which I would have liked to be there with him. Talked to him. Asked him what he was feeling. Asked him what he was thinking. His return from his Long Walk is one of those times. When Yeshua returned from his time in the wilderness, there was no turning back. He was the chosen one. He knew where he was going.

His responsibility was to lead the world to salvation through his own suffering, overcoming any doubts, shedding blood and guts and dying…for us.

That is why I choose to follow him.

LEAD BY EXAMPLE

YESHUA THE SMALL UNIT LEADER:
FOLLOW ME

CHAPTER 15

I. Lead By Example

> *Anyone who intends to come with me has to let me lead. You're not in the driver's seat; I am. Don't run from suffering; embrace it. Follow me and I'll show you how. Self-help is no help at all. Self-sacrifice is the way, my way, to finding yourself, your true self. What kind of deal is it to get everything you want but lose yourself? What could you ever trade your soul for? (Matthew 16: 24-26, MSG)*

I cut my teeth on combat during the Panama Invasion in 1989. I was a corporal leading men in combat. After the jump, and after we had what we needed at the assembly area, a squad of men and a machine gun team, we moved to our first objective. Gunfire was sporadic but I didn't let it distract me. I knew exactly where we needed to go. Between us and our objective was a guard shack with a guard who kept popping his head up. We needed to get past him so we could get a foothold in the first target building that we were tasked to secure.

He popped up again, and this time he had a gun. He fired off a few rounds and ducked back down.

It looked to me like he only had a pistol. What was he thinking? We had a full Ranger squad ready to obliterate him and his guard shack.

He did it again; a few rounds popped over our heads. We returned fire but he was behind thick concrete cover.

I hollered over to Ranger Hale, our M249 Squad Automatic Weapon (SAW) gunner, to light him up. The first burst from the SAW was high, over the roof of the guard shack. I hollered to Hale again, "Bring your fire down!" This time his rounds hit the roof of the guard shack.

I switched over to Ray, with the team's M203 grenade launcher. "End this now, Ray!" I yelled. He scored a direct hit inside the guard shack. Anything in there would be pulverized.

"Follow me," I hollered. We advanced online and swept past the guard shack. It was empty.

Suddenly, to my left I saw a Panamanian soldier lying on the ground, on his stomach, facing away from me with his hands on his head. He really startled me, and I raised my rifle, switched the selector lever from safe to fire and began to apply pressure to the trigger.

He was shaking. I saw the pistol lying in the grass a few feet from his hands. I was sure this was the same guy who seconds earlier was shooting at us from the guard shack. I thought, "Well, he escaped the grenade but he's getting it now." I squeezed my trigger a little more.

He was whimpering. As I applied more pressure to the trigger, my mind was conflicted. It was like I had an angel on one shoulder and a devil on the other.
"Kill him," the devil said.

"Clearly, he's a noncombatant," the angel said.

"He was just trying to kill you," the devil said.

"He's surrendering," the angel said.

"This is war," the devil said.

Yeshua the Small Unit Leader: Follow Me[134]

 "Follow Me" is the official motto of the US Army's Infantry.[135] It is the prescribed command by which the corporal leads his squad, the basic Infantry unit.[136]

"Follow me" are the simple words Yeshua used to lead his disciples.[137]

Small unit leaders are expected to lead by example. Regardless of the danger, the small unit leader is

---

[134] David Scott Stieghan, "'Follow Me!': A Brief History of the Infantry School Shoulder Patch," Lessons from the Past, Fall 2021, https://www.benning.army.mil/infantry/magazine/issues/2021/Fall/pdf/15_Stieghan.pdf. "Follow Me" is the prescribed command by which the corporal leads his squad, the basic Infantry unit. The Infantry itself says to the Amy as a whole "FOLLOW ME."

[135] Albert N. Garland, "Army Combat Branches: Infantry," Encyclopedia.com, accessed March 21, 2023, https://www.encyclopedia.com/history/encyclopedias-almanacs-transcripts-and-maps/army-combat-branches-infantry.

[136] Stieghan, "'Follow Me!': A Brief History."

[137] Mark 1:17; Matt. 4:19.

expected to lead from the front. His men are expected to follow.

Yeshua lived as a simple man. He lived a life of humility and grace, first as a student and then as an apprentice laborer for his father Joseph.

When it came his time to lead, he prepared his disciples for what lay ahead. He developed them so they were ready for the worst. He empowered them and emboldened them. He led them with humility and grace.

When we read the accounts of Yeshua calling his disciples, we may get an unrealistic view of what likely would have occurred. Yeshua was not mystical. He spoke in the common language of the day. He told stories that were intended to be simple and commonly understood in order to communicate very difficult concepts.

He didn't mesmerize an audience with his gaze or woo them with his magical voice. He did not glide smoothly across the sometimes harsh landscape of the Middle East. He walked and sweated and stumbled. He did not have a built-in supernatural compass or map. He walked from town to town on the routes prepared for him.

I don't think he used his supernatural powers to fully understand the background and resume of the disciples he chose. He chose twelve men. The first three disciples Yeshua chose were fishermen.[138] The next one was a tax collector.[139] At daybreak, after spending a full night in prayer, he chose the rest of his team.

> *Jesus went up on a mountain to pray, and he prayed to God all night. At daybreak he called together all of his disciples and chose twelve of them to be apostles. Here are their names:*
>
> > *Simon (whom he named Peter)*
> > *Andrew (Peter's brother)*
> > *James*
> > *John*
> > *Philip*
> > *Bartholomew*
> > *Matthew*
> > *Thomas*
> > *James (son of Alphaeus)*
> > *Simon (who was called the zealot)*

---

[138] Luke 5:1–11.
[139] Luke 5:27–28.

> *Judas (son of James)*
> *Judas Iscariot (who later betrayed*
> *him)*[140]
> *(Luke 6: 12-16, NIV)*

He settled on twelve men. And one of those men betrayed him. One of these chosen men literally sold him for a few silver coins.

More to the Story

The first few disciples were followers of John the Baptist before they began to follow Yeshua.[141]

These were the recce guys; they knew how to gather intelligence. John likely walked the routes that Yeshua would later walk, making notes about the directions and the most efficient paths to take. The recce guys would have built relationships in towns and briefed innkeepers, rabbis, grocers, and other people throughout Israel so they were prepared to meet Yeshua when he would visit their village.

---

[140] Luke 6:12–16 (New International Version).
[141] John 1:35–42.

They built rapport. John was tasked with "*preparing the way for the Lord.*"[142] I don't believe these words were meant solely for preparing hearts and minds for Yeshua. I believe this phrase includes work—hard work. John and his followers would have built footbridges and identified fording points that Yeshua and his disciples would later use. The recce guys would find the fording sites and then pass the bridge building duties over to the engineers; they knew how to build stuff.

These types of mundane details are not discussed in depth in the Bible, but if we use the test that I've discussed numerous times already, it makes perfect sense. How do things actually work in this world? Was Yeshua walking about willy-nilly, making plans by the seat of his pants?

Too often we have an image of "laid back Jesus." That is total nonsense. Yeshua's coming was announced in the Garden of Eden, moments after Adam and Eve sinned.[143] For thousands of years, prophecies were shared that would allow the Jews and ultimately the Gentiles to recognize the Messiah when he arrived. For thousands of years, the Jews

---

[142] Mark 1:3.
[143] Gen. 3:14–15.

followed meticulous customs and excruciatingly detailed rules and laws in preparation to receive the Messiah.

Yahweh laid out the exact dimensions of important items throughout the Bible: Noah's ark, the tabernacle, the Ark of the Covenant, the temple, the exact dress of the priests.

He gave extremely specific details about notable events throughout the Bible: take this many men, say this, blow your trumpets here, wait until I give you a sign.

So why do we have this sense that when Yeshua came, he was mostly winging it?

Yeshua came with a very specific purpose, and had only a couple of years to get it done. There was no time to wander about, get lost, and waste time trying to find food or lodging.

He was on a mission.

II. Lead By Example

The angel must have grown tired of trying to appeal to my sense of mercy and said, "The night is young. There will be plenty of killing." This last statement swayed me. It was logical.

The man on the ground became our first enemy captured. We passed him off to another team and I lined up my squad and said, "Follow me," as we got back to work.

The fighting continued into the morning and then things began to settle down. In the lull, I sat down next to Hale and said, "Hey man, I need you to be on target with your rounds. And when I say bring your fire down, bring your fire down."

He didn't look at me, but hung his head and said, "I don't think I can do it."
"Do what?" I asked.
"I don't think I can kill another man," he said quietly.
I was enraged. I pushed him. I punched him. I yelled at him.

"What about us? Your team? You need to protect us!"

"I don't think I can do it," he repeated.

I pushed him again. I screamed at him:"You're finished! Pack your stuff. You are not a Ranger!" I yelled, "NOT a Ranger! You are a disgrace!" I stormed off and told our Platoon Sergeant what had happened.

Hale was removed from the platoon, taken off the line, and continued the rest of the deployment doing menial support tasks like handing out chow and cleaning our gear.

I was disgusted with Ranger Hale for over thirty years, until I started writing this story down for this book.

I can look back at that time and realize that I was afraid of failure. I was afraid that Ranger Hale's actions would reflect badly on me. My desire to be a tough guy Ranger Team Leader absolutely overshadowed the fact that Hale was struggling with something.

I wanted to be a monster hunter and I was ready to crush anyone who wasn't with me 100%. That is the danger of becoming a monster hunter. You have to learn how to turn it on and off. Sometimes it takes a monster to defeat another monster, but I had not yet learned how to switch back and forth. My lack of empathy for Ranger Hale was monstrous. I feel ashamed of it now.

Ranger Hale, you are out there somewhere, and I want to apologize. I didn't prepare you. I didn't develop you. You weren't ready. I felt like you had failed us. But in fact, I failed you.

I was your Team Leader, and I lacked humility and grace.

Ranger Hale, wherever you are, I am sorry, and I wish you well.

APPOINTMENT IN SAMARRA

WEST BANK

GAZA

BOUNDARIES:
REAL AND IMAGINED

CHAPTER 16

I. Appointment in Samarra[144]

> Because you're not yet taking God seriously," said
> Jesus. "The simple truth is that if you had a mere
> kernel of faith, a poppy seed, say, you would tell
> this mountain, 'Move!' and it would move. There
> is nothing you wouldn't be able to tackle.
> (Matthew 17:20, MSG)

"Please do your best to bring him back alive," I told
Ihsan. "We really want to speak with him, but do

---

[144] "The Appointment in Samarra," retold by W. Somerset Maugham,
1933 (Kansas State University, 2000), https://www.k-state.edu/english/baker/english320/Maugham-AS.htm.

whatever you've gotta do. I don't want any of your guys getting hurt."

"No problem," Ihsan replied. "The Wolf will get him. Easy."

I wasn't so sure but I had faith in him.

Our Iraqi partners located a High-Value Target (HVT) named Natham, from the Al-Marsoumi tribe. This tribe was dispersed around Iraq but mainly between the cities of Samara and Baghdad. In fact, this HVT was the most wanted target for all of the 1-66 Armor Regiment that was part of the 4th Infantry Division at Ft. Carson, CO.
This guy was responsible for the deaths of numerous American soldiers and countless Iraqis from improvised explosive devices and car bombs. For the better part of a year, 1-66 Armor hunted this man. They could not pin him down.

The Iraqi Battalion Commander, Lieutenant Colonel Ihsan, with whom I was partnered, personally knew this terrorist. They had played in the same soccer (football) club together as children. He knew exactly where he was. He was hiding in Baghdad and Ihsan was sending his best guy to get him. Lebeed was nicknamed "The

Wolf." He was fearless, brutal, smart, and could find anyone we asked him to find. Lebeed was a monster hunter.

The CIA wanted Natham Al-Marsoumi. The commander of all coalition forces wanted him. No one could seem to track him down.

I told my bosses that our Iraqi partners could easily capture Natham and bring him back to Samarra. We could then drive him up to Tikrit and anyone who wanted to speak with him could. My boss balked at the idea and denied the mission. Baghdad was in a different battlespace. Our Iraqi force in Samarra was forbidden from traveling to Baghdad without the proper approvals, even if the drive from Samarra to Baghdad is only about two hours.

The rule up at higher headquarters was that there was no boundary crossing without all Battlespace owners approving it.
The next Battlespace Owners Meeting was later in the week. I explained the dilemma to Ihsan, but he could not comprehend it. There was no boundary. How could we pretend there was one? He asked me to allow him to go.

Ihsan implored, "I don't understand. This man is very dangerous. I know where he is right now. I can have him back here before morning."

Natham was with a mistress in Baghdad. I reiterated the situation to my commander but he continued to say no. I told Ihsan to go anyway.

The Wolf cornered Natham as he left a restaurant with his mistress, stuffed him in the trunk, and returned to Samarra. He called me when he got in and I asked him to come over to our compound. The Wolf drove a small sedan and when he pulled up to the compound, he was chain smoking cigarettes like he always did. Flicking a stub out his driver's window, he pointed to the trunk and popped it open from the inside of his car. "Got him," was all he said.

I walked around to the back of the car and there was Natham, hog tied with flex cuffs, uncomfortably contorted with his hands and feet tied together behind him. It must have been a hell of a ride from Baghdad.

Boundaries: Real and Imagined

There are a few things in the account of Yeshua's life that always puzzled me and made me pause and ask,

"Why did he say this? This doesn't seem to make sense."

Teachers I have had over the years did their best to answer my questions, and most of them were answered well enough. I am not saying all things can be explained. Belief in this story requires belief in the supernatural-—miracles, higher beings, resurrection, eternal life, and many smaller details.

I am not asking you to start believing in the supernatural if you don't already, but what I am asking is that you enjoy learning the real, practical, and even mundane details of this story that make it special. Once you see that this story is special, perhaps then you can begin to entertain the supernatural side of it.

Let's dig into a couple of these phrases and comments in the Story that have always seemed odd to me. In a bunch of instances, following miraculous healings, Yeshua instructed the healed person or their family not to say anything about it.

Don't tell a soul what happened in this room.[145]

Jesus urged them to keep it quiet.[146]

Then Jesus became very stern. "Don't let a soul know how this happened." But they were hardly out the door before they started blabbing it to everyone they met."[147]

Jesus dismissed him with strict orders: "Say nothing to anyone. Take the offering for cleansing that Moses prescribed and present yourself to the priest. This will validate your healing to the people." But as soon as the man was out of earshot, he told everyone he met what had happened, spreading the news all over town. So Jesus kept to out-of-the-way places, no longer able to move freely in and out of the city. But people found him and came from all over.[148]

It always seemed odd to me that Yeshua told so many of the people he healed to be quiet about it. When I asked some of my teachers and pastors

---

[145] Luke 8:56.

[146] Mark 7:36.
[147] Matt. 9:30–31.
[148] Mark 1:43–45.

about this oddity, I was not satisfied with the answers I received. It's not that the answers were necessarily wrong, they just didn't satisfy my instinct that there was more to the story.

I've concluded that there was a very practical reason for Yeshua to limit the fanfare about his miracles. It was politics, and first-century politics were brutal.

Yeshua already knew his fate and needed some time to develop his disciples before he could surrender himself to the political leaders.

More to the Story

As I was digging into the common explanations for why Yeshua told people not to talk about their miraculous healing, I began to feel frustrated. The answers were so religious sounding. And some of them, I am sorry to say, seemed absolutely tone deaf and inconsiderate.

I remember some people tried to explain it to me by saying that Yeshua did not want people to focus only on his miracles and overlook his real reason for coming into the world—to save us from our sins. They further explained to me that Yeshua feared people's attention would be distracted by the miracles he performed instead of the more important aspects of his ministry.

They emphasized that Yeshua came as a prophet and a teacher, and that people should not be attracted to him only for the sake of the miracles he performed.

What?

What are your primary concerns if you are in the hospital today, or suffering from pain, mental illness, or even depression? You are in pain. You are suffering. And that is precisely the biggest problem with religion today. We are so haughty with our demand for you to focus on the law and then the gospel that we fail to address what you need right in the moment. Comfort. Kindness. Healing. Protection.

Jesus healed people because that was their immediate need. He wasn't afraid that they would miss the "more important aspect of his ministry." He knew they could not hear the promise of a new life when they were deafened by fear, pain, and suffering.

Feed the hungry. Clothe the poor. Attend to the widows and orphans. Does anybody remember those instructions? Too often the church today gets bogged down in politics and prosperity. Yeshua was not concerned with politics that way, and he certainly never promised wealth on this earth if you followed him.

In fact, he promised the opposite.[149] Yeshua knew he would suffer, and he knew his disciples would suffer too. He was worried about his guys. They were mostly young men. Some were likely still teenagers.[150] The disciples were susceptible to getting caught up in political traps and Herod was very well known for his treachery.[151]

He was not known as Herod the Great because he was a good man, but because he was a prolific builder. He was a narcissistic lunatic who left megalithic monuments to himself across his kingdom.[152]

---

[149] Mark 1:43–44.
[150] https://www.gotquestions.org/how-old-were-Jesus-disciples.html
[151] Luke 13:32.
[152] https://en.wikipedia.org/wiki/Herod_the_Great

Herod Antipas was very much like his father: a psychopath.[153] He is the one who imprisoned John the Baptizer and ultimately chopped his head off because his mistress's daughter wanted it as a reward for her sexy, provocative dancing.[154]

He ended up being the only one of the Herod dynasty to meet Yeshua face to face. During that meeting, on the night of Yeshua's betrayal, torture, and looming execution, Herod Antipas wanted Yeshua to perform for him, to entertain him with his magic. Herod wanted to show off to his friends but Yeshua refused to "perform" so was sent back to Pilate for his final sentencing. We will dig deeper into this story later.

If you cross-reference the times when Yeshua did not want the healed person to speak of the miraculous event, they occurred in the region under Herod Antipas's control. He was an egomaniacal and paranoid ruler, always fearful of losing control of his subjects and wary of any potential successor, including his wives and children.

---

[153] https://en.wikipedia.org/wiki/Herod_Antipas
[154] Matt. 14; Mark 6.

Capernaum was a border town just a few miles from the Jordan River.[155] It was officially under the rule of Herod Antipas, but little attention was paid to it. Because of its border location, Capernaum had a thriving tax economy and had a Roman garrison nearby to ensure this source of revenue for Rome continued to flow. This border town is where many of the miracles of Yeshua took place.

Yeshua and his ministry could easily have been perceived as a threat to the stability of Herod's tetrarchy. At a minimum, as we see during the Passion Week, Yeshua had become a fascination for Herod, a novelty that grew in curiosity over time.

Yeshua needed time and space to share his message and grow his followers. He needed a couple of years, without interruption from Herod and the Romans, until the time was right. His followers needed time to fully grasp the revolutionary ideas he was sharing with them.

Practically speaking, this is a very pragmatic move. It brings me comfort. Yeshua was protecting his

---

[155] https://en.wikipedia.org/wiki/Capernaum

followers. Just as when we must weigh our decisions and choices, Yeshua needed to do so as well.

Did he seek divine counsel? I think he did, but it is clear through his prayers in Gethsemane that all these things were not revealed to him. I believe Yeshua received divine counsel in much the same way that it is afforded all of us—a gift that most of us do not even recognize.

Yeshua prayed. He fasted. He surrounded himself with people he trusted and loved.

Yeshua walked in duty and faithfulness. I believe he knew his fate was going to be terrible and painful, but he did not know the exact hour of this fate. So, like us, he did his best. And what he did was enough for all of us. We can rest in that thought. We are expected to do our best, but Yeshua has already purchased our freedom for us. We simply need to accept his gift.

II. Appointment in Samarra

We had Natham Al-Marsoumi but no American force wanted to take him. We didn't capture him the right way. We didn't follow the rules correctly. We crossed boundaries without clearing it appropriately. US Forces refused to place him in their jail so I held Natham in our jail for a few days.

He, Ihsan, and Lebeed were all friendly. They talked, smoked cigarettes, and even kicked the soccer ball around a bit, for old time's sake. Natham seemed relieved to be in an "American" jail. He was worried what would happen to him if I handed him directly to the Iraqis. He was very cooperative. He laid out, in great detail, the burgeoning insurgency. He really was just a money guy, not a real threat, but he knew everyone, and had access to an incredible amount of information. He was short, chubby, and soft. Not a monster.

Still, no Americans wanted to meet with him. We even invited him into our house to eat some warm meals and play darts. We recorded everything he was telling us and sent daily reports to higher command with the expectation that they would in turn pass the intel to the CIA and coalition forces.

After about a week passed, I was ready to hand him to Ihsan and Lebeed for his final judgment. I sent up one last report and explained that I was letting

Natham go and releasing him to the Iraqis the next day.

Finally, US Forces relented and asked us to drive him to Tikrit for in-processing into the prison there. We drove to a nondescript building on the sprawling Forward Operating Base in Tikrit. We rang the doorbell and were met at the front door by a young man in civilian clothes.

"Can I help you?" he asked.

"Yeah, I'm Captain Tiegs, we just drove up from Samarra with this prisoner. I was told to bring him here."

"Got it," the young man answered. "Come in and please wait here." He pointed to a living area behind him with a big screen TV, Xbox, cushy furniture, and a few coffee tables strewn about.

We came in and sat down. It was me, Ihsan, Lebeed, Natham, and one of my intel/security guys. We sat there for half an hour and then helped ourselves to some of the snacks nearby.

In the middle of some peanuts and Coke, a man with a beard entered the room and hollered, "Who are you?! What are you doing here? You can't be in here?! You need to get out of here! Who are these guys? You can't be in here?!"

I was trying to answer him but he grew louder and redder, like he was losing control.
Lebeed and Ihsan continued to eat peanuts. I held up my hand and said, "Take it easy, man. I'm Captain Tiegs. I have a prisoner here for you."
"Which one is the prisoner?" the bearded man asked me.

I was incredulous. "Um, the one in the hood and the handcuffs, who do you think?"
"Who are these two?" he asked, pointing to Lebeed and Ihsan.

"They're the ones that captured him."
"You can't be here. They can't be in here," he said again.

"Ok, I get it, we were invited in. Where do you want us to go?"
The bearded guy led us back to the porch. "Wait here," he said.
We stood on the porch for a while and then sat down on the steps.

Eventually another man came out and said, "I'm here to sign for the prisoner." He pushed a clipboard with some paperwork to my chest. "Please sign here."

I signed the document and asked if he would want to speak with Lebeed, or Ihsan too.

"No, we just want him."

With the paperwork signed, I handed Natham Al-Marsoumi to the man standing in front of me and left.

I headed over to Advanced Operating Base (AOB) where my commander lived and worked. As soon as I entered the AOB, some MP's met me and I was read my rights for violating the boundaries. I broke the rules. It was unacceptable. My team and I were placed on suspension.

Boundaries. Some are real and some are fake. Some are necessary to maintain peace, and some are simply designed to exploit others.

Shortly after the end of World War I, the nation we call Iraq was established.[156] For nearly 400 years prior

---

[156] https://en.wikipedia.org/wiki/History_of_Iraq

to World War I, the provinces that would be formed into Iraq were distinct, semi-autonomous provinces ruled by the Ottoman Empire. The provinces were unique in religion, tribal loyalties, and even cultural norms. Shiites, Sunnis, and Kurds co-existed under the Ottoman rule that balanced the complexities of the local clan and tribal alliances.

When the Ottoman Empire chose to partner with Germany, they sealed their fate as World War I ended. Their empire was quickly dismantled and rewritten. The British took pencil to map and created a whole new set of countries.

Back in 2004, the United States was just beginning to come to terms with the fact that the "victory" in Iraq was not a "Mission Accomplished."

Insurgents and Al Qaeda were pivoting to a drawn-out, underground war. Some of us recognized this early on, especially those of us who were partnered with Iraqi forces who truly understood their home-field advantage in outmaneuvering the insurgents and staying one step ahead of Al Qaeda.

Unfortunately, US military leaders would not even consider the idea of decentralized operations with

Special Forces teams empowering and enabling Iraqi forces to fight and win their own way.

Some of the Iraqi men I fought with over the years were truly impressive. They were patriots in every sense of the word. They knew what they were fighting for.

Relatively young, most of them were between nineteen and thirty-five years old and they saw an opportunity to rewrite Iraqi history and return it to a place of honor on the global stage. Iraq and Babylon were ancient dynasties, responsible for advancements that spread to the entire world, but this was ancient history. For generations, Iraq was abandoned, nearly forgotten, left to despots.

I will never forget the Iraqi men who partnered with us, agreed to follow me into combat, and trusted me with their lives and the lives of their families and children. It truly was an honor to fight with these men and try to help them realize a new future.

We fought hard and won each battle we fought together.

I went on to fight battles in other places and with other partners while they stayed and defended their communities.

We never lost hope.

This story took place when we were turning the tide against the insurgency in Iraq. It didn't matter if neither of our countries quite understood what was happening yet.

But we did.

My job, and our detachment, was to fight the insurgency in the Salah ad Din Province, based out of Samarra. My job was to build a cohort of US Special Forces and Iraqi troops to hunt, capture, and kill insurgents. The training alone forges bonds with each other but fighting together in combat forges an even stronger and deeper bond.

A unique bond.

One that I shared, at the time, with more Kurdish and Iraqi soldiers than US soldiers.

In combat, there is plenty of time to wait for the conditions to be right for attacking. So we would spend hours together, talking, eating, planning, waiting to set out on a mission.

Each one of the Iraqi leaders had a nickname that they wanted to be called by. It was more than a nickname, it was a name that embodied their spirit, the name was an example of how they saw themselves and wanted to be seen.

Each name was an animal renowned for its strength, speed, or cunning. Ihsan was the Falcon.

Lebeed was the Wolf.

We also had the Eagle, the Jaguar, and the Panther One was simply known as the Sergeant Major and one of the leaders was actually named Saddam Hussein.

He could not live that one down and we jokingly called him the President.

This was not the only lighthearted title. There was a young man who was about six feet, five inches tall and weighed at least 230 pounds who we called the Donkey. His size resembled the size of a donkey, but also, his job was logistics and he moved supplies all over Samarra for us.

He was a donkey.

The lighthearted nicknames were rare. The titles of Wolf, Eagle, Falcon, Panther, and Jaguar were to be taken deadly seriously.

And our team honored that in full.

Often when we were waiting for an operation to begin, we would play darts. We would shoot darts for hours

as we talked and laughed. We would shoot darts as a
respite between planning, preparing, and worrying.
Late into the night we would play, waiting for our
enemies to go to sleep so we could descend upon them
in the night like birds of prey and apex predators.

We were in Samarra over Thanksgiving and Christmas
of 2003 and ushered in the New Year and even
celebrated Easter in 2004 there. Each of these holidays
are unforgettable to me. For Christmas that year, I had
asked my wife to buy some darts with unique fletching
for each friend. The fletching had images of each
animal: Falcon, Wolf, Jaguar, Panther, and one with
the Sergeant Major rank on it.

On Christmas night, before we headed out on a
mission, the Iraqi leaders opened their gifts.

They could not have been more delighted or honored.
With tears in their eyes, they appreciated the gesture.
They knew we understood how important these names
were to them.

Live or die, it would be part of their legacy.

They were also extremely moved that a woman far
away in America might also somehow understand, in a
small way, what they were going through, what they
were fighting for.

Most of these brave men are no longer with us. Most
of them were murdered after the United States

prematurely exited Iraq and ISIS emerged from the ashes of the Al Qaeda insurgency.

Somehow, unfortunately, global media, especially American media, never bothered to truly care about the Iraqi people and certainly never told the story of patriots like these men. Everyone was too busy wrangling for political power and simply twisted and turned the events of the war to fit their narrative. The real devastation was to the Iraqi and Kurdish people, two groups we still use and abuse today to fit a political narrative.

This story of Natham Al- Marsoumi was when I knew that we would not succeed in Iraq. We created boundaries that did not exist. We needed to have those lines drawn so we could feel like we were in control. But we were not in control. We were never in control. We *are* never in control.

Religions build fake boundaries. Religions hide behind the fake boundaries they build. Religions are too quick to go to war to defend their pretend boundaries.

There are no boundaries between us and God. We should not pretend there are. Boundaries should always be real and never imagined.

I think about these men often, all of them Muslims. My prayer is that we see each other again in the next life. Any sense of abandonment long forgotten.

And we play some darts together. And talk long into the night. But this time, hopefully a few of the disciples will join us. Maybe Yeshua will swing by and throw a few bullseyes too. And we will all feel like brothers with no boundaries between us.

WE ALL NEED VALIDATION

PAN'S GROTTO:
CONSTERNATION TURNS TO CONFIDENCE

CHAPTER 17

I. We All Need Validation

*So speak encouraging words to one another.
Build up hope so you'll all be together in this,
no one left out, no one left behind. I know
you're already doing this; just keep on doing it.
(1 Thessalonians 5: 10-11, MSG)*

"We are jumping too low for that reserve chute to even open. Why are we wearing them?" One of my guys asked.

"Dude, do I look like I'm in charge of this invasion?" I asked him.

"Corporal, seriously, what are we wearing them for?"

His question was valid and I didn't have an answer for him. I didn't want to say it was because we were told to so I replied, "I don't know about you, but this thing covers my balls. Not saying it will suck up too many rounds but it sure feels better having something covering my balls as we hang it out there, knees to the breeze, with dudes shooting up at us. Don't ya think?"

He nodded and smiled. "Duly noted," was all he said.

When we were alerted to come in to work, it had taken us all by surprise. We were scheduled to go on Christmas leave that next day, Monday, and we only got block leave every three years over Christmas. None of us were expecting a call to come in and prepare for war.

When we got to the barracks, all of the pay phones were disassembled and there were new MP's manning the gates with multiple checkpoints set up all around Hunter Army Airfield. We had no idea what we were called in for and had no idea where we might be heading.

It was only after we switched on CNN did we realize that we were bound for Panama. They were plainly stating that the 82nd Airborne and the US Army Rangers were preparing to invade Panama to oust the dictator, Manuel Noriega.

So much for surprise.

We were expected to remove him from his dictatorial position, ensure he met justice, dissolve his crony forces, and offer order and freedom to the citizens of Panama.

As time went on, the situation on the drop zone became more dire. The Panamanian forces knew we were coming. Noriega knew we were coming.

Rigged up in the plane, we got a final intel dump. The airfield we were about to jump into was a mess. The runway was littered with obstacles and the end of the runway had ZSU 23-4s waiting for us and other anti-aircraft weapons.[157]

_____

[157] https://en.wikipedia.org/wiki/ZSU-23-4_Shilka

All of us in the front and middle of the stick turned around to look at the poor bastards that were at the end of the stick. They would be landing right on top of those guns.

I turned and smiled at an old friend in the back of the airplane. He shook his head, smiled, and flipped me the bird.

I shrugged, smiled, and returned his bird.

It was time to jump into the unknown.

Pan's Grotto: Consternation Turns to Confidence

While on earth, Yeshua was very selective of what he spoke about when, where, and to whom. His messages, while universal, were tailored to each audience.

He was very careful and conservative in sharing the stories of his miraculous powers in the areas controlled by Herod Antipas. He was much more open and encouraging for people to share

testimonials of his power in Philip's tetrarchy, with
Caesarea Philippi as its capital, but not always.
There is a story in which he warns his disciples to
remain silent about his power and his true identity
in Philip's empire:

> *When Jesus came to the region of Caesarea
> Philippi, he asked his disciples, "Who do people
> say the Son of Man is?"*
>
> *They replied, "Some say John the Baptist;
> others say Elijah; and still others, Jeremiah or
> one of the prophets."*
>
> *"But what about you?" he asked. "Who do you
> say I am?"*
>
> *Simon Peter answered, "You are the Messiah,
> the Son of the living God."*
>
> *Jesus replied, "Blessed are you, Simon son of
> Jonah, for this was not revealed to you by flesh
> and blood, but by my Father in heaven. And I
> tell you that you are Peter, and on this rock I
> will build my church, and the gates of Hades
> will not overcome it. I will give you the keys of
> the kingdom of heaven; whatever you bind on*

*earth will be bound in heaven, and whatever
you loose on earth will be loosed in heaven."*
**Then he ordered his disciples not to tell
anyone that he was the Messiah.**[158] *(Matthew
16:13-20, NIV)*

More to the Story

This is a unique case where Yeshua ordered his
followers to be silent about his identity in Philip's
tetrarchy. Why did he want his disciples to be quiet?
Where were they? What was happening at this
place?

They were at a place called Banyas (Panias) in
Caesarea Philippi.[159] At this site, there was a series
of pagan temples cut into the limestone cliff face,
with one of them an edifice over the Grotto of Pan.

The Grotto of Pan and the activities around it were
seriously twisted. Pan is the half-goat, half-man god
of the wild and outdoors.[160] He was believed to
govern the seasons and was therefore connected with
fertility. His sexual exploits were legendary, and

---

[158] Matt. 16:13–20 (New International Version).
[159] https://en.wikipedia.org/wiki/Banias
[160] https://en.wikipedia.org/wiki/Pan_(god)

worshiping him was a free-or-all. Being outdoors excused much of the behavior that would otherwise violate social norms, even of an ancient pagan society. This place was crazy. Worshipping Pan included buying time with temple prostitutes, child sacrifice, and even bestiality with the goats was accepted as a form of worship.

The site at Panias was a pagan worship site for centuries. Even prior to the Hellenistic influence and the renaming and rededicating the area to Pan, it was a location where Baal was honored in a similarly sexually depraved manner.

If you follow the stories in the Old Covenant, Baal is the archenemy of Yahweh and the Israelites. Some believe that Panias is the same location known as Baal Gad or Baal Hermon. During the forty-day mission that Joshua and the spies were tasked with, they would have passed through this area in the final days before they needed to return to the Israelite camp and report their findings to Moses.

Baal Gad is the northernmost point to which Joshua's conquests extended after they entered the Promised Land and established a kingdom for the twelve tribes of Israel. In Yeshua's time, the names and events associated with this place would not have been forgotten.

Caesarea Philippi was a bustling place, a fascinating blend of the natural environment and a very modern city.[161] The Panias worship site just outside the city would have had a constant flow of visitors and tourists with ceremonies and debauchery peaking at certain holidays. We cannot be certain if Yeshua and his disciples were there during a high holiday, but I think it is very possible.

I can imagine Yeshua sitting on the hillside overlooking the chaos below when he asked his disciples what I will paraphrase:

Look at the confusion down there, the chaos, the debauchery, the panic. For centuries people have been coming here looking for answers, seeking good fortune, blessings, and getting caught up in the hype of this manipulation. How many temples, idols, and shrines can you see from here? Bestiality and child sacrifice have stained this place. I take pity on the suffering below as we sit here, some of us feeling superior and judgmental, but do not be so quick to

---

[161] https://en.wikipedia.org/wiki/Caesarea_Philippi

feel special. You know some of the stories, but you still need to learn the rest of the story. Who do people say that I AM?

Who do you think that I AM?

The disciples answered him as best they could, but there was still some confusion. Yeshua was recognized as a prophet and the Messiah, the Son of God, but the disciples did not fully understand what it truly meant to be the Son of God.

This story was a meaningful point in Yeshua's ministry. Here he introduced the disciples to what was coming. He tried to make them understand that his life would end in suffering and dying but that he would rise from the dead after three days in the grave.
They didn't get it.

Yeshua's praise for Peter is usually the highlight of this story, and rightfully so, but the last line, "Then he ordered his disciple not to tell anyone that he was the Messiah," has always made me pause. Why did he say that? Why did Yeshua order his disciples to keep this information to themselves?

This was supposed to be a moment of revelation for the disciples but they didn't get it. They didn't quite "know" him yet.

Panias was a place of chaos, frenzy, panic, and confusion. This revelation would not have calmed things down or been received calmly. This was a quiet moment for the disciples to ponder. This was not the time to hasten violence. This was a time when saying nothing was the right answer.

We do not know what happened immediately after this, but looking at the story in Luke, it appears as if they were just entering Caesarea Philippi and had not yet completed what they went there to do.

Perhaps Yeshua was there to visit with Veronica, the woman whom he healed from her twelve-year bleed in Capernaum.[162] [163] Perhaps he simply went there to pray over the city and ask the Spirit to do His work there and in the surrounding towns. When Yeshua traveled, he spent time with people. He let people get to know him.

---

[162] https://en.wikipedia.org/wiki/Saint_Veronica
[163] Luke 8:42–48. There is a tradition that this woman was named Veronica and lived in Caesarea Philippi.

In the Hebrew culture, knowledge and experience are much more intertwined than in western culture. To truly "know" something, you must live it, experience it, and not just intellectualize it.

The Hebrew verb "to know" means to encounter, experience, and share in an intimate way. "To know" denotes an act involving concern, inner engagement, dedication, or attachment to a person. It also means to have sympathy, pity, or affection for someone.[164]

People needed first to know that Yeshua was worthy of their faith and trust.

Then they needed to know that they were worthy of the gift he offered them.

The disciples needed to be encouraged that they, too, were worthy. They didn't recognize that they were the select few who were following in the footsteps of all the Jewish heroes who preceded them.

---

[164] Marvin R. Wilson, *Our Father Abraham: Jewish Roots of the Christian Faith* (Grand Rapids, MI; Dayton, OH: William B. Eerdmans Publishing; Center for Judaic-Christian Studies, 1989).

These young men needed to be instilled with confidence. Things were about to get much harder.

Much more would soon be asked of them.

II. We All Need Validation

On that muggy night, after exchanging middle fingers, we leapt from C141 aircraft at a low altitude of 500 feet and landed on a drop zone that was hotly contested by the Panamanian Defense Forces (PDF) manning it.
The PDF were quickly overpowered, and our mission of securing the necessary airfields to bring in follow-on firepower was accomplished with relatively little loss of life. After a couple of weeks of intermittent fighting, we returned home satisfied with our part in the mission.

We were awarded the coveted combat star to affix to our jump wings. This bronze star denotes that its wearer parachuted into combat against an armed enemy. This is what we all thought at the time; the actual requirement is simply parachuting into a combat zone.

Regardless of why we thought we were getting awarded the combat star, some of the men began to grumble and were vocal in their opinion that we did not deserve it.

We held ourselves to the standard of the men who went before us, parachuting into occupied territory during World War II or parachuting behind enemy lines during the Vietnam War. In both conflicts, paratroopers suffered incredible casualties.

Some of the Vietnam high altitude jump teams disappeared completely, last seen hitting the wind from thousands of feet above the combat zone.

We did not feel worthy.

These discussions lasted for several weeks, even after we were ceremoniously awarded our combat stars. Many Rangers did not affix them to their uniforms but quietly tucked them away in wall lockers and boxes.

Eventually, a group of veterans from World War II came to visit, and during discussions, in between exchanging war stories, someone mentioned our unease with wearing the combat jump star on our uniforms. I will never forget the weathered and hunched World War II veteran who calmly asked, "Did you know what was awaiting you on that drop zone?"

We told him that we knew there would be resistance; we knew we would have to fight our way off the drop zone to assemble and wage our offense.

"But did you know the full extent of what the enemy had in store for you?" he added.

We did not.

"Would it have mattered?" he asked wisely.

It would not have mattered.

The old veteran concluded, "If Satan and all of his evil hordes had been awaiting you on that drop zone, would you have still jumped?"
Every one of us agreed that yes, we all would have jumped. It did not matter what awaited us.

"Why didn't it matter?" he continued to press.

It didn't matter because we fight for each other. We fight for our brothers. We fight because we love our teammates and would rather die than let one of them down.

"That," he said, "is why you should proudly wear that combat jump star. It is not what was actually required of you on that particular night, but for the mere fact that it never would have mattered. You are Rangers. You carry yourselves as Rangers. You fight as Rangers, and live or die, you can be rewarded for your unflinching courage to meet whatever lies before you as a Ranger."

From that day onward, we wore our combat stars with pride. We wore those badges for the men who went before us. Many of those men were asked to sacrifice more than was asked of us.

We did not fail in our mission. We did what was asked of us. We fulfilled the proud lineage of the Rangers who had gone before us. We lived to fight another day and pass our stories down to the next generation.

We finally felt worthy. Soon, more would be asked of us.

FIGHT TO YOUR LAST BREATH

I'M OK, YOU'RE OK!
IT'S GOING TO BE OK!

CHAPTER 18

I. Fight to Your Last Breath

> *I'll be with you. I won't give up on you; I*
> *won't leave you… Strength! Courage!*
> *Don't be timid; don't get discouraged. God,*
> *your God, is with you every step you take.*
> *(Joshua 1: 5-6, 9, MSG)*

When we attend to a wounded soldier, one of the
things we are taught to say immediately is, "You are
going to be OK."

Saying this was as important as knowing how to
apply a pressure dressing, splint a fracture, open an
airway, or properly place a tourniquet. If you were

being evaluated in training on your field medical skills and did everything technically right but never said to your patient, "You're going to be OK," you would fail that task.

That simple sentence can literally be the difference between life and death, hope and despair.

I have experienced it firsthand. As I've rendered aid to young men who were badly shot, blown up, or with body parts torn off, I would say to each of them, "You're going to be OK."

Not all of them would be OK. Some would live. Some would die. But it was my responsibility to give them that one tiny bit of assurance, no matter how bleak things really were.

One man died in my arms. He was a friend.

The streets in Iraq are often very poorly lit, especially in the middle of a war. Returning to Samarra from Tikrit, we were driving along a dangerous stretch of road and we were all on high alert. Without warning, the HMMWV jeep in front of me began to flip and roll, and roll, and roll.

The top gunner, a seasoned Special Forces Master Sergeant, disappeared in the dust. The trail vehicle in which I was sitting quickly arrived at the scene.

We secured the crash site with a perimeter of soldiers, not sure what would happen next. We prepared for a complex ambush while simultaneously tending to the wounded.

As I got nearer to the overturned vehicle, wheels still spinning, I could see where the Master Sergeant lay. It was Ferg. He had been thrown a good distance and was lying motionless in the gravel on the side of the road. His hands appeared to be folded, almost like he was just taking a nap.

I hoped he had been thrown clear of the wreck and had sustained little damage but my hope was in vain.

He had taken the full weight of the vehicle on his chest as it rolled. Being the top gunner manning the machine gun, he was half in and half out of the vehicle before it flipped and began rolling. It had all happened so suddenly. He was crushed.

I knelt beside him to check his pulse. It was incredibly faint. I told him he was going to be ok. He was not breathing, either. I placed my mouth on his and began to try to breathe for him.

In the trauma classes I had attended, you alternate breathing for the patient and compressions on their chest. But this was not a training scenario. This was real.

He did not have a chest left. Every bone appeared to be broken. Even my slightest touch produced a weird crackling sound like I was crushing a bag of thin potato chips.

I didn't know what to do, so I just kept trying to breathe for him. His chest would slightly rise with each of my breaths but little else was happening. I also prayed that God would save him. I prayed that he would not die. Not here. Not like this.

Then a strange thing happened. This place on the side of the road just outside Samarra, Iraq became a thin place. God planted a thought in my head that sounded like, "Let him go, he really is OK."

I got mad. I yelled to no one in particular, "No, I will not let him go, he's not OK." I continued to breathe into his mouth and lungs.

The complex ambush we were expecting did not occur.

In this thin space, I could sense a couple of angels standing there.[165] I couldn't see them clearly, but I could kind of see them faintly. I spoke to them softly, "Help me. Please help me save him." But they just stood there with their hands folded. It looked like they were just patiently waiting.

And then in this thin space, I could hear Ferg say, "It's time for me to go. It's ok. Let my wife know that I love her."

Then I could see him standing there, not quite clearly visible, just like the angels. And Ferg, like the angels, was looking down on me. I was still on my knees. I nodded and said, "OK." And then he took one last breath. It was not one of my breaths, it was

---

[165] Lacy Clark Ellman, "Thin Places, Holy Spaces: Where Do You Go to Encounter God?," *A Sacred Journey* (blog), accessed March 21, 2023, https://www.asacredjourney.net/thin-places/.

his breath. It was a long, slow inhale and a long, slow exhale.

And then his spirit left his body. Ferg and the angels that were standing with him simply floated away. And this thin space simply felt peaceful.

This earthly journey for him was over. He was beginning a new journey where I could not go.

Not yet.

I'm OK, You're OK: It's Going to Be OK

Shortly after Yeshua finished his mission in Caesarea Philippi, he went through what is known as the Transfiguration. He chose a couple of disciples to get to "know" him more deeply.

Here is the account of the Transfiguration from Matthew:

> *Jesus took Peter and the brothers, James and John, and led them up a high mountain. His appearance changed from the inside out, right*

*before their eyes. Sunlight poured from his face.
His clothes were filled with light. Then they
realized that Moses and Elijah were also there
in deep conversation with him.*

*Peter broke in, "Master, this is a great moment!
What would you think if I built three
memorials here on the mountain—one for you,
one for Moses, one for Elijah?"*

*While he was going on like this, babbling, a
light-radiant cloud enveloped them, and
sounding from deep in the cloud a voice: "This
is my Son, whom I love; with him I am well
pleased. Listen to him!"*

*When the disciples heard it, they fell flat on
their faces, scared to death. But Jesus came over
and touched them. "Don't be afraid." When
they opened their eyes and looked around all
they saw was Jesus, only Jesus.*

*Coming down the mountain, Jesus swore them
to secrecy. "Don't breathe a word of what
you've seen. After the Son of Man is raised
from the dead, you are free to talk."*

The disciples, meanwhile, were asking questions. "Why do the religion scholars say that Elijah has to come first?"

Jesus answered, "Elijah does come and get everything ready. I'm telling you, Elijah has already come but they didn't know him when they saw him. They treated him like dirt, the same way they are about to treat the Son of Man." That's when the disciples realized that all along he had been talking about John the Baptizer.[166] (Matthew 17:1-13, MSG)

The disciples still didn't really get it.

More to the Story

The traditional location of this story is Mount Tabor in Israel.[167] But I doubt the story happened here. Like some other sites in Israel, people say, "We know it didn't happen here, but it should have." This is said tongue in cheek, but also accurately reflects the sentiment of many visitors at special sites. Some of these remarkable sites look like a lump of dirt while others are overly ornate and

---

[166] Matt. 17:1–13 (The Message).
[167] https://en.wikipedia.org/wiki/Mount_of_Transfiguration

overcrowded. Mount Tabor is neither of these. It is a peaceful garden, with a beautiful church, high on a hilltop with a breathtaking view. It is one of my favorite sites to visit in Israel, even if the Transfiguration did not happen here.

The most likely location for the Transfiguration is Mount Hermon, the highest point of Israel. Banyas and Pan's Grotto were situated on a lower shoulder of Mount Hermon, so it also makes sense that this event happened shortly after the events of the previous chapter.

Of all the important figures in the Bible, why do you think it was Moses and Elijah who showed up? Remember how we explored the idea that Yeshua went to Mount Sinai during his forty days of fasting? If he did, he likely would have met with Moses and Elijah and God Himself. These men are intricately connected with Yeshua and his Father, Yahweh.

Moses was the deliverer of Israel from their oppressors.[168] He was given the power to perform miracles. He was the intercessor between the

---

[168] Deut. 34:10–12.

Israelites and God. Moses was saved from a massacre that was intended to wipe out the Israelite infant boys.

Moses grew up in Egypt, as part of the ruling Pharaoh's own family. Moses was a prince, a nobleman, but he became an outcast and had to flee Egypt. Later, Yahweh called him to service from a burning bush on Mount Sinai.[169]

Moses was emboldened and encouraged to take on the mission set before him. He returned to Egypt and demanded freedom for all the Israelites. It was not an easy task, but he eventually succeeded and led the Israelites on the exodus from Egypt to reclaim their inheritance in the Promised Land.[170]

Along the way, they stopped at the foot of Mount Sinai. Yahweh descended and called Moses to meet with Him at the top of the mountain.[171] Moses was there with God for forty days and forty nights. He didn't eat any food or drink any water.[172] God spoke with Moses face to face, as two men would speak to

---

[169] Exod. 2–3. , https://en.wikipedia.org/wiki/Moses
[170] Exod. 7–12.
[171] Exod. 19:20.
[172] Exod. 34:28.

one another. At one point, Moses asked to see Yahweh in His full glory, and Yahweh agreed to reveal a little more of Himself to Moses.[173] God passed through a cleft between two rocks to share just a quick glimpse of His back. When Moses finally came down from Mount Sinai, the skin of his face glowed because he had been exposed to a glimpse of God's glory.[174]

Moses had met with God, face to face.
Elijah is another man who met with God, face to face.

After death threats from the king and queen, Elijah walked forty days and nights, all the way to Mount Sinai. When he got there, he crawled into a cave and went to sleep.[175] God awakened him and told him to stand in the opening of the cave. He wanted to reveal Himself to Elijah.

> *A hurricane wind rips through the mountains and shatters rocks but God wasn't in the hurricane.*

---

[173] Exod. 33.
[174] Exod. 34:39.
[175] 1 Kings 19:8–9.

After the wind came an earthquake, but God wasn't in the earthquake.

After the earthquake came fire, but God wasn't in the fire.
After the fire came a gentle and quiet whisper. This whisper was God.[176]

When Elijah heard the quiet voice, he muffled his face with his great cloak, went to the mouth of the cave, and stood there.

And then Elijah spoke with God, which emboldened and encouraged him to take on the mission set before him. He returned to his duties in Israel, found Elisha, and began to prepare Elisha to follow in his footsteps.

Remember how Elijah's life ended? He was swept up to heaven in a fiery chariot.

Do you remember how Moses's life ended? God commended him for preparing Joshua to lead after him. And then God personally buried Moses.

---

[176] 1 Kings 19:11–13.

The Transfiguration was the fulfillment of many different promises and an intersection of these incredible heroes.

Can we try to guess what Yahweh, Moses, Elijah, and Yeshua were talking about?

We will never know for sure, but I think the conversation was meant to encourage Yeshua. Right after this event, Yeshua was emboldened and encouraged to take on the mission set before *him*.

It was *his* time.
Perhaps Yahweh repeated similar words of encouragement that he had shared with Joshua many years before.

> *Be strong and very courageous. Be careful to obey all the law my servant Moses gave you; do not turn from it to the right or to the left, that you may be successful wherever you go. Keep this Book of the Law always on your lips; meditate on it day and night, so that you may be careful to do everything written in it. Then you will be prosperous and successful. Have I not commanded you? Be strong and courageous. Do not be afraid; do not be discouraged, for the*

Lord your God will be with you wherever you go.[177] *(Joshua 1:5-9, NIV)*

Everyone needs encouragement when times get tough, even Yeshua did. Following this event, he began the slow march toward the events that led to his torture and crucifixion.

This story should embolden you and encourage you to take on the mission set before you, whatever it may be.

II. Fight to Your Last Breath

I want to encourage all of you who are hurting, feeling hopeless, feeling despair: "You're going to be OK." Hang on for one more minute. Breathe. Hang on for one more hour.

We used to call it the "golden hour." If we could get a badly wounded soldier to the appropriate level of care in an hour, their chances of survival skyrocketed.

---

[177] Josh. 1:5–9 (New International Version).

"You're going to be OK."

Stay alive for one more hour. Breathe. Fight one more day.

If your soul is OK, you're going to be OK.

The story about Ferg has a side to it that I rarely talk about. The reason we were even on the road from Tikrit to Samarra was that I was returning from an ass-chewing by my boss. My Operational Detachment Alpha (ODA) was fighting nearly every day to first survive and then to expand our reach and bring the fight to the enemy. Our aggressiveness and Operational Tempo (OPTEMPO) were unique and my boss, the Company Commander, simply could not keep up and he began to feel uncomfortable. He applied control measures to slow us down but we continued to press the fight. I did my best to communicate to him that a strong offense was our best defense but it just didn't compute with him.

He was safely tucked away on the giant military base in Tikrit, far from danger and the ever looming tribal insurgency and burgeoning resistance led by Al Qaeda. I was a brash captain and may not have been as tactful as I should have been with a superior officer.

Keep in mind, this was 2004, we didn't have reliable email and radio comms were kept to a minimum. We communicated through short encrypted data bursts. This was a very difficult way to express anything that required some nuance.

The situation where our Iraqi partners "violated" the boundaries and went to pick up an HVI was one of the events that strained things nearly to the breaking point. I honestly don't remember the official reason why I was summoned from Samarra to Tikrit, but what I got was an ass-chewing. And apparently the ass-chewing had to be in person.

I took a few members of my team and we drove to Tikrit. I met my commander, he summarily chewed my ass, banished me to an extra bedroom for a few hours and then told me to return to my base in Samarra.

Ferg volunteered to ride back with us. He wanted to check out Samarra.

I was glad to have him.

He stood tall in the gun turret, taking it all in.

I was behind him in my HMMWV stewing. The scolding didn't really sting, it was the absurdity of it all. We were in Iraq to fight.

And win.

I sat with my thoughts, just wanting to get back to Samarra. Get back to my men.

Then Ferg's vehicle began flipping and I knew things were not going to be ok.

You want to know a little secret?

I am still not ok.

MAKE IT HAPPEN

THE ENEMY GETS A VOTE:
IF THEY REALIZE IT OR NOT

CHAPTER 19

I. Make It Happen

At the right time I'll make it happen. (Isaiah 60:22, MSG)

We flew to a loiter spot to get closer to the target.

After watching the Al Qaeda leader for hours, we began to see a pattern emerge with his movements. We figured that we had a window of about seven minutes to be able to catch him in between villages with their maze of structures and canals through which we did not want to try to navigate. We had to thread this needle and get him while he was in the open desert. It was safer for us, and it was safer for the peaceful villagers who did not deserve to be caught in the middle of this fight.

I asked the flight lead to put the helicopters down to conserve fuel, expecting to sit there for only a few minutes. The flight armada circled and then landed on a small plateau between two streambeds.

This landing spot was odd.

We had been working with this flight crew for months, and we were precisely dialed in. Things were so in sync that we rarely even needed to speak. The complex drill of a mixed aerial and ground attack had become almost second nature to all of us. But something didn't feel right.

We almost always landed in a place where we had a clear line of sight, which translates into clear shooting lanes out to 300 meters or so. Setting down between the dry streambeds only gave us about 200 meters of clear sight on two sides and only about seventy-five meters of clear sight on the other two sides.

I was about to get on the radio and ask why we were landing there, but hesitated.

I rationalized a few things. We would only be there a few minutes. It wasn't that bad a spot.

Surely if it was an unsafe location the Sergeant Major or one of the team leaders would protest.

I waited for a few seconds as the dust kicked up and the helicopters began to settle into the sand. No one came up on the net and we settled into our usual ground formation. I certainly didn't want to come across as the worrywart know-it-all officer. If these more experienced operators were fine with it, I'd be fine with it.

Any concern quickly slipped from my mind. Besides, it was quite cold, and we all had to relieve ourselves in a seriously bad way. The blades were still spinning when the men poured out of the helicopters. If I hadn't also had to pee so badly, I would have thought we were assaulting something. A team walked around the perimeter and checked for any threats we may have overlooked, and any residual apprehension about our temporary LZ drifted away. We settled into the usual priorities of work, relieve yourself, drink water, check your weapons and equipment, conduct any minor maintenance you needed to address, and have a quick bite of food. And of course, start goofing off in that interesting way that men do in the middle of combat. One-liners started coming across the radio that were soon followed by arguments about the best type of pizza. We seemed to be evenly split on whether pineapple belongs on top of pizza or not.

We continued to monitor the target as he seemed to be attending to mundane things in and around his walled compound. One ISR platform replaced another, and we bided our time waiting for an opportunity to pounce.

During a routine diagnostic, one of the helicopter crew chiefs indicated that something was malfunctioning. We had two choices: send the bird back for repairs, or send another one of the smaller aircraft back to our base to get the requisite part. The helicopter could fly, it just wasn't going to be able to perform some of the aerial acrobatics that were required for our attack profile. It would be 45 minutes of ground loiter before we would have the part back, and then a few more minutes to conduct a mechanical swap.

Our temporary LZ just became more permanent. I don't remember giving it any more thought than that.

We wanted to change our plan to conduct a hard point assault on the compound of the targeted individual. After watching him for many hours, we concluded that he was there alone. Even if he were armed, he would be no match for our team. Higher command was not fond of daylight hardpoint raids, but I argued that it was a safer move than waiting for nightfall and sending in a team that no longer had the situational awareness that we had earned.

We got approval for the daylight assault, and we began to switch our focus to the details of that task. We needed to reconfigure the air load, a few guys needed to make some small adjustments to their gear, and we needed to meet in the middle of the perimeter to "rock drill" the plan in the sand so everyone knew specifically where they were going, what their specific tasks were and what we expected the helicopters to do while we were on the target.

The men were beginning to assemble in the center of the perimeter. Some of us had our weapons with us; some of us left them sitting in the helicopter. A few of us had on our body armor only because the radios were attached to the plate carrier, and it was often easier just to leave it all on.

We were in various levels of disrobing. Because of the bitter cold, we were wearing layers of insulating clothing, heavy jackets, and heavy gloves. We needed to shed a bunch of layers in preparation for the assault. Like those first minutes of a cold morning run or swim, you must bear the cold at first because soon enough, your body will heat up and the sweat will begin to pour.

We expected our target to see and hear the helicopters a few minutes out and make a run for it. We needed to be prepared for a foot chase.

I was standing on the south side of the perimeter as one of the team leaders began to sketch out the objective in the sand. My helmet and rifle were about 20 meters away, sitting in the helicopter. One of my top layers was shed, draped over my shoulder. I struggled to keep my balance as I removed a bottom layer. My overpants were down around my ankles when a machine gun opened fire just to my rear. Bullets were ricocheting into our perimeter from two different locations. My first thought, rather senseless, was, "Are they shooting at us?"

The Enemy Gets a Vote: If They Realize it or Not

Yeshua knew that his mission would end in his death, but his disciples had a difficult time fathoming that fact.

After the experience of the Transfiguration, the disciples gathered in Galilee. Yeshua once again tried to explain to them what was coming. He said to them,

> *"The Son of Man is going to be delivered into the hands of men. They will kill him, and on the third day he will be raised to life." And the disciples were filled with grief.*[178] *(Matthew 17: 22-23 NIV)*

As the disciples started to come to terms with Yeshua's true identity, they simply could not imagine his time was already short.

---

[178] Matt. 17:22–23 (New International Version).

Yeshua's mission took him through Judea, Samaria, and the surrounding areas to reach the people there. He healed the sick, preached repentance and redemption, cast out demons, taught many parables, and let the people get to know him. He continued to demonstrate a life of service, fasting, and prayer.

The disciples assumed more and more responsibility and the pace of the ministry accelerated. Yeshua sent out seventy more disciples to spread the good news.[179] His popularity grew and the crowds became almost unmanageable.

But not everyone was a fan.

Herod, the Pharisees, and many of the priests grew more jealous. A plot to get rid of this nuisance declaring himself the Messiah grew. They feared they would lose their power if Yeshua's teachings continued to spread.

The Sanhedrin, the priests, the Pharisees, and the Sadducees of 33 A.D. were power mongers, rich, and consumed by their own egos.

---

[179] Luke 10.

Yeshua ran out of patience for them quickly. After being invited to dinner with one of the Pharisees, Yeshua, exasperated with their pride and hypocrisy, said:

"I've had it with you! You're hopeless, you Pharisees! Frauds! You keep meticulous account books, tithing on every nickel and dime you get, but manage to find loopholes for getting around basic matters of justice and God's love. Careful bookkeeping is commendable, but the basics are required.

"You're hopeless, you Pharisees! Frauds! You love sitting at the head table at church dinners, love preening yourselves in the radiance of public flattery.
Frauds! You're just like unmarked graves: People walk over that nice, grassy surface, never suspecting the rot and corruption that is six feet under."

One of the religion scholars spoke up: "Teacher, do you realize that in saying these things you're insulting us?"

He said, "Yes, and I can be even more explicit. You're hopeless, you religion scholars! You load people down with rules and regulations, nearly breaking their backs, but never lift even a finger to help...

"You're hopeless, you religion scholars! You took the key of knowledge, but instead of unlocking doors, you locked them. You won't go in yourself and won't let anyone else in either."

As soon as Jesus left the table, the religion scholars and Pharisees went into a rage. They went over and over everything he said, plotting how they could trap him in something from his own mouth.[180] *(Luke 11:42-54, MSG)*

All the antagonists were now united on one side. The Pharisees, Sadducees, Temple Leaders, and Herod were all plotting to arrest Yeshua. They still needed to get the Romans on their side.

Yeshua knew they were plotting, but he was not finished with his mission. He needed to make one

---

[180] Luke 11:42–54 (The Message).

last trip to Jerusalem. The highest holiday of the
year was coming. The Passover celebration would
bring hundreds of thousands of visitors to Jerusalem.
Yeshua and his disciples would be among them. The
disciples had no idea, but Yeshua knew that this
would be his last visit to the holy city.

> *Now Jesus was going up to Jerusalem. On the
> way, he took the Twelve aside and said to
> them, "We are going up to Jerusalem, and the
> Son of Man will be delivered over to the chief
> priests and the teachers of the law. They will
> condemn him to death and will hand him over
> to the Gentiles to be mocked and flogged and
> crucified. On the third day he will be raised to
> life!"[181] (Mark 20:17-19, NIV)*

The disciples could not understand this clear
warning. Yeshua's popularity was at a crescendo, and
they couldn't see how this could ever end, let alone
so soon. People were being healed, demons were
being driven out, Yeshua was raising people from
the dead. How could this end so soon?

---

[181] Mark 20:17–19 (New International Version).

As the miracles became more stunning, the religious leaders felt more threatened. They began to concoct the idea that Yeshua was an existential threat to Israel. They convinced themselves and others that he had to die, or they might face the wrath of Rome. After Yeshua brought Lazarus back from the dead, Caiaphas himself stated,

> *"It is better that one man die for the people than that the whole nation perish."*[182]

After this declaration, there was no turning back. Their vote was cast.

Although Yeshua and the disciples lay low for a few weeks, supporters of the Sanhedrin in the city of Jerusalem were on high alert, awaiting Yeshua's return for the festivals. When Yeshua arrived on Palm Sunday, greeted like a king, with throngs of people cheering him as the Messiah, his fate was sealed.

Following his triumphant arrival, Yeshua, the Lamb of God, spent four days in Jerusalem speaking to the people in parables about justice, dedication,

---

[182] John 11:49–52.

stewardship, and love. He was infuriating the Sadducees and Pharisees. They were ready to strike, but were held back because they were afraid of the crowd supporting Yeshua.[183] They were filled with rage but did not want to be reckless.

The Pharisees, Sadducees, and Chief Priests were unified in their mission to destroy Yeshua. They got everything they needed in order and waited for the right place and right time to spring their ambush.

More to the Story

It is important to note that throughout Israel's history, there had been others who claimed to be "Messiahs," such as Judas of Galilee and Theudas, who are mentioned in the Book of Acts.[184] There were charlatans, rebels, and zealots who were continually threatening the tenuous balance that Jewish leaders maintained with the Romans. And Galilee was the region most directly connected to these rebels. So Yeshua easily fit into this narrative of rabble from the north that needed to be silenced.

---

[183] Matt. 21:45.
[184] Acts 5:35–37.

It seems obvious now, but as this story was unfolding, the ending was not clear. Yeshua came to earth to die, and somebody was going to ambush him, but the individual characters in this story always had a choice. I have moments of sympathy for the Pharisees, Sadducees, Chief Priests, and the Romans. Even Judas. They were merely pawns in this incredible game. They had no idea that they were dealing with the real Messiah, the Son of God. They were the bad guys and didn't even recognize it. The moment they sprung their trap, they were already doomed and didn't even know it.

My sympathy passes quickly. All these men had a choice to make; they had their own vote to cast. At any time, they could have rewritten their own personal ending.

They did not have to try to kill Yeshua.

Some of the men were blinded by hate and pride.

Others were consumed with apathy and indifference.

II. Make It Happen

Another machine gun burst ricocheted around us. "They were definitely shooting at us," I quickly deduced.

Keep in mind, this was about my eighth combat tour, so even as I describe how nonchalant we were, bordering on laziness, we were very attuned to a gunfight. As the first burst of machine-gun fire splattered rocks and bullet shrapnel at our feet, the men sprang into action.

Thoughts rushed my mind: get to the helicopter, it's where your rifle is; get these helicopters in the air; protect them—we can't afford to get one of them shot up. I can't believe these guys, whoever they are, have the balls to try to ambush us. Do they not know this will not end well for them?

An RPG flew past the lead helicopter, narrowly missing its main body. Uh oh, I realized, they have rockets, too.

I got to the helicopter and started to guide the flight lead. "Get these birds up and out of here. We'll assault through the ambush. Get a team on the helos and create an aerial base of fire for us to maneuver under."

Instinctively, the entire troop got online and returned fire, suppressing the area where the enemy fire was coming from, creating a window for the helicopters to spin up and begin their counterattack.

We continued a steady rate of fire as the helicopters lifted off to a safe distance. To my relief, even though some of the birds had sustained some bullet holes, nothing critical was damaged. They lifted off smoothly, with two helos each having a gun team on board, rising behind us, and covering our forward assault.

I calmly ordered, "Attack, attack, attack," and the ground teams began their maneuver.

It was flawless, a synchronized movement that was wholly lethal in its intent. The enemy ambush line began to break and run.

I knew three things: we had shifted the momentum; they could not outrun us or our marksmanship; and they certainly were not going to outrun the helicopter teams.

The chase was on.

The trap they tried to spring on us had backfired. They paid with their lives. As I inspected their lifeless bodies, I almost felt sorry for them. What were they thinking? How did they think they would win this fight? They were no match for us.

My sympathy slipped away rather quickly. They had cast their vote. They did achieve a level of surprise, but they did not understand who we were. Did they think they could win?

I imagined these men plotting. They must have seen us land. They observed us and decided that we were vulnerable. They got all of their equipment in order and recruited a few more men to support them. They waited until they felt they had the element of surprise. And then they attacked us.

What were they thinking?
I stood over one of the dead men for a few minutes and really did feel sorry for him. Did he have a family? He was so young. Did he know who I was? Had he ever heard of our specialized unit? Would any of it have mattered?

They didn't have to attack us.

These men were blinded by hate and pride.

We left them lying in the mud and went back to our helicopters. We still had a mission to complete.

I had known better than to land where we did that day, but we did it anyway. Everyone else knew better, as well, but we did it anyway.

We knew better than to sit there so long but we did it anyway.

Once we were attacked, everyone sprung into motion but then there was a hesitation. It wasn't long but I could feel it. I waited a few seconds for one of the Team Leaders or the Team Sergeant to start barking out instructions. We needed to counterattack immediately.

We quickly established an assault line and returned fire but no one was moving. We were static.

We needed to attack.

I waited, expecting to hear one of the NCO's take charge of the counterattack. The radio remained silent.

It felt really weird to me. I had never before commanded the team to attack. They just did it naturally.

It was strange. I will never forget the feeling.

I looked to my left and the men were online. I looked to my right and the men were online.

But nobody began the counterattack. No one was maneuvering.

I pressed my radio "talk button" and said "Attack, Attack, Attack."

That was all it took.

The men did what they always did and the speed, surprise, and violence of action were unleashed on the men who dared try to kill us.

Things were back to normal; the deadly precision and aggressiveness of the team were on full display.

I stood and watched it unfold, still somewhat perplexed.

What happened?

To this day I don't know what happened. Maybe the men would have gotten unstuck moments after I stepped in.

It was the first time that I ever needed to prod the team to action. It was also the last time.

When I think back on it, I am still perplexed. It was a glitch in the system, a hiccup, a disturbance in the force. I don't know if anyone else in the team sensed it or not.

We never spoke about it.

However, the experience reinforced something that I already knew to be true: when it is your time to step up and lead, be ready.

DON'T STAY DOWN
GET BACK UP

CHAPTER 20

I. Don't Stay Down, Get Back Up

God-loyal people don't stay down long; Soon they're up on their feet, while the wicked end up flat on their faces. (Proverbs, 24:16, MSG)

The helicopter flared, swirling the desert sand, and obscuring the village below, but I could still see the objective clearly below me.

Something wasn't right. There was a tower on the roof on which we were planning to land. There was still enough space to land the helicopter, but the tower with its attached loudspeakers was concerning, and I wondered how I'd missed that detail.

We were about to assault a mosque.

We were out of time; we couldn't turn back now. As shocked as I was, I was sure the men inside the mosque were going to be even more surprised.

Everything was moving fast.

The helicopter's skid lightly pressed against the lip of the building.

Mosques were generally off limits, and strong evidence, validation, and a compelling story were required to mount an attack on one. But it was too late to abort now.

Our target was a suicide bomber and intelligence reported a car laden with explosives was somewhere in this small village.

We needed to find him and neutralize the car bomb, or innocent people could die.

Assaulters jumped onto the roof and enveloped the building. I had to send a situation report to my boss.

"Boss, this is Jeff, we are assaulting a mosque," I said into my mic, like I was going for a walk in the park.

I knew he would have questions, but time was against me. I unplugged my radio lines from the helicopter and followed the men. I had more important things to concentrate on. I would deal with the fallout in due time.

How had I missed the clues?

Reaching the sanctuary entrance, I passed about one hundred pairs of sandals. This may not end well, I thought. I hadn't heard any shooting yet, so maybe the assaulters secured the room without a fight.

How could we find the bomber among 100 men? We had a few clues, but we didn't know the whole story. How would we identify him?

The Clues Are There: You Have to Seek Them Out

The twelve disciples were on a mission that they still did not fully understand. They knew of some of the grumblings and conflict with the powerful men in Judea, but they did not see how close the end was. They felt like their adventure was still only beginning.

None of them were recognizing the clues. They weren't seeking them out. They were occupied with day-to-day activities. The mundane can often mask the clues. Routine can create complacency.

Conversely, big events, holidays, and anticipating exciting happenings can also obscure your ability to see clues that may be right in front of you.

It was time for the Passover festival in Jerusalem, and all attention was on this monumental annual event.

> *Jesus told his disciples, "You know that Passover comes in two days. That's when the Son of Man will be betrayed and handed over for crucifixion."*

> *At that very moment, the party of high priests*
> *and religious leaders was meeting in the*
> *chambers of the Chief Priest named Caiaphas,*
> *conspiring to seize Jesus by stealth and kill him.*
> *They agreed that it should not be done during*
> *Passover Week. "We don't want a riot on our*
> *hands," they said.*[185] *(Matthew 26: 1-5, MSG)*

This warning to the disciples had little effect. They were busy. They were preoccupied. They did not appreciate how much the powerful men of Jerusalem hated Yeshua, and wanted him dead.

A few days later, the disciples were seated at the Passover meal and Yeshua repeated his warning.

> *During the meal, he said, "I have something*
> *hard but important to say to you: One of you is*
> *going to hand me over to the conspirators."*
>
> *They were stunned, and then began to ask, one*
> *after another, "It isn't me, is it, Master?"*

---

[185] Matt. 26:1–5 (The Message).

Jesus answered, "The one who hands me over is someone I eat with daily, one who passes me food at the table. In one sense the Son of Man is entering into a way of treachery well-marked by the Scriptures—no surprises here. In another sense that man who turns him in, turns traitor to the Son of Man—better never to have been born than do this!"

Then Judas, already turned traitor, said, "It isn't me, is it, Rabbi?"

Jesus said, "Don't play games with me, Judas." During the meal, Jesus took and blessed the bread, broke it, and gave it to his disciples:

Take, eat.
This is my body.

Taking the cup and thanking God, he gave it to them:

Drink this, all of you.
This is my blood,
God's new covenant poured out for many people for the forgiveness of sins.

"I'll not be drinking wine from this cup again until that new day when I'll drink with you in the kingdom of my Father." (Matthew 26:21-29), MSG

More to the Story

How did the disciples miss the clues that by the following day, Yeshua would be dead, his beaten body lying in a grave? They just couldn't see how all of this would end.

We can draw comfort from their willingness to continue this adventure not knowing how it would end. The same challenge is there for us. We can look back and see that Yeshua doesn't remain in the grave.

But what about our story? Are we living like we truly believe all of it? Are we busy? Distracted?

The disciples were no different from us. They needed Yeshua's wisdom, grace, love, and encouragement daily.

In my reading, praying, and researching, I cannot discover anything special about the disciples. There is likely something somewhere, but I haven't found it. I would hypothesize that these twelve young men fulfilled something that is long lost to time. Perhaps they represented each of the original tribes of Israel. Perhaps they were the fulfillment of promises made long ago to men and women who were faithful to Yahweh. I am sure there is more to the story than we realize.

Whatever their importance, they clearly did not understand the full scope of Yeshua's true mission as the sacrificial lamb. Even as they sat at the table during the Last Supper, they didn't realize the incredible fulfillment of the Old Covenant that was unfolding before their eyes.

Without being intimately familiar with the Passover tradition, you cannot fully appreciate the beauty, complexity, and finality of the Lord's Last Supper, and how it ended the necessity of the Passover requirements and animal sacrifice once and for all.

Plenty of scholars have debated whether the Last Supper was the Pesach meal, the night before Pesach, or simply a normal Jewish evening meal with friends.[186]

Pesach, or Passover, was a ritual with details dictated directly from Yahweh for the Israelites who were still in slavery and bondage to the Egyptians.[187] The first Pesach was conducted the evening of the tenth plague in Egypt, when the Angel of Death visited all the homes and judged each family. If found wanting, the penalty was the life of the first-born son. The first-born son was sacrificed from each family as a punishment for the disobedience of the Egyptian people and their Pharaoh.

Each Israelite home covered its threshold with the blood of a sacrificial lamb and the Angel of Death passed over these homes, declaring them worthy of grace and redemption.[188] On the evening the Angel of Death "passed over" the homes in Egypt, Yahweh told

---

[186] Jonathan Klawans, "Was Jesus' Last Supper a Seder?," *Bible History Daily* (blog), Biblical Archaeology Society, November 15, 2022, https://www.biblicalarchaeology.org/daily/people-cultures-in-the-bible/jesus-historical-jesus/was-jesus-last-supper-a-seder/; Jonathan Klawans, "Jesus' Last Supper Still Wasn't a Passover Seder Meal," *Bible History Daily* (blog), Biblical Archaeology Society, March 19, 2021, https://www.biblicalarchaeology.org/daily/people-cultures-in-the-bible/jesus-historical-jesus/jesus-last-supper-passover-seder-meal/.
[187] Exod. 12.
[188] https://en.wikipedia.org/wiki/Passover

the Israelites fleeing Egypt to grab everything and leave. Yahweh directed them to not "even let any leavening touch the dough". Just "eat in a hurry" and go. In compliance, the Israelites grabbed their belongings and fled toward the land Yahweh was preparing for them.

Yahweh also directed that this ritual was to become an annual tradition for the Israelites to remember His judgment, justice, grace, and mercy. Yahweh delivered Israel from their bondage and slavery and ushered them into the Promised Land. He also told them to commemorate this feast by getting all yeast out of their homes for seven days. This became known as the Feast of Unleavened Bread, with Pesach (Passover) being only one day of this festival.

The Pesach was celebrated every year by the Israelites, with strict adherence to Yahweh's original decree. Some slight alterations crept in when Israel was conquered, exiled, and when the temple was destroyed, but for the most part, the ritual never changed.

In Yeshua's time, the temple was standing, and all Jews were required to offer a sacrifice in the temple during

Pesach.[189] Because the number of people required to offer a sacrifice was so large, some believe that the priests split up the times for each group of people to offer their lamb. The Galileans were asked to offer their lambs on Thursday and eat the Passover meal on Thursday night (the fourteenth day of the month Nisan).

This would leave Friday for the Judeans to sacrifice and dine on Friday night. This is a possible explanation for the timeline of Yeshua's passion week and how he ended up hanging on the cross at the exact time the Passover sacrificial lamb was laid upon the altar not far from where he was crucified.

We know that the Passover ceremony began in the temple at 6:00 a.m. and the first sacrificial lambs were brought to the altar and sacrificed at 9:00 a.m. The second sacrifice was at 12:00 noon. At the end of the ceremony, the lambs that each family sacrificed were taken home and prepared for the feast that night.

On Thursday, the disciples were tasked to prepare for the meal. Some were taking care of the sacrifice while others were cleaning the room and preparing to cook. I

---

[189] https://en.wikipedia.org/wiki/Passover_sacrifice

am not sure which of the disciples were good cooks, but as with all groups of men, there would only have been a couple of them who had a knack for it.

For some reason, I doubt it was Peter. He doesn't strike me as the culinary type. Cutting off ears seems to be more his thing.

One disciple was not preparing for the upcoming meal, but instead was conspiring with the Jewish leaders to arrange for Yeshua's arrest. On one hand, I find this incredible and I feel really bad for Yeshua. He knew this betrayal was coming, yet he accepted it in full humility. On the other hand, I find comfort in the fact that even in Yeshua's small circle of friends and confidants, within his twelve-man group, one of them was a two-faced snake.

Why do we expect more than he got? Betrayal is part of life.

During the Passover meal, Yeshua skipped aspects of the traditional Passover service and created a new covenant that is routinely practiced across the world, known today as Holy Communion.

Yeshua used the unleavened bread as a metaphor for his body, sacrificed for all of us.

He gave his life for us.

As part of the Passover meal tradition, a piece of unleavened bread (matzoh) is broken off (called the afikomen) and hidden somewhere in the house. At the end of the meal, the children search for the afikomen and the one who finds it is given a reward. The bread is brought back to the table and is eaten by all the guests.[190]

Some scholars believe that in Yeshua's time, the afikomen represented the promised Messiah (HaMashiach), the promised and expected deliverer of the Jewish people. The tradition was that the matzoh, when whole, represented all of Israel. The afikomen, the part that is broken off and hidden, represents the Messiah that is hidden.[191] When the afikomen is found and brought to the table, the guests celebrate its return.

---

[190] https://en.wikipedia.org/wiki/Afikoman

[191] "The Passover Symbols and Their Messianic Significance," Jews for Jesus, March 1, 2021, https://jewsforjesus.org/learn/the-passover-symbols-and-their-messianic-significance.

When Yeshua held up the afikomen that night, he said, "This is my body," he was making a shocking claim to be HaMashiach, the promised and expected deliverer of the Jewish people.[192]

Throughout the Passover meal, guests partake of four different glasses of wine. In some traditions, there is a fifth glass that is not consumed, but left untouched.[193] On that night, when the third glass was to be consumed, Yeshua took that third glass and used it as a complementary metaphor to the afikomen, and designated it as the ritual remembrance of the blood he was about to shed for the redemption of all people.

This was revolutionary. It must have blown the minds of the disciples and guests. They were expecting the traditional Passover meal with all its prescribed rituals and traditions and suddenly Yeshua pivoted. You can see the confusion as the discussion rapidly devolved to an argument about which of the disciples was greater, missing much of what Yeshua was trying to teach them.[194]

---

[192] Rich Robinson, "Passover: Why Is This Night Different Since Yeshua Observed It?," Jews for Jesus, November 1, 1983, https://jewsforjesus.org/publications/issues/issues-v03-n02/passover-why-is-this-night-different-since-yeshua-observed-it/.

[193] https://en.wikipedia.org/wiki/Passover_Seder

[194] Luke 22:24.

None of them fully grasped that this was their last meal together.

As the disciples were processing these revelations, another bomb dropped. One of them was going to betray Yeshua.

I can imagine his heartache as he waited to be betrayed. I can imagine his heartache as he realized the disciples just didn't get it. They could not see the clues.

He was running out of time.

II. Don't Stay Down, Get Back Up

"This was going to be a mess," I thought. "How are we going to identify our guy?"
I entered the prayer room of the mosque. Assaulters surrounded the perimeter and 100 local men knelt in the center. We had rapidly and violently interrupted their devout and solemn ritual.

Ninety-nine men turned around, twisting their necks, staring at the invaders in confusion. Everyone was completely quiet. You could hear a pin drop.

How would we recognize this guy? How would we find him? Every man in the room stared at us except one. That was him. I knew it instantly.

The assault team leader saw it at the same time I did, and he moved directly to him.

One man was out of place; he still faced forward. Only the back of his head was visible. He knelt as if in repose, and did not flinch. The assault team leader called over the radio and two assaulters weaved through the mass towards the man pretending to be pious.

They pushed him to the ground with one assaulter on each arm, still concerned that he may have a detonator to a car bomb in one of his hands. After they were confident that he was unarmed, they put steel handcuffs on him, blindfolded him, carefully walked him past all the other devout men, and moved him outside. The other men remained stoic. No one said a word.

Beneath the prayer rug in front of where our man had been praying, an assaulter found a vehicle key fob, and some very tightly folded papers.

Moving him to a secure corner of an outbuilding, we began to interrogate him. He gave us his name, but it did not match the name of the bomber we were looking for.

We brought various men from inside the mosque outside and questioned them, one by one, but no one was willing to speak with us about the suspected bomber.

I paced back and forth between the interrogations. The men in the mosque stubbornly feigned ignorance, while the suspected bomber sat in the corner of the outbuilding, adamant about his innocence.

Maybe we had the wrong man. I had missed the clues about this structure being a mosque; maybe I'd missed something else.

The outbuilding was a small shed that housed a few tools and a couple of sickly-looking goats. A young boy walked up to the entrance of the small building, right up to one of our heavily armed operators, and tried to explain that he needed to feed the goats inside. We let the boy inside, not only to feed his goats, but to get a good look at the man sitting quietly in the corner.

We asked the boy if he knew that man, and the boy stated flatly that the man had arrived only that morning. His parents told him to be wary of the man, as they suspected he might be Al Qaeda.

Our suspected bomber finally broke demeanor. It was slight, but he looked up at the boy as soon as he said Al Qaeda.

We didn't miss it.

Our intel guys and our interpreters deciphered the coded messages on the papers we had found. The way the notes were folded reinforced that they were Al Qaeda messages, a standard technique that reduced a normal sheet of paper to no bigger than the tip of your finger.

The evidence was beginning to add up.

There was no way our small force could search this entire town. Our only lead was the key fob for an unknown car.

Our explosives and intel experts thought it unlikely that the vehicle was fully rigged to detonate yet. Their normal procedure was to set it up right before use.

So we took a chance.

Assaulters began walking the streets around the mosque, while the team leader pressed the button as if he had lost a car in a mall parking lot.

We flinched with every press of the key fob. Finally, we heard a faint beeping. We were getting closer.

"We got it," came a call on the radio. "By the river."

We found the car at the edge of the village. Our explosives expert confirmed the contents without incident and destroyed the explosives and the car.

"Jackpot," I said over the radio. I was sure we had our man.

We loaded the bound and blindfolded bomber into the helicopter and lifted off in another swirl of dust and debris.

Mission complete.

Then, I remembered my job still wasn't done. How had I missed all the clues? I still had some explaining to do to my boss.

COLLATERAL DAMAGE

THIRTY PIECES OF SILVER:
A SMALL PRICE TO PAY

CHAPTER 21

I. Collateral Damage

God rescued us from dead-end alleys and dark dungeons. He's set us up in the kingdom of the Son he loves so much, the Son who got us out of the pit we were in, got rid of the sins we were doomed to keep repeating. (Colossians 1:13-14, MSG)

"What's the current CDE limit?" I asked.

"I think it's in the mid-20's still but will confirm ASAP," our lead intel analyst answered.

"And what are we thinking is on target–non-combatants?"

"A couple of women and a few children. No more than ten."

"Roger that, I'll call the boss."

I dialed up the Commander and laid out the intel in detail, highlighted the danger if we did NOT kill this Al Qaeda leader, and confirmed with him that the CDE (Collateral Damage Estimate) limit was still at 22.

He approved the mission.

We were about to drop two bombs, five hundred pounds each, on the target building with the crosshairs on it we were watching on the ISR feed. It was the middle of the day, too dangerous to assault the compound with our helos. Plus it was too far away, too much could happen en route. We knew where he was right then and there.

He was in our crosshairs.

There were no adults outside, only children. I couldn't really tell what they were doing. It looked like the kids were playing some kind of game, almost like Duck, duck, goose. Some were seated in a circle as others chased each other around the circle. I hoped that maybe the pressure from the bombs would toss the kids to safety. I didn't think it was likely but hoped for it anyway.

"Bombs will be TOT (Time Over Target) in 3 minutes," the voice on the radio squawked.

I sat still, drinking some lousy coffee.

"Bombs away," came the next call.

Any second now and the ISR screen would white out with the bombs exploding near simultaneously. I sipped my coffee again and grimaced just a little bit. Not enough for anyone to notice.

In warfare, we look at collateral damage and proportionality. Collateral damage is damage to things that are incidental to an intended military target. It can include damage to civilian property, incidental loss of civilian life, injury to civilians, or a combination thereof.

Proportionality is the concept of balancing collateral damage in relation to the concrete and direct military advantage anticipated in a military action.[195] Collateral damage limits are not constant. They will go up or down as the ebb and flow of war goes on and with the value of a targeted individual.

The collateral damage associated with capturing or killing Osama Bin Laden was very different from some unnamed terrorist in the far reaches of Iraq or Afghanistan.

---

[195] https://en.wikipedia.org/wiki/Just_war_theory

I can remember numerous times, sitting in the Tactical Operations Center, waiting on the collateral damage guidance. We would have a High-Value Target (HVT) located and we were prepared to drop a bomb on his head, but only if we could meet or stay below the command guidance for collateral damage.

Obviously, dropping a precision-guided bomb onto an HVT was much safer for us than landing on his roof and engaging in a close-quarters gunfight.

We would wait for the number. Usually, it made sense. Sometimes it did not. Early in the Iraq war, the collateral damage threshold was in the twenties and thirties. By the end of the war, it was zero.

I want to make sure you understand this. We were permitted to kill a high-value target, even if it meant the death of 10, 20, or sometimes 30 others. It was considered collateral damage. It was proportional.

A bomb could kill hundreds of innocent people in a single blast, while our targeting was precise. The technology of our bombs and missiles allows them to be incredibly accurate, but we also accept collateral damage.

As time went on, collateral damage became less and less necessary. But it is always part of war. If the collateral damage on the target we were looking at was too high, we would sit and wait until some people left the building and then we would bomb it.

Or we would go in by ourselves. No bombs. Just man on man. This could be dangerous for us, but we also understood something important and accepted it. We were collateral damage, too.

When conducting a hostage rescue, the collateral damage we were willing to accept in our own ranks was not even calculated. We would attempt the rescue, whatever the cost.

Thirty Pieces of Silver: A Small Price to Pay

Who was the traitor?

Perplexed, the disciples argued as Judas slipped away to complete his betrayal.

Judas had cast his vote earlier. While the disciples were preparing for the big Passover feast, Judas was selling his soul for some silver.

Here is how Luke describes it:

> *The Feast of Unleavened Bread, also called Passover, drew near. The high priests and religious scholars were looking for a way to do away with Jesus but, fearful of the people, they were also looking for a way to cover their tracks.*
>
> *That's when Satan entered Judas, the one called Iscariot. He was one of the Twelve. Leaving the others, he conferred with the high priests and the Temple guards about how he might betray Jesus to them. They couldn't believe their good luck and agreed to pay him well. He gave them his word and started looking for a way to betray Jesus, but out of sight of the crowd.[196] (Luke 22: 1-6, MSG)*

And Matthew tells the story here:

---

[196] Luke 22:1–6 (The Message).

> *That is when one of the Twelve, the one named*
> *Judas Iscariot, went to the cabal of high priests*
> *and said, "What will you give me if I hand*
> *him over to you?" They settled on thirty silver*
> *pieces. He began looking for just the right*
> *moment to hand him over.*[197] *(Matthew 26:*
> *14-16, MSG)*

More to the Story

What was going through Yeshua's mind while all of this was happening? Do you think, as a mortal man, he was disappointed, upset, or even angry with Judas?

Righteous anger is not a sin. I am sure he was raging inside. Not at Judas but at the sin involved in this treachery. We cannot claim he experienced true humanity without also accepting the feelings and emotions that go along with being human.

A betrayer, allowed into the inner circle, plotting against his teacher for personal gain. The plot twist is painful to watch as it unfolds.

---

[197] Matt. 26:14–16 (MSG).

Betraying him for thirty pieces of silver. That's an odd detail, isn't it?

This is another precise detail loaded with meaning and depth. The first reference to thirty pieces of silver can be found in the ancient Hebrew writings, instructing that the payment to the master of a slave gored by an ox should be thirty pieces of silver.[198] Yeshua was sold as a common slave to be delivered to his executioners.

Thirty pieces of silver.[199]

The irony would not have been lost on anyone there, including the men who "bought" him.
A simple slave was one without any real talents but simply a laborer or a servant. Yeshua was sold into the hands of the religious politicians of the day for the price equivalent to a low-level slave.

This was not random. The religious leaders chose this amount to denigrate and demean Yeshua and let Judas know immediately that they were not there to bargain. They wanted Yeshua gone.

---

[198] Exod. 21:32.
[199] https://en.wikipedia.org/wiki/Thirty_pieces_of_silver#

During Yeshua's life, there was a complicated relationship between the Jewish religious leaders and the Roman political leaders. Where these two systems were in sync was to oppress and subjugate the commoner in taxes, guilt, and fear.

The Pharisees, Sadducees and Priests were the powerful men of their era. They were not interested in seeing this power balance disrupted.

Yeshua came to free the oppressed. They feared that Yeshua's teachings would bring great wrath from their Roman overseers.[200] It did not take them long to decide it was better to get rid of Yeshua than to risk civil war or an uprising against the Romans, for which they were not prepared.[201] They rationalized that it was better for one man to be sacrificed than risk a Roman backlash on the masses.

They felt that it was time for Yeshua to die. They tried to pretend that Yeshua was simply collateral damage.

He was collateral damage that they could accept.

---

[200] John 18:14.
[201] John 11:49–50.

II. Collateral Damage

In both Iraq and Afghanistan, we always carried with us a COMPFUND (COMPensation FUND) of cash. We usually had about ten to fifteen thousand dollars on us to pay cash for any collateral damage that we felt deemed compensating. We also had a form that we could leave with the civilians left on target that they could fill out to make a claim for more compensation.

I don't remember using it very often. We were incredibly precise with our assaults. I remember paying a few times for broken gates or doors to families that were stuck in the middle between us and the terrorists. Often, the terrorist would hole up in an innocent bystanders home and any damage we ended up causing the home, we would do our best to pay for.

We didn't have any standard amounts but we had general guidelines of what everything was worth.

A nice metal gate was worth a few hundred bucks.

A door was about fifty bucks.

A goat was a hundred bucks.

A cow was about a thousand.

A child was about twenty-five hundred.

That's how much a child's life was worth in Iraq. It was even less in Afghanistan.

I never had to pay for the death of a child but I was prepared to. Not only was I prepared to pay, I was prepared to haggle over the cost. This is hard for people to understand and can certainly sound cold, insensitive, callous, or even evil. But it is not, I assure you.

War creates markets. Many of those markets are illicit. In our desire to compensate families for their losses, we did not want to create a market for dead women and children. Al Qaeda, ISIS, and the Taliban routinely placed women and children on target, not just because they knew we would be extra careful but so they could get a pay out.

There was a target in Afghanistan where the Taliban slaughtered a family, including a pregnant woman in a building that was adjacent to a target building that Coalition Forces raided one spring. The village elders, prodded by the Taliban, demanded compensation. Coalition Forces denied that they had anything to do with the deaths. I was called in for my opinion and prompted a simple solution. I asked about the caliber of the bullets that were found at the site. If they matched US/NATO Forces' rounds and casings then we had some more digging to do. If they were AK47 rounds or other Soviet era munitions we knew the Taliban was responsible.

To know one's surprise, the rounds were not US or NATO rounds.

A two star general officer paid the village elders anyway. To make matters worse, the Commander apologized, sacrificed a goat to show his remorse and publicly rebuked US Forces.

This scapegoat that was offered that day did more harm than I think he realized. But those of us in the thick of it knew immediately.

More women and children would be murdered and friendly forces would get framed.

All for a few bucks.

The world had an opportunity to provide women and children in both Iraq and Afghanistan safety, security, opportunity, and hope. We had the opportunity to help both of those nations rewrite their future with freedom, prosperity, and equity.

We squandered it.

Their political leaders squandered it.

The numbers of lives lost in both of the wars is tragic. We offered each country hope and opportunity only to let it dissolve into chaos and evil.

Much of the collateral damage still lies in the minds of those who served.

It is strange to think of Yeshua as collateral damage, but in a way he was. To appreciate this, you must first recognize that we are at war.

The devil is dead set on destroying all of us, and all he must do is lead us into temptation. Pride, greed, lust, envy, gluttony, anger, and sloth are all self-inflicted and only lead to destruction. We allow ourselves to be held hostage by our own sinful desires. But Yeshua is our rescuer. He is a one-man hostage rescue team— prepared to die that we may live.

He rescued us and He allowed himself to be collateral damage for us.

22

INSHALLAH

BETRAYAL IN THE GARDEN:
GRACE UNDER PRESSURE

CHAPTER 22

I. Inshallah

> *A false witness will not go unpunished, and*
> *whoever pours out lies will not go free.*
> *(Proverbs 19:5, NIV)*

"Play it again, please," I said. Listening to the recording for a second time, it was unmistakable: Captain Arkhan was planning to kill me.

We were scheduled to meet the following week at a restaurant outside of Kirkuk, Iraq, and he was plotting an ambush.

The phone intercept was clear. He was covering all his bases. Bombs were going to be placed in the plants outside the main entrance to the restaurant, and if they didn't do the trick, Arkhan had arranged for a couple of thugs to be near enough to finish me off.

I wasn't surprised. I knew this guy was playing both sides, and we were trying to build a case against him. We were sure that he was responsible for the recent deaths of the Iraqi partner force soldiers we trained and fought with. We just couldn't quite prove it yet.

Arkhan was clever. He was a paid informant for multiple US Intelligence Agencies and gave just enough credible information to remain vetted, in their good graces, and most importantly, on their payroll.

We shared our concerns with both the intelligence agencies and the US Army commander on the nearby airfield that was the Forward Operating Base (FOB) for most of the military forces in the region. The intelligence personnel were more than dismissive–they were straight-up rude about our concerns and basically ordered us to keep quiet. The Army commander was a lot more receptive, but said there was very little he could do without the appropriate evidence to back it up.

We were told to let it go. I understood.

But I didn't let it go.

Betrayal in the Garden: Grace Under Pressure

Betrayal cuts deep and the pain lasts a long time. If the betrayer is someone you care about, it hurts even worse and the pain never goes away.

Throughout the week before his betrayal, Yeshua preached at the temple from early in the morning until late in the day. He would spend his evenings on the Mount of Olives, not far from the temple, and sometimes even spend the night there.[202]

Yeshua knew he was running out of time. His close friend had already sold him out.

---

[202] Luke 21:37.

He tried to enjoy his last meal with his friends but the pressure was mounting and the hour of betrayal was near. When the Passover meal concluded, Yeshua and the disciples walked down the hill, across the Kidron Valley, and over to the Mount of Olives, stopping at the Garden of Gethsemane, one of their favorite places.

Luke records the events this way:

> *Jesus went out as usual to the Mount of Olives, and his disciples followed him. On reaching the place, he said to them, "Pray that you will not fall into temptation." He withdrew about a stone's throw beyond them, knelt down and prayed, "Father, if you are willing, take this cup from me; yet not my will, but yours be done." An angel from heaven appeared to him and strengthened him. And being in anguish, he prayed more earnestly, and his sweat was like drops of blood falling to the ground*

> *When he rose from prayer and went back to the disciples, he found them asleep, exhausted from sorrow. "Why are you sleeping?" he asked them. "Get up and pray so that you will not fall into temptation."*

*While he was still speaking a crowd came up,
and the man who was called Judas, one of the
Twelve, was leading them. He approached
Jesus to kiss him, but Jesus asked him, "Judas,
are you betraying the Son of Man with a kiss?"*

*When Jesus' followers saw what was going to
happen, they said, "Lord, should we strike with
our swords?" And one of them struck the
servant of the high priest, cutting off his right
ear.*

*But Jesus answered, "No more of this!" And he
touched the man's ear and healed him.*

*Then Jesus said to the chief priests, the officers
of the temple guard, and the elders, who had
come for him, "Am I leading a rebellion, that
you have come with swords and clubs? Every
day I was with you in the temple courts, and
you did not lay a hand on me. But this is your
hour—when darkness reigns."*[203] *(Luke 22: 39-
53, NIV)*

---

[203] Luke 22:39–53 (New International Version).

More to the Story

It was a dark night and a dark hour.

Why does evil always gravitate to the dark? We talk about the thin spaces where the barrier between heaven and earth is thin.[204] There are also dark places where the barrier between earth and hell is thin. But these places don't last. A little light can chase away the dark in an instant. Darkness can only survive if the light allows it to.

Yeshua allowed the darkness to descend on this garden spot that was special to him. I am sure he could sense the evil descending on him and his friends, but the disciples were oblivious. They simply could not grasp that this was their teacher's last night as a mortal man on earth. Yeshua continued the routine he had established earlier in the week as if it were any other night, so what could possibly be wrong?

There are a couple of interesting things to consider about the short walk from Mount Zion to

---

[204] Ellman, "Thin Places, Holy Spaces."

Gethsemane and the time of prayer and betrayal that followed.[205]

I always wonder what it was like to be there that evening—to walk at the side of Yeshua on that fateful night of betrayal?

The Kidron Valley is a deep valley that separates Mount Zion and the Temple Mount from the southern slope of the Mount of Olives.[206] During the seasonal rains back then, the Kidron turned into a raging river. As the seasons shifted, it would have been reduced to a brook, then an intermittent stream, and then a dusty wash like it is today.

Yeshua was betrayed, arrested, judged, and crucified in the month of Nisan, which is the month of April. The rainy season in Jerusalem is in the winter, and by March the rains begin to wane. Pending unseasonable weather, it is likely that the Kidron would have been a flowing stream running through the valley but not much more.

---

[205] William D. Edwards, "On the Physical Death of Jesus Christ," *JAMA* 255, no. 11 (March 1986): 1455–63, https://doi.org/10.1001/jama.1986.03370110077025.
[206] https://en.wikipedia.org/wiki/Kidron_Valley

So, to set the scene, Yeshua and the disciples walked beside the stream, the sound of the water giving off a comfortable, soothing feeling. This time of year would have been perfect to enjoy the valley, in contrast to the summer's cracked, barren, dry streambed which would have elicited a very different feeling.

An evening walk down the winding road from Jerusalem to Gethsemane would have been pleasant for most of the group, but for Yeshua, it must have felt like he was a condemned man walking to his execution.

Gethsemane means the "place of the olive press." This location would have been a familiar and favorite place for Yeshua to visit in solitude. When you visit these locations today, you can see the remnants of the garden, and a short distance away, the cave that was used to house an olive press.

Yeshua and the disciples reached the Garden of Gethsemane, unlocked the olive press cave, and had some time to themselves. Maybe they picked up where they left off in the upper room and sang some songs, but the night was growing more somber for Yeshua.

You can still visit the olive press cave next to the Garden of Gethsemane.[207] It is a place where you can pray, sing, or simply contemplate that night so long ago. Today the olive trees, while much less numerous, gnarled and twisted, still solemnly stand watch over the garden just like they did over two thousand years ago.

In 70 A.D., when Titus destroyed Jerusalem, he turned the city into rubble. Because olive trees were so sacred and important to the Jews, he also destroyed many of them, leaving only razed stumps.[208] But olive trees are hearty, they can regenerate themselves. Even if the tree is severely damaged, if the roots are still intact, they can survive and live thousands of years. Some of the olive trees in the garden today likely witnessed the events of that night.

When you visit the Garden of Gethsemane, you can touch the olive trees and feel their ruggedness and solemnity. You can kneel next to the rock where Yeshua prayed and experience its barrenness and loneliness.[209] You can feel the pain that still

---

[207] https://en.wikipedia.org/wiki/Gethsemane
[208] https://en.wikipedia.org/wiki/Siege_of_Jerusalem_(70_CE)
[209] https://en.wikipedia.org/wiki/Church_of_All_Nations

emanates from this cold stone. It becomes incredibly personal.

It is also a place where you can experience the grace of God. The cold stone and quiet garden also has a lightness about it that you can enter into and find peace. It is one of my favorite places on the planet. It's a special place that can heal you, if you allow His light to rest upon you.

Yeshua took Peter, James, and John on a short walk from the cave to a place amongst the olive trees to pray. The rest of the disciples remained in the cave where it was warm and dry. Possibly a small fire was already burning, making it more comfortable for them.

Yeshua left the three disciples and moved to a familiar place where he was expecting a heavy discussion with his Father. He went off in the cold and prayed alone.

Nights in desert countries can be very cold, and Jerusalem, sitting at an elevation of 2,500 feet and surrounded by cold stone, can get down to the 40s (less than ten degrees Celsius) in early April.

Yeshua must have been shivering. I think of the exertion from his earnest prayers, the sweat drying on his skin. He must have been shivering not from fear, but from that strange lack of control that happens when your body is damp, and you prepare to meet danger head-on.

He asked for some comfort and his father sent him an angel. This gift only offered temporary relief. Yeshua still needed to do what he was sent to do.

The Bible briefly mentions that his sweat was mixed with blood as he prayed.[210] This medical oddity was a clue to the events of that night, and is wholly supported by the accounts written about it in the gospels. Bloody sweating is called hematidrosis.[211] It is usually associated with blood disorders, but it may occur in individuals suffering from extreme levels of stress, fear, and intense mental contemplation.[212]

Most of the cases reported have been in men condemned to execution. There are multiple mesh-like blood vessels around the sweat glands that constrict under the pressure of great stress. Then, as

---

[210] Luke 22:44.
[211] Edwards, "On the Physical Death of Jesus Christ."
[212] https://en.wikipedia.org/wiki/Hematidrosis

the anxiety passes, the blood vessels dilate to the point of rupture and seep into the sweat glands. As the sweat glands produce sweat, they push the blood to the surface and secrete droplets of blood mixed with sweat. In some cases, blood can ooze from the eyes and nose, as well.

This process was precisely what Yeshua experienced in the garden. He commented to his disciples how he felt overwhelmed with anguish, sorrow, and trepidation. When he went off to pray in solitary anguish, he prayed so hard that he constricted his blood vessels. When the angel was sent to comfort him, his anxiety lifted, allowing his blood vessels to dilate and ultimately seep out as his blood mixed with sweat as he continued to pray.

As Yeshua prayed, blood droplets mixed with sweat rolled down his face. Blood clogged his breathing and blurred his vision.

Looking back toward Jerusalem, even if blurry, he could see part of the temple and the highpoint of the temple complex. This high point was the very spot where Satan tempted him years earlier.[213]

---

[213] Matt. 4:5–7.

He had passed that test.

This same pinnacle location is where tradition holds that James, Yeshua's little brother, would be murdered. James was given the choice to denounce his brother or be hurled down from the temple. If the fall didnt kill him, the people would stone him to death. James stood up for his brother and chose death instead.[214]

But this night, no one seemed to be sticking up for Yeshua. He felt alone.

This specific spot where Yeshua was praying was the same place David prayed when he was betrayed by his son Absalom and his close friend Ahithophel.[215]

The scene for Yeshua's betrayal in the garden had been set a long time ago. In the upper room, before the disciples began to murmur amongst themselves, wondering which of them would be the betrayer, Yeshua repeated David's prayer but no one seemed to catch it. Yeshua flatly stated,

---

[214] *Eusebius Ecclesiastical History*, vol. II, trans. J. E. L. Oulton (Cambridge, MA: Harvard University Press, 1932).
[215] 2 Sam. 15:13–37.

> *"He who ate my bread has lifted his heel against me."*[216]

The scripture Yeshua referenced was what David wrote a thousand years earlier,

"Even my close friend in whom I trusted, who ate my bread, has lifted his heel against me."[217]

Yeshua was speaking about Judas and David was speaking about his betrayer, Ahithophel. David wrote this psalm after crossing the Kidron and directing most of his followers into the wilderness to flee persecution. He ordered some of his followers back to Jerusalem, including the Levites (the priests) with the Ark of the Covenant while David waited and prayed for guidance from God.[218]

David's son was betraying him.

One of David's best friends, a man he trusted, was on his son's side and was coming for him.

---

[216] John 13:18 (New American Standard Bible).
[217] Ps. 41:9 (NASB).
[218] 2 Sam. 15.

David was prepared to do whatever God asked of him—return to Jerusalem and face his betrayers or flee into the desert.

Yeshua repeated this prayer. Three times he prayed to his Father, asking him if there was any other way. Was there any way to avoid the upcoming pain, torture, and temporary abandonment from his Father?[219]

Like David, a thousand years earlier, he was prepared to do whatever God asked of him—return to Jerusalem or flee into the desert.

An angel appeared to Yeshua to encourage and strengthen him but also to bring him the bad news. This was it. This was his night of suffering.[220]

Yeshua accepted that this was it. He got his answer. He was to return to Jerusalem.

And then he saw the mob. They were coming for him.

The route from the upper room, or anywhere from the city of Jerusalem, is winding as it descends to the

---

[219] Mark 14:32–42.
[220] Luke 22:43.

Kidron Valley. A mob of men with torches and clubs could be seen from a far-off distance.

The disciples in the Gethsemane cave would not have seen the soldiers approaching, and the three who fell asleep would not have seen Judas approaching, either, as he led the mob into the garden.

But Yeshua would have seen them long before they got to him. As the mob, led by Judas, continued toward him, he woke the disciples and prepared to meet his betrayer.

The mob crossed the Kidron. He knew this would be the biggest test of his life. He knew what he needed to do but could he surrender Himself? Willingly?

Yeshua prayed that he would not stumble. He prayed that he would have the courage to hand himself over and honorably withstand the torture and crucifixion forthcoming.

It was indeed a dark night. It was certainly a dark hour.

Yeshua woke the disciples. As he patiently waited to meet his betrayer and the mob bent on violence, he was resolute in knowing that when the day was through, if he could stay the course and not stumble, his mission would be accomplished.

II. Inshallah

Arkhan was playing both sides and on top of that, he was trying to kill me.
This was not cool.

We decided to take the matter into our own hands. Arkhan was a traitor. I was relieved to know beyond a shadow of a doubt where we stood with him, and that he was planning to betray us in less than a week. This gave us just enough time to hatch a plan of our own.

We positioned cameras outside of the restaurant meeting place with the hopes of catching the bomb makers placing the bombs in the planters and thereby collecting the evidence we needed to sway our US partners.

Unfortunately, we did not see any nefarious activity, so we decided we would call at the last minute with an excuse and invite Arkhan to our safe house to conduct the meeting there instead of the restaurant.

We notified our Kurdish partners of our plan, and they were very interested. Arkhan was a wanted man in Kurdistan. The plan was to lure Arkhan to our place, interrogate him, and then hand him over to the Kurds to be whisked across the "Green Line." This imaginary boundary is the demarcation line between the Kurdish northern provinces and Iraq. The city of Kirkuk was less than fifteen minutes from this boundary line and was still a largely contested city.

Three of our Kurdish Peshmerga partners arrived that morning. We concealed their car in the garage and hid them in the basement until we were ready to hand over Arkhan. Through our interpreter, I called Arkhan and apologized that I would not be able to meet at the restaurant that day, but could meet a little later if he was available. When he asked where I wanted to meet, I invited him to our safe house. I asked him if he needed an address, and he snidely remarked that he knew where we lived.

I was under no impression that we were hiding from everyone, but we were living in a low-profile neighborhood, somewhat vulnerable to a direct and concentrated attack. Other than some barriers and gates that blended in with other wealthy neighbors, we were largely hiding in plain sight. So, I took Arkhan's comment in stride and wanted to allow him to feel arrogant and "in the know."

We were expecting him to arrive at our house in a car with just him and a driver/bodyguard. To our surprise, he showed up with a full security detail consisting of two civilian vehicles with four bodyguards each and a couple of police pick-up trucks with about 20 police officers armed with AK-47s and Glock pistols.

Our guards stopped the convoy at our gate and called me on the radio to tell me that our plan had a wrench in it. We quickly brainstormed a plan and walked out to meet Arkhan at the gate.

I explained to him that we simply could not allow all these armed men and Iraqi vehicles into our compound and asked him to allow me to escort him to our house and catch up on the details we were meeting about. He insisted that his driver be allowed to drive through our gate and right up to the front door of our house and then his driver would be dismissed to join the rest of the security team. I relented.

We opened the gate and Arkhan drove into our compound, parking near our front door. This was about 30 meters from the gate, and in plain view of the rest of the police outside. They watched as he exited his car. He took a long look around at our compound security and greeted me with a kiss on each cheek. We entered the house. He asked about lunch and said that we could still order food from the restaurant at which we had originally planned to meet. The restaurant had already started cooking the meal in anticipation of our visit, and he thought it would be a shame for the food to go to waste. I asked him if one of his men could pick it up and we could eat it right in our dining room. He agreed, and sent his driver/bodyguard back to the rest of his team with instructions to go get the food and deliver it back to us as quickly as possible.

We walked into the dining room and sat across from each other at the table. I had a couple of my teammates with me, along with an interpreter. Arkhan spoke English pretty well, so the interpreter was just there as a backup. I wasted no time in telling him that I knew about the plot to kill me at the restaurant and that he had better come clean with how he was playing both sides or I would send him to Kurdistan to receive justice there.

He didn't flinch a bit. I could see that he was thinking it through, but his demeanor remained flat. I tried to read his thoughts. Should he call my bluff? Was he holding a losing hand? Did I really know what I told him I knew?

He called my bluff.

"Captain Jeff," he said, "We are brothers. We have broken bread together. We have fought Al Qaida together."

"Yes. Yes, we have." I said, "But you also killed some of the Iraqi troops working for me, continue to murder Iraqis sympathetic to our mission, and to top it all off, you had a very real plan to kill me today."

He smiled ever so slightly.

"I don't understand what you are talking about," he said. He was intently trying to read my face and body language.

I calmly said, "Arkhan, I am not in the mood for you to waste my time. Answer my questions directly or I will call the Kurdish Asayish (intelligence) officers who are waiting in the basement right now."

I pointed to the radio on the table. Arkhan studied it. He began to realize that I was not bluffing, but he still did not have a single demeanor hit.

He was a fox. He was calm, cool, and calculating.

But so was I.

I had this fox in a trap.

"What do you want to know?" he asked. I can only imagine how quickly his mind was racing, trying to figure a way out of the trap that he had walked into.

I repeated a few direct questions to him, but he continued to play games with me.

"Arkhan," I said, "This is the last time I am going to ask you. I don't care if you live or die tonight. There is a very good chance that you will not see tomorrow. If you do live through the night, I expect that it will be extremely painful, no matter how much or how little you decide to cooperate." Arkhan's level gaze never faltered.

"What I do know," I continued, "is that this morning was the last time you will ever see your wife."

This comment seemed to rankle him just a bit. I could see a very subtle demeanor hit. His eyes narrowed and his brow wrinkled momentarily. He reached into his jacket and both my teammate and I quickly put our hands on our pistols.

He pulled his hand out of his jacket and placed his palms forward, in front of his chest, and asked, "Do you mind if I smoke?"

I reached across the table and pulled out a pack of cigarettes and a lighter from his jacket's left breast pocket. We both leaned back as he lit a cigarette. His confidence was returning.

The minor hiccup in composure was smoothed over. He was ready to accept his fate. He took a drag, slowly, and looked me straight in my eyes. He didn't blink.

"This is your last chance," I stated flatly. "Stop playing games. I am the only one who can save you. Your life is in my hands right now," I continued, "and I hope you have come to realize that I don't care if you live to see another day. In fact, I would be quite pleased if you were executed tonight."

Arkhan continued to inhale and exhale slowly as the cigarette hung loosely from his lips. My patience had run out.

"Do you want to live or die?" I asked.

"Inshallah," he said quietly.

"Inshallah" is an Arabic term that means "if God wills."[221]

---

[221] https://en.wikipedia.org/wiki/Inshallah

I bowed my head for a moment and then looked him directly in the eyes. "Are you sure, are you ready?"

He nodded slightly and took another drag on his cigarette.

I picked up the radio and called our friends up from the basement. You could hear them thundering up the stairs.

Arkhan could hear it too. He stared straight ahead, avoiding my gaze.

As two men crashed through the dining room door, I could see Arkhan's eyes widen a bit, but he stayed still. He did not put up a fight.

The driver returned from the restaurant with the food and stood at the gate, waiting for us to let him in. One of our guys went out to meet him and brought him and a couple of other Iraqis into the house to drop the food off in the kitchen. I popped my head out of the dining room door and thanked them for the meal, pretending that Arkhan was still in there with me. "Please take some drinks back out with you for everybody," I offered.

I closed the door and waited for them to leave. Most of the team then gathered in the kitchen and began to eat the meal Arkhan had purchased for us. It was the typical Arab meal of rice, lamb, kebob, chicken, lentils, bread, and more. It was especially delicious because of the irony of it all.

We knew how we were going to finish off this plan, but we were stuck in the middle for the moment. The security detail was still outside, and Arkhan's car was plainly still parked in our driveway. We didn't have all the details worked out yet. We needed to figure out a plan so we could finish up this kidnapping.

One of the guys pulled out a whiteboard the size of a poster and we started to brainstorm ideas again. We landed on something simple and a bit silly, but we thought it would work.

The guys pulled our gun trucks out of the garage and parked them squarely between Arkhan's Mercedes and the security detail milling about smoking and drinking outside our gate.

The charade was that we were cleaning the trucks. The trucks were American military HMMWVs, each with a cupola for mounting a heavy machine gun on top.

They were pretty high and seemed to obscure Arkhan's vehicle enough. One of our guys got in Arkhan's car and moved it out of view of the security detail.

Our compound had a front and back entrance. To get to the front entrance, you would have to wind your way through some narrow streets of a neighborhood, but the back exit had a straight shot to the main road leading out of Kirkuk, northeast, toward the green line.

This was the exit Arkhan had already been moved through by the Kurds over an hour earlier. He was handcuffed and locked in the trunk, well on his way to a Kurdish prison. He should have been nearly there by now.

After confirming that no one had noticed Arkhan's car move, two of our guys drove it out the back gate, closely followed by two more of our guys in one of our low signature cars, a blue BMW.

We were back on track with the original plan.

They drove Arkhan's Mercedes up to a bad part of town called Bajawan, a part of town that Arkhan should not go to alone. This part of the town consisted of a tribe in rivalry to Arkhan's. Tribal enmity often resulted in violence and reciprocal murders.

Our team, dressed in local Iraqi garb with the appropriately colored headdresses called keffiyehs, parked Arkhan's car by the side of the road and got into the blue BMW, leaving Arkhan's blood-stained keffiyeh in the driver's seat. The blue BMW did a wide U-turn and as they passed Arkhan's Mercedes, riddled it with AK-47 bullets, making it look like Arkhan had been ambushed with a drive-by shooting.

We did all of this in broad daylight.

My team sergeant and I waited in the TOC and monitored everything on the radio. It was going smoothly, just as we had planned. We started to feel confident that we were about to pull this off. Then the radio squawked a report of a drive-by shooting in Bajawan.

All American forces were issued a BOLO (be on the lookout) for a blue BMW that was last seen heading west.

My heart sank.

I called our team on the radio. "How far out are you?" I asked.

"We are about seven minutes out." I was relieved to hear.

I warned them about the BOLO and reinforced that the biggest threat they faced was running into an American patrol, and to get back to the house as quickly and directly as possible. Skip the evasion route and beeline it back home.

The seven minutes seemed to drag on, but the team eventually cruised right through the back gate and drove directly into the garage. Part of our team was already in the garage, getting the paint sprayer set up. We would have that blue BMW turned into a green one within the next hour.

We heard more reports come in over the Coalition Forces radio. They recognized the abandoned vehicle as Arkhan's. The vehicle was riddled with bullets. There was blood, but no bodies.

Arkhan was missing.

The kidnapping was almost finished, but we had another problem. The security detail was still waiting outside our front gate. They didn't know Arkhan was missing.

I walked out to the security detail with more refreshments just as the team rolled up the hoses and returned our gun trucks to the garage.

"Oh," I said, "I didn't realize you guys were still here. Didn't any of you go with Arkhan when he left?" I asked.

All of them looked perplexed. The security lead looked panic-stricken. Not only was what I was saying to them confusing, they were just noticing that Arkhan's car was no longer where they thought it was.

I said, "Arkhan left over an hour ago. I thought you would leave together. He got a call on his radio and had to cut our meeting short."

"Where did he go?" the security lead asked.

I told them I wasn't sure, but thought I had heard the name of Bajawan over his radio.

"What?" the security lead was even more panicked. "He can't go there without us!"

"I know," I said, "That is a tough neighborhood. Is there anything I can do?" I asked.
They declined further refreshments and hurriedly loaded their vehicles. They sped off toward Bajawan. Little did they know that they were driving 180 degrees in the wrong direction from where Arkhan actually was.

They would not find him. He betrayed us. And for that, he would pay.

It was not clear how all of this would end, but we were prepared to accept any repercussions.

"Inshallah."

It was beginning to get dark outside. We would wait to see what the light of the morning would bring.

23

COURAGE AND COWARDICE

THE PRIEST'S TRIAL:
A KANGAROO COURT

CHAPTER 23

I. Courage and Cowardice

Consider it a sheer gift, friends, when tests and challenges come at you from all sides. You know that under pressure, your faith-life is forced into the open and shows its true colors. So don't try to get out of anything prematurely. Let it do its work so you become mature and well-developed, not deficient in any way. (James 1:2-4, MSG)

"You're OK. You're gonna be OK. We're gonna get you outta here." Scott kept repeating to Anthony as he plugged the numerous holes in his body.

Anthony was spraying blood from multiple locations, we prioritized the spray coming from the main artery under his right arm and the spraying blood coming from the main artery in his left pelvis. Pelvic bleeds are very difficult to stop. Scott, our EOD expert, was addressing the armpit bleed as I kneeled heavily on Anthony's pelvis while still engaging the enemy in the target building. Their machine guns continued to strafe the courtyard. My guys on the roof were almost ready to breach.

I kept looking down at Anthony to see if he was still alive.

At the height of the engagement, not only was I in a direct fire fight with the insurgents barricaded in the building, not only was I working to manage the fight as a whole, not only was I trying to figure out if Anthony was alive and if we could keep it that way, there was a man off my left shoulder, about twenty meters away, who kept peeking around an open doorway.

I kept trying to plunge some rounds deep into the target building but did not have a clear path. I started to consider conserving my ammo for whatever may come next. Other team members had better vantage points. I threw a couple of hand grenades into the target building but quickly ran out. Other team members with a satchel charge had already climbed on top of the target building roof, and were about ready to drop it inside.

The satchel charge would end this fight in one fell swoop.

And then that unknown man kept poking around the corner. I yelled at him to go inside. I yelled in English so I'm sure he couldn't understand but I waved him inside as well. Then a woman popped out too. I assumed it was his wife. She stood squarely in the threshold of the door silhouetted from the light inside their home.

I watched my team, I watched Anthony, I watched him. I radioed the Sergeant Major.

"The team on the roof is about ready to breach. Prepare for fire in the hole. I've got one MAM messing around behind me. No weapon observed. Can't tell if he's good or bad."

"Copy all," Mark said, "We are moving casualties back to the trucks now."

"Roger."

The unknown male crouched behind his wife and continued to poke out from behind her. His head would pop up over her shoulder, and then down by her waist, by the time he started sneaking between the folds of her burqa, I got really suspicious.

I shifted from my right knee to my left knee to keep the pressure on the wound. When he was finished with Anthony's armpit, Scott took over on the pelvic wound, packaged Anthony, and moved him to a slightly more covered position.

I turned to see how much longer before the team on the roof would have a hole cut big enough to drop the charge into. It looked like they were just about there. I was about to radio Mark, the Sergeant Major, again when the hair on the back of my neck stood up and I spun around to face the woman in the doorway.

"You've got to be kidding me," I thought.

The Priest's Trial: A Kangaroo Court[222]

The plot of history's most famous assassination was unfolding.

The mob of Roman soldiers and Jewish police armed with lanterns, torches, clubs, swords, and restraints descended upon the disciples. Judas stepped forward and kissed Yeshua on both cheeks, using the

---

[222] https://en.wikipedia.org/wiki/Kangaroo_court

predesignated sign so the soldiers could identify Yeshua in the darkness.[223]

Yeshua was betrayed with a kiss.

Peter fought back, cutting the ear off a man named Malchus.

Yeshua quickly reattached the ear and surrendered himself to the mob.

Yeshua, the Lamb of God, was bound, bruised, and brought back across the Kidron. He was marched up the steep incline toward Mount Zion and ultimately to the home of Caiaphas,[224] where he would be tried. He was lowered into one of the holding cells, where he waited. These cells were designed to hold Jewish prisoners until the Sanhedrin, the priestly council, could assemble to preside over the case.

Yeshua awaited his first inspection and interrogation. Alone.

---

[223] Matt. 26:47–50; John 18:2–11.
[224]
https://en.wikipedia.org/wiki/Church_of_Saint_Peter_in_Gallicantu

Annas interrogated Jesus regarding his disciples and his teaching. Jesus answered, "I've spoken openly in public. I've taught regularly in meeting places and the Temple, where the Jews all come together. Everything has been out in the open. I've said nothing in secret. So why are you treating me like a traitor? Question those who have been listening to me. They know well what I have said. My teachings have all been aboveboard."

When he said this, one of the policemen standing there slapped Jesus across the face, saying, "How dare you speak to the Chief Priest like that!"

Jesus replied, "If I've said something wrong, prove it. But if I've spoken the plain truth, why this slapping around?"

Then Annas sent him, still tied up, to the Chief Priest Caiaphas.[225] *(John 18:19-24, MSG)*

Once Yeshua was in front of Caiaphas, it was more of the same.

---

[225] John 18:19–24 (The Message).

The chief priests and the whole Sanhedrin were looking for evidence against Jesus so that they could put him to death, but they did not find any. Many testified falsely against him, but their statements did not agree.

Then some stood up and gave this false testimony against him: "We heard him say, 'I will destroy this temple made with human hands and in three days will build another, not made with hands.'" Yet even then their testimony did not agree.

Then the high priest stood up before them and asked Jesus, "Are you not going to answer? What is this testimony that these men are bringing against you?" But Jesus remained silent and gave no answer.

Again the high priest asked him, "Are you the Messiah, the Son of the Blessed One?"

"I am," said Jesus. "And you will see the Son of Man sitting at the right hand of the Mighty One and coming on the clouds of heaven."

The high priest tore his clothes. "Why do we need any more witnesses?" he asked. "You have heard the blasphemy. What do you think?"

They all condemned him as worthy of death. (Mark 14:55-64, NIV)

Yeshua's fate was sealed.

More to the Story

Replacing Malchus's ear was the last miracle Yeshua performed before his resurrection. We never hear about Malchus again. There must be something more there, but I haven't found it yet.

One simple explanation might be that Yeshua was protecting Peter. Peter should have been arrested that night. He cut a guy's ear off. Why wasn't he arrested? Maybe because Yeshua put it back on.

How would the soldiers explain this one to the high priests? What would have happened if they had arrested Peter and stood before the court? They would have had to admit that Yeshua miraculously replaced an ear. That wasn't going to go over well.

This trial was designed to show Yeshua as a charlatan, a fraud, a liar, and a blasphemer. How would a miracle performed just minutes earlier get folded into this process?

This was Yeshua's time to complete his mission. There was no room for this type of interference and confusion, so Peter was free, and followed the mob at a distance.[226]

The plot to arrest and try Yeshua that night was planned by a select few men. Trying to cram this process in before the Sabbath and the Passover observances was a significant oversight. They were forced to act quickly. This event occurred late at night. Many members of the Sanhedrin must have been awakened from a sound sleep and told to hustle to Caiaphas's palace.

It is not clear how many Sanhedrin members were able to muster, but it is highly doubtful that they reached the legal requirement of a full quorum to be able to make a binding decision over this matter.[227]

---

[226] Mark 14:54.
[227] Charles Souvay, "Sanhedrin," Catholic Encyclopedia, New Advent, accessed March 21, 2023, https://www.newadvent.org/cathen/13444a.htm. A legal quorum varied but it usually consisted of 23 members. There were usually 71 members in the Sanhedrin.

The Sanhedrin, the ruling council of the Jews, was permitted under Roman rule to handle many offenses and violations internal to their community without any Roman intervention or oversight. The Sanhedrin was an influential and powerful group, but their power was limited. They could conduct trials and sentencing, even sentencing someone to death, but the Romans would not delegate the right to carry out any executions.

The Sanhedrin also had Jewish laws to which they were subordinate. For example, they could not conduct trials at night or during festivals. If they did conclude with a death penalty, they were required to wait overnight before passing the final sentence. The court location for all trials was designated to be the Hall of Hewn Stones on the temple grounds. The law also required that two or three witnesses had to agree on all the details. Any false witness found to be lying would receive the same sentence as the person on trial.[228]

As you read the account of this sham trial, see how many violations you can point out.

---

[228] Douglas O. Linder, "The Sanhedrin," Famous Trials, accessed March 21, 2023, https://www.famous-trials.com/jesustrial/1054-sanhedrin.

Most of the Sanhedrin had no idea what was going on, but should have seen right through this nonsense. They, like most governing bodies, were overwhelmed with peer pressure and individuals lacked the courage to speak up for what was right. A few of them likely tried to intervene, but things were already in motion.

Yeshua was inspected three separate times. His first official inspection was with Caiaphas, who had been the high priest for over a decade. Caiaphas was an adept politician who had figured out how to get rich and exert power while working as a stooge for the Romans. His father-in-law, Annas, was the high priest before Caiaphas, but he fell out of favor with the Romans. Annas no longer held any official position, but his deep corruption and intimidation was a heavy influence on Caiaphas and the court.[229]

This brief interview with Caiaphas provided time for the Sanhedrin to assemble. At daybreak, Yeshua was brought before the rest of the council, with Caiaphas presiding.[230] The Jewish leaders needed a quick conviction. They needed the process completed if they were going to get this case before the Roman governor,

---

[229] https://en.wikipedia.org/wiki/Caiaphas
[230] Luke 22:66.

Pilate, before the Passover sacrifices resumed in a few hours.

Bound and beaten, Yeshua was brought before the assembly. He remained silent as Caiaphas interrogated him.

The paid witnesses were brought in so the Sanhedrin could file charges against Yeshua that would excite the Romans. They needed charges serious enough not only to garner the attention of the Roman rulers, but also to raise such alarm that the Romans themselves would choose to execute this lowly rabbi.

The proceeding was quickly turning into a circus because none of the claims made any sense, and none of the witnesses were credible.

Yeshua remained silent.

He stood alone. The mock trial wasn't working well. Exasperated, the high priest finally stood up and asked Yeshua if he was the Messiah.

This time, Yeshua answered. "*I am.*"

Then he added, *"And you will see the Son of Man sitting at the right hand of the Mighty One and coming on the clouds of heaven."*[231]

There must have been an audible gasp, followed by shouts of blasphemy and demands for immediate justice.

The high priest dramatically tore his garments in protest and disgust. The men in the room were infuriated.

It was blasphemy.

At first glance, Yeshua's reply seems a little convoluted, doesn't it? But it is not convoluted at all. In fact, it is extremely clear, powerful, and potent–especially if we rewind this story a few hundred years.

Yeshua was repeating scripture from the Book of Daniel, written nearly 600 years prior to this trial. The prophet Daniel wrote about a vision he had:

> *And there before me was one like a son of man, coming with the clouds of heaven. He approached the Ancient of Days and was led into his presence.*

---

[231] Mark 14:61–62.

He was given authority, glory and sovereign
power; all nations and peoples of every language
worshiped him. His dominion is an everlasting
dominion that will not pass away, and his
kingdom is one that will never be destroyed.[232]
(Daniel 7:13-14, NIV)

For some at the hearing, those who simply didn't understand what was happening, this reply may have seemed ironic. Yeshua, the prisoner, was declaring his sovereignty?

But to others, the scholars, it would have been like a punch in the gut. He stood before them quoting the prophet Daniel and declaring his divinity. A divinity they feared. Their angry reaction clearly betrayed their fear.

Meanwhile, Peter was in the courtyard outside of the ad hoc courtroom betraying Yeshua in a different way. This courtyard sits inside a beautiful compound just on the edge of the Jewish sector of Jerusalem, overlooking the tough Arab neighborhood Silwan.[233] You can stand in this courtyard and imagine the events that took place

---

[232] Dan. 7:13–14 (New International Version).

[233]

https://en.wikipedia.org/wiki/Church_of_Saint_Peter_in_Gallicantu

there. You can also descend an ancient stairway and stand before the holding cells, wondering which of them may have held Yeshua that night. The holes are dungeon-like, somber, and menacing.

Peter was bold enough to follow the mob from the Garden of Gethsemane up to the "kangaroo court," but here his boldness was shaken. He stood in the courtyard warming himself by a fire when a small crowd enveloped him. A servant girl confronted him and accused him of being one of Yeshua's followers.

He denied it.

Another girl pressed him further. He denied it again. They didn't let up, commenting on his Galilean accent. Peter really panicked and began cursing.[234]

Denying Yeshua a third time, the words were not even fully off his lips when Peter heard a rooster crow. At this same moment, Yeshua was being led to another room near the courtyard, he turned to look at Peter. Peter's heart sank. He was filled with shame and *"went outside and wept bitterly."*[235] Peter, the "rock that the church will be built upon," crumbled after a few questions from a servant girl.

---

[234] Matt. 26:69–75 (NIV).
[235] Luke 22:62 (NIV).

Peter was having a terrible night.

An hour earlier, he overreacted as a tough guy in the garden and cut off a young man's ear. A few hours before that, he had been filled with pride during the Passover meal and was mildly chided by Yeshua. He warned Peter of the events that would unfold that night, the impending betrayal and the denial before the rooster crows.[236]

Peter was devastated.

He had betrayed his rabbi and to make it even worse,

Yeshua had tried to warn him but he did not listen.

This story gives us a glimpse again of what Yeshua knew before it happened.

He knew he would be betrayed by Judas that night.
He knew Peter would deny him.
He knew he would be found guilty and nailed to a cross.

His courage was amazing.

---

[236] Luke 22:31–34.

Peter, on the other hand, buckled under the slightest pressure. But you know what he did? He repented, had a good cry about it, and regrouped.

Peter became one of Yeshua's mighty men. He boldly traveled the world to spread this story, one that he lived through—a story that was later called the Gospel.

He survived earthquakes, beatings, torture, and was ultimately murdered for his belief in Yeshua.[237] Legend has it that Peter was crucified, just like Yeshua, but with a twist. To honor his savior, he asked to be crucified upside down. He felt that he was not worthy of dying in the same manner as Yeshua.[238]

How's that for a comeback?

Yeshua was likely being shuffled between the dungeon and the rooms where he was getting ridiculed and abused when he caught the eye of Peter as the rooster crowed. We can only imagine that the divine side of Yeshua looked at Peter with grace and compassion, but we can also imagine that the human side of Yeshua looked at Peter in disappointment and sadness.

---

[237] https://en.wikipedia.org/wiki/Saint_Peter
[238] Acts of Peter, XXXVII

One of his best friends denied him, betrayed him, on a night when he needed him most.

Yeshua was fully abandoned by all his friends to experience the rest of this trial on his own.

II. Courage and Cowardice

"You've got to be kidding me," I said to myself again.

The MAM behind me was between the woman's legs peeking out at me. I couldn't see if he had a weapon or not. He looked a little confused. She looked scared.

I had enough of this nonsense and made a split-second decision. I told myself, "Don't hit the woman."

I raised my rifle, shifted slightly into a better firing position from my knee and aimed low. My intent was to either have a direct hit into the unknown male's face or skip some rounds into him. I steadied my rifle and prepared to kill this man when he disappeared from between the woman's legs. She stood there in the doorway as I placed some rounds in the door jamb around her. The woman disappeared in a flash out of my view.

Just as I was processing this, the radio barked "Fire in the hole, Fire in the hole." I instinctively dropped down closer to the earth and behind the wheel well of the car that was protecting me. The explosion was impressive. The satchel charge collapsed the building in an instant, crushing the Al Qaeda terrorists inside as it fell. A dust cloud kicked up and obscured the target building. Operators didn't waste a second and were converging on the target from three different directions immediately.

I ran over to the doorway, peered into the room and saw the man and his wife crouched in the corner with a baby in her arms. I yelled at them to stay put and was returning to my "safe" spot behind the car when something caught my eye in the bushes. Something moved.

If you are not envisioning this happening in the dark of night, my mistake. This is all happening at two o'clock in the morning. The only light anywhere is the dim glow coming from one or two of the buildings in the compound.

I raised my rifle again, flipped my selector level to fire, and applied pressure to the trigger. The bush moved again and I could make out the ACU pattern that was standard issue to American soldiers.

It was an American soldier.

I lowered my weapon, put it on safe, and asked him, "Are you OK?"

"Yes," he said, "Is it over?"

"Yes," I answered, "Come with me, let's get you home."

I was awestruck and conflicted. I felt sorry for this poor kid who got in over his head. He was clearly terrified.

But I was really pissed off, too. I could've gotten killed and he would've just laid there watching the whole thing.

That's what he did. In his fear, he just laid there and watched everything and didn't do a single thing to lend a hand.

I'm not sure what happened to that kid. I never got his name. I sure hope he got out of the Army shortly after this event. It pains me to think that he could still be in, likely a Master Sergeant or Sergeant Major by now telling "No shit, there I was" stories.

Or maybe he turned himself around. Maybe he faced his cowardice and, like Peter, became bold.

Maybe he is a great NCO out there coaching, mentoring, and leading a new generation of soldiers.

Either way, my job was to get him home alive and that's what I did.

24

FINISH THE JOB

PILATE'S CHOICE:
NOBODY'S PERFECT EXCEPT HIM

CHAPTER 24

I. Finish the Job

> *Consider it pure joy, my brothers and sisters,*
> *whenever you face trials of many kinds, because*
> *you know that the testing of your faith produces*
> *perseverance. (James 1:2-3, NIV)*

"Can this thing go any faster?" I joked to the flight lead. "We gotta get him before he reaches that compound."

"We're pedal to the metal. One minute out," the flight lead answered.

"Dang, this is gonna be another close one," I thought.

The Taliban terrorist leader we were after did not present himself where we could pluck him off the battlefield that day. We had an armada of helicopters, but we needed some open space between him and any built-up area so we could swoop down and nab him.

We loitered out in the cold desert for most of the day. We got the rotors spinning and stutter-stepped a few times thinking that he would break the limits of the village, but he never did.

As the daylight began to wane, the young man who was driving our target around the village all day got on a motorcycle and headed out into the open desert.

We decided that capturing this guy would be better than going home empty-handed. We could interrogate him and find out what his boss had been up to all day.

The helicopter armada formed up behind him and the chase was on. In a wide-open desert, four helicopters don't sneak up on you. Even trying to use any map-of-the-earth techniques, a couple of minutes out from contact they can hear you and see you.

He saw us and tried to make a run for it.

The two star high ranking officer had been sitting right behind me most of the day. My position was on a plastic cooler in the center of the helo facing the cockpit. I could see through the windshield and also had a computer in front of me that I watched intently. The two star high ranking officer had been on this cooler with me all day, looking over my shoulder.

The officer had been supportive and inquisitive, asking questions on who, what, when, where, and why we did what we did. This was somewhere around the hundredth time we'd conducted a raid on that rotation and probably somewhere around my two hundredth time leading a raid with this team. It wasn't an easy one. We spent a lot of time in the freezing cold desert waiting for the target to break into an open space where we could nab him only to settle for his driver.

The two star high ranking officer asked me why we were going after the driver and I explained that he was in every meeting that the Taliban commander had been in that day. He would likely have some valuable information for us.

"But we don't know who he is?" asked the officer.

"No, we do not."

"And you feel ok about killing him?"

I thought that question was weird and maybe even a little passive aggressive.

"We aren't planning on killing him, we are planning to capture him."

"What if he resists and shoots at us or the helicopters?"

"Well, then we kill him."

"And you're ok killing someone we don't know just because he shot at us?"

Now it was getting really weird.

"Yes," I said. "The enemy always gets a vote. If they decide to fight us, they die."

At this point, I was too busy orchestrating this assault and the two star officer returned to watch mode.

Many raids are uneventful. You gain the advantage and convince your opponent to give up. We talk, and everyone lives happily ever after.

Raids like that are quite common but don't make it into a book. It's the equivalent of you taking your trash out to the curb every Monday. There's no story there. But the day that you take the trash to the curb and a mountain lion or a bear is waiting to confront you? Now that's a story.

It's like that.

The unknown Taliban driver leapt off his motorcycle and started running for the lone building that offered him some cover. As soon as he jumped off the motorcycle, I could see the ammo vest he was wearing including the magazines loaded into it, his AK-47 slung over his shoulder. All of this was concealed under a heavy winter coat but when he ran it flew open and we could see this wasn't going to be a boring trash run. He was loaded for bear. We were close enough to see two hand grenades drop behind him as he fled. We assumed that they were live and the helicopter made a quick jolt away from the impending explosions and came to an abrupt landing.

The grenades did not explode.

All the men on the right starboard side of the helo jumped to the ground before it even settled and began running toward the target building that the Taliban fighter had just disappeared into. I followed right behind them. The men on the port side of the helo, including the two star high ranking officer, got off and waited for the helo to take off again. As soon as it did, the team ran to the target building. The other helo landed and I watched them running toward us, filling in from the right, but the two star officer was left standing in the desert by himself.

The distances were not that far. One assault team was already on the wall of the compound, the other team was about twenty meters back, running our way.

The high ranking officer just stood there by himself.

I looked at the target building, then the assault team, then back to the officer.

As I always did, I asked myself where I needed to be on this objective to influence success. What did I need to start doing or what did I need to stop doing?

Quickly I concluded that I needed to stop worrying about the assault–the Sergeant Major had that well under control–and start worrying about the high ranking officer.

No sooner had I concluded that when he started jogging away from the objective, one-hundred and eighty degrees away from where the rest of us were focusing. He moved about twenty to thirty meters and stopped again.

I radioed the Sergeant Major and said, "You got this, I'm going to link up with the boss." I ran to the officer and kneeled down next to him.

"What's up sir?" I asked.

"What's happening?" he said. I was confused. What did he mean "what's happening," he'd seen it all unfold right next to me.

"Well sir, as luck would have it, we caught up to this guy just as he got to this compound. Looks like he is going to fight. Did you see his AK and rack when he ran?"

"Just because he has an AK doesn't mean he's bad," the high ranking officer replied.

Before I could agree or disagree with his logic, I heard the burst of an AK-47 come from the compound. Then another. And finally one more when things went silent.

"Jackpot EKIA," soon followed on the radio.

"Now what's happening?" the officer asked again.

"Looks like he put up a fight. He's now dead. The team is continuing to clear the building and the rest of the compound. We are pushing a sniper team up that hill to get an overwatch between us and the village up ahead."

"I didn't see a village," he responded.

"It's about 600-800 meters away. It's on the other side of the IV line." An IV line is an InterVisibility line that is a terrain fluctuation, often very subtle, that masks observation from one side to another.

"Kenny will get up there so we don't get any surprises."

The high ranking officer and I sat there together in between a clump of rocks as the assaulters continued to work.

He watched intently from behind his night vision goggles and continued asking more questions.

It didn't seem like I could satisfy his questions. It seemed to me that somehow, he felt this Taliban fighter was innocent and we should not have killed him.

He was not into it at all.

It seemed to me like the high ranking officer was ready to get back home and just wanted to wash his hands of this whole matter.

Pilate's Choice: Nobody's Perfect Except Him

The first inspection and interrogation was complete. Yeshua, although innocent and pure, received a death sentence from the Jewish leaders. Still, the Jews had to convince the Romans that Yeshua deserved death. The Sanhedrin needed to bring Yeshua before the Roman authorities, to Pontius Pilate, the governor, for final sentencing.

Dawn was breaking and Pilate would have been awake, starting his morning routine. This would be a big day as the Sabbath before the Passover was always a busy time in Jerusalem, and a dangerous time for Roman soldiers.

Here is how John tells the story:

> *They led Jesus then from Caiaphas to the Roman governor's palace. It was early*

morning. They themselves didn't enter the palace because they didn't want to be disqualified from eating the Passover. So Pilate came out to them and spoke. "What charge do you bring against this man?"

They said, "If he hadn't been doing something evil, do you think we'd be here bothering you?"

Pilate said, "You take him. Judge him by your law." The Jews said, "We're not allowed to kill anyone."

Pilate went back into the palace and called for Jesus. He said, "Are you the 'King of the Jews'?"

Jesus answered, "Are you saying this on your own, or did others tell you this about me?" Pilate said, "Do I look like a Jew? Your people and your high priests turned you over to me. What did you do?"

"My kingdom," said Jesus, "doesn't consist of what you see around you. If it did, my followers would fight so that I wouldn't be handed over to the Jews. But I'm not that kind of king, not the world's kind of king."

Then Pilate said, "So, are you a king or not?"

Jesus answered, "You tell me. Because I am King, I was born and entered the world so that I could witness to the truth. Everyone who cares for truth, who has any feeling for the truth, recognizes my voice."

Pilate said, "What is truth?"[239] *(John 18: 28-38, MSG)*

What is truth? Pilate knew full well that this charade was not about finding the truth. He didn't fully understand why the Jewish leaders were so upset with this simple rabbi, but he was tired of the game already. He had more important things to do.

Pilate instructed the Jewish leaders to come in and state their case, but they refused to enter Pilate's palace because it would make them unclean for the upcoming Passover meal. They didn't have time to visit the mikvah to wash so Pilate had to walk outside and meet with them on the steps of his fortress.

---

[239] John 18:28–38 (The Message).

He was just getting more annoyed with the whole thing. He told them to deal with it, judge Yeshua, and sentence him according to their own laws and the leeway that Rome had granted Israel.

But the Jewish leaders sought a death sentence. They wanted Yeshua executed, and for that they needed Rome's authority. They needed to make Pilate care, and they knew exactly what to say.

> *"We have found this man subverting our nation. He opposes payment of taxes to Caesar and claims to be Messiah, a king."*[240]

> *"He stirs up the people all over Judea by his teaching. He started in Galilee and has come all the way here."*[241]

These allegations piqued Pilate's interest for a few reasons. He could not chance another misstep with Rome. He had made some blunders previously that agitated the Jews, and his bosses in Rome took note. They allowed him to remain in power but they

---

[240] Luke 23:2
[241] Luke 23:5

warned him that he would get fired if he screwed up one more time.[242] He could not afford a new commotion. Pilate also saw an opening to pass the buck. Being that Yeshua was from Galilee, he could send him over to Herod for a hearing.

This was Yeshua's second inspection.

> *When Pilate heard that, he asked, "So, he's a Galilean?" Realizing that he properly came under Herod's jurisdiction, he passed the buck to Herod, who just happened to be in Jerusalem for a few days.*

> *Herod was delighted when Jesus showed up. He had wanted for a long time to see him, he'd heard so much about him. He hoped to see him do something spectacular. He peppered him with questions. Jesus didn't answer—not one word. But the high priests and religion scholars were right there, saying their piece, strident and shrill in their accusations.*

> *Mightily offended, Herod turned on Jesus. His soldiers joined in, taunting and jeering. Then*

---

*they dressed him up in an elaborate king
costume and sent him back to Pilate. That day
Herod and Pilate became thick as thieves.
Always before they had kept their distance.*[243]
(Luke 23:6-10, MSG)

Herod was disappointed. This magic man was
boring. He had better things to do. So, Herod sent
Yeshua back to Pilate.

Pilate's ploy to pass the buck didn't work so he was
ready to give Yeshua a stern warning and send him
on his way.

*Then Pilate called in the high priests, rulers,
and the others and said, "You brought this
man to me as a disturber of the peace. I
examined him in front of all of you and found
there was nothing to your charge. And neither
did Herod, for he has sent him back here with
a clean bill of health. It's clear that he's done
nothing wrong, let alone anything deserving
death. I'm going to warn him to watch his step
and let him go."*[244] *(Luke 23: 13-17, MSG)*

---

[243] Luke 23:6–10 (The Message).
[244] Luke 23:13–17 (MSG).

The mob became incensed. They were overcome with bloodlust and wanted Yeshua executed. Things were escalating out of Pilate's control. He had one last card to play.

Now it was the governor's custom at the festival to release a prisoner chosen by the crowd. At that time they had a well-known prisoner whose name was Jesus Barabbas. So when the crowd had gathered, Pilate asked them, "Which one do you want me to release to you: Jesus Barabbas, or Jesus who is called the Messiah?" For he knew it was out of self-interest that they had handed Jesus over to him.

While Pilate was sitting on the judge's seat, his wife sent him this message: "Don't have anything to do with that innocent man, for I have suffered a great deal today in a dream because of him."

But the chief priests and the elders persuaded the crowd to ask for Barabbas and to have Jesus executed.

"Which of the two do you want me to release to you?" asked the governor.

"Barabbas," they answered.

"What shall I do, then, with Jesus who is called the Messiah?" Pilate asked.

They all answered, "Crucify him!"

"Why? What crime has he committed?" asked Pilate.

But they shouted all the louder, "Crucify him!"

When Pilate saw that he was getting nowhere, but that instead an uproar was starting, he took water and washed his hands in front of the crowd. "I am innocent of this man's blood," he said. "It is your responsibility!"

All the people answered, "His blood is on us and on our children!"

Then he released Barabbas to them. But he had Jesus flogged and handed him over to be crucified.[245] (Matthew 27: 15-26, NIV)

---

[245] Matt. 27:15–26 (New International Version).

Although faultless, pure, and without blemish, Yeshua failed his third inspection.

More to the Story

With hundreds of thousands of pilgrims coming up to Jerusalem for the Passover holiday, there was a heightened threat of revolt during this time, and Pilate kept a close watch on the activities in the city. Pilate's main residence was down in the coastal town of Caesarea Maritima, about a two-day journey from Jerusalem, but he would travel with additional troops to Jerusalem for the high holy days. When in Jerusalem, he had a palace that once belonged to Herod, but it is my belief that on the days surrounding Passover, he remained in his opulent quarters near the Praetorium and the Antonia Fortress.[246] [247] [248]

No one knows for sure, but as a soldier and a commander, I know where I would have been. Commanders are taught to position themselves where they can best influence any situation and maintain awareness. No good commander would be

[246] https://en.wikipedia.org/wiki/Herod%27s_Palace_(Jerusalem)
[247] https://en.wikipedia.org/wiki/Praetorium
[248] https://en.wikipedia.org/wiki/Antonia_Fortress

on the other side of the city from his troops and from the potential flashpoints on a day like this.

Any unrest that led to violence in Jerusalem would cost Pilate his job and potentially his life. Pilate was already on thin ice. With his lack of understanding of the Jewish culture, traditions, and their unwavering adherence to their religion, he had brought unwanted attention down upon himself from Rome and could not afford to do so again.[249]

The Romans could barely stand the Jews. The Roman Empire was held together by each conquered land assimilating and adopting Greek and Roman customs. They wanted homogeneity across their empire. This adherence to Roman laws and customs allowed for the Roman Empire to last for centuries. If a region did not acquiesce and assimilate, it would be subjugated or destroyed.

Judea and the Jews were not easy to categorize. They did not assimilate, but they also were not rebellious. They were strange people with weird customs and a mostly peaceful religion that Rome tolerated. The

---

[249]https://en.wikipedia.org/wiki/Pontius_Pilate, Josephus, *The Jewish War*; Josephus, *The Antiquities of the Jews.*

Jews acquiesced just enough to avoid destruction, but not enough to where Rome was ever comfortable with the Jewish self-rule arrangement.

This self-rule allowed the Jewish leaders to take care of many of their own social and legal issues but restricted them with others, requiring Roman counsel on many things including capital punishment.

Yeshua was brought before Pilate early in the morning and the Roman Prefect interviewed him.
Pilate seemed a little annoyed about the whole thing.
It was early in the morning, and he certainly had plenty of things to do that day—better things than to get in the middle of some silly religious squabble of the Jews.

Blasphemy? What did he care about that nonsense?

We can only imagine what was going through Pilate's mind. They wanted this guy executed? For what? Pilate had likely heard about Yeshua, but could not recall anything illegal or threatening. All he could remember about Yeshua was that he was some kind of prophet or preacher, a healer or magician, a teacher or a rabbi. To the best of his recollection, Yeshua never even spoke poorly about Rome.

In fact, wasn't he the one who, when asked about taxes, said, *"Give Caesar what is his, and give God what is his"?*[250]

Pilate couldn't care less about this sorry peasant teacher in front of him, but he fully understood that the intent of the Jewish politicians was to wipe Yeshua and his movement from the annals of history.

Knowing the fickleness of the Jewish leaders and their emotional overreaction to things, he figured he had a way out of this that would satisfy all the parties involved:

He offered a trade.

During the Feast of Unleavened Bread, Pilate complied with a Roman tradition where the governor released one prisoner, and forgave their debt.

Pilate offered the violent criminal Barabbas.

The name Barabbas in Aramaic means either "son of the father" (bar abba) or it may mean "son of the teacher" (bar rabban).[251] If Barabbas' father was a

---

[250] Mark 12:13–17 (The Message).
[251] https://en.wikipedia.org/wiki/Barabbas

Jewish teacher or leader, and well known, he may have been known as "son of the teacher" (bar rabban). There is also a longstanding tradition, supported in the Book of Matthew, that Barabbas's first name was Jesus (Yeshua).[252] Yeshua Barabbas. Yeshua son of the Father.

It is also likely that Barabbas was a Sicarii. The Sicarii were a group of Jewish zealots, or radicals, who were recognized by the long dagger (a sica) they would carry with them.[253] [254] They would use this dagger, hidden in their robes, to assassinate Roman soldiers and leaders. One of their tactics was to mingle in a crowd of people, often during festivals like Passover, and assassinate their victims, stabbing them viciously, and then disappearing back into the crowd.

Barabbas was probably a thief and a criminal, but he was still a rebel zealot for the Jews, and he would do their dirty work for them. So, while he was a dangerous man, an unclean man, he was also respected by many for his zealotry and his courage to fight on behalf of his people. Barabbas may have even received

---

[252] Matt. 27:16–17.
[253] https://en.wikipedia.org/wiki/Sicarii
[254] https://en.wikipedia.org/wiki/Sica

compensation from the Jewish leaders for his acts of violence.

To some, Barabbas was a messianic warrior, viewed by many as a necessary evil, someone necessary to usher in a new freedom and reign that had been promised to them for centuries.

Someone like Barabbas is what many of the Jews were looking for, a brave and bold messiah who could overthrow the tyranny of the Romans.

This is the choice Pilate gave the crowd: Who do you want to set free:

Jesus Barabbas, the robber, murderer, insurrectionist? Of the Sicarii? The terrorist?

Or Jesus the Messiah, the Miracle worker, the Anointed One, the Teacher?

The irony in this detail is staggering. Not only did these two men standing before Pilate, sentenced to death, share the same name, but they shared the same mission.

Yeshua Barabbas was a freedom fighter for the Jews. He fought to deliver his people from their oppression. He fought to usher in the long-awaited king.

Yeshua HaMashiach was the deliverer of the Jews. He was sent to redeem his Father's people and lead them to a new kingdom. He *was* their long-awaited king. But this Yeshua, Yeshua of Nazareth, did not fit the people's expectations. They were anticipating an earthly king, one who was a direct descendant of David. They were anticipating a warrior who would restore the Kingdom of Israel.

Yeshua of Nazareth was a huge disappointment to them. He spoke of a kingdom not of this world. He could not, *would* not be the promised messiah.

Their choice was clear: Free Barabbas. Crucify Yeshua HaMashiach.

Pilate just wanted to get on with the day. No more games.

He just wanted to wash his hands of the whole matter.

II. Finish the Job

It had been a long day.

There were not going to be any interrogations that night.

The man we wanted to capture and question decided to fight back so he died, instead.

As we loaded back into the helicopters, we were told over the radio that the original Taliban leader we had been hunting all day had walked away from the village and was lying in an open field about four kilometers away from anything that might serve as cover.

Was this going to end up being our lucky day?

We flew back to the Tactical Operations Center (TOC) to figure out what was happening. I was a little concerned that this might be a come-on, an ambush.

As I moved from the helicopters to the TOC, I felt a hand on my shoulder. It was the high ranking officer who had been hanging out with us all day. He said to me, "I don't think this is a good hit."

"What do you mean, sir?" I asked.

"There's too much confusion about what is going on. It's late. It's been a long day," he said.

"But that's why we are here at the TOC, to take a break, clear things up and see if we should go get him or not.".

He squeezed my shoulder and said, "I'm sure you'll do the right thing, Major." This time he used my rank. There was a lowly oak leaf cluster on my uniform. This guy was wearing two shiny stars on his uniform.

I was confused. Did he want me to turn this off? Did he want me to skew the discussion with the team leaders and the flight leads? One thing I knew for sure, he had had enough combat for one day.

There is much more to this story, but I will simply say that combat is not a spectator sport. Especially for two star officers. He might have been in charge, but he really did not understand this world we were in. If you want to mix it up with seasoned commandos, the least you can do is not get in the way.

He was done for the night. We were not. I was not going to suppress the truth.

We went into the war council with the team leaders and evaluated the objective. It was unanimous. We were ready to go get this guy.

The high ranking officer once again placed his hand on my shoulder and this time said, "Young major, I guess I didn't make myself clear the first time. This is not a good hit. Let it go. You have to know when to let something go and try again another day."

I kept my demeanor stoically, but inside I was seething. I wasn't trained to be an Assault Force Commander so I could let terrorists go. I was an Assault Force Commander assessed, selected, trained, and entrusted to accomplish the mission.

We were expected to do things others could not. Or would not. We were expected to finish the job.

Oppressors Beware. Our enemies feared us because we were relentless, precise, deadly. Professionals.

There was certainly a disconnect in expectations. I called my boss and told him that we were going to pass on the target that we had been chasing all day. I was embarrassed to make the call, but we had clearly been outvoted by the two star officer.

Leaving the phone on speaker, I explained to the Ranger Colonel that we were on our way back to base. He was dumbfounded. How could we pass this up?

He had known me back when I was a buck sergeant. "What's going on?" he asked. "This isn't like you," he continued. "Is everything OK?"

"Yes, everything is fine," is all I said.

As I waited for the two star officer to say something, there was just dead air. Incredulous, the Ranger Colonel relented. "OK, I'll see you when you get back here to base."

The high ranking officer never said a word. He turned and walked out.

To remain silent amidst false accusations and painful quiet as you feel belittled is a difficult thing. That's why I include it here. My blood boils retelling this story. I felt degraded.

But time has passed. Just as I accuse this high ranking two star officer of not understanding the world I was in, I certainly did not understand the world he was in.

I did not understand why he wanted to wash his hands of the whole matter.

I have got to stop being angry about this. None of us are perfect.

Every time I read Yeshua's silence, I am humbled. He was blameless.

He was perfect.

He endured all this injustice with pure grace. He is the Lion of Judah. He allowed himself to be the Lamb of God. He could do things no one else could or would. He was expected to complete the mission for us.

He was born to die.
For me.
For us.

NO ROOM FOR HATE

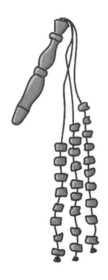

EXACTOR MORTIS:
THE OPPRESSOR OF DEATH

CHAPTER 25

I. No Room for Hate

> *He was pierced for our transgressions, he was crushed for our iniquities; the punishment that brought us peace was on him, and by his wounds we are healed. (Isaiah 53:5, NIV)*

"Permission to engage?" Kenny asked on the assault net.

"Engage at will," I answered.

A shot rang out.

"What's happening?" the two star high ranking officer asked.

Once again, I was confused. He was sitting here with me, watching and hearing all of this unfold.

"We have a Taliban element assembling and getting ready to maneuver on Kenny and Scott."

Another shot rang out.

Kenny came up on the radio. "Engaged one MAM with an RPG. He fell and another picked it up. Engaged him too."

"What's happening?" the officer asked again.

I'm a professional soldier. Cold and calculated in my approach to combat. Our enemies are not innocent until proven guilty. It's quite the opposite. I'm not a cop. We collect the evidence of their guilt and assume their guilt as we develop a plan to capture them or kill them.

We absolutely are the judge and jury deciding life and death for our enemies.

This is not a light responsibility and one that I have always carried with incredible respect and honor. The battlefield is not the place to be merciful and gracious toward our enemies. We protect innocent men, women, and children. The non-combatants are safeguarded. We will lay our lives down for them. We get between them and our enemies. Our job is to die before they do.

But when an enemy shows his colors and votes, he pays. He fights, he dies.

Kenny and his spotter got to the top of the hilltop, overlooking the intervisibility line and directly into the village nearby.

"In position," he reported over the radio on the assault net.

The Taliban identified Kenny and his spotter up on the hill and were discussing a plan to move around in the low ground to ambush him. It was getting darker–when Kenny switched to his night vision goggles, he could see even more. He could see men congregating right where they said they would.

We knew exactly what the Taliban were up to. They were going to assemble at the base of a big oak tree and then maneuver to the north in the low ground to kill Kenny. They were waiting for someone named Ahmed to arrive with an RPG before they set out.

Kenny could see it all.

Ahmed arrived with the RPG.

"Permission to engage?" Kenny asked on the assault net.

"Engage at will," I answered.

Kenny could clearly see what was going on. We all clearly understood what was going on.

Except the high ranking two star officer.

"What's happening?" he asked again.

"Kenny is engaging the Taliban."

"How do you know that they are Taliban?" he asked.

"They are assembling like soldiers with AK-47s, machine guns, and RPGs. They're Taliban."

"What if they are just citizens protecting their village?"

I could see that we were looking at this event from two very different points of view.

Another sniper shot rang out.

"How long is this going to go on?"

"As long as Kenny can positively ID a threat, he is free to engage. EOD is prepping the motorcycle with a charge and then we will move to exfil."

"You're going to destroy the motorcycle?" the two star officer asked. "Is that necessary?"

"Sir, the Taliban care more about that motorcycle then they do the guy that just got killed driving it. Motos are hard to come by and need to be registered, licensed, etc. They hate that. They'd rather lose ten guys before losing a motorcycle."

Another sniper shot rang out.

Exactor Mortis: The Oppressor of Death[255]

Their minds were made up. The mob made the conscious choice to murder Yeshua. Unwittingly, they were participating in God's plan to sacrifice His only son to atone for the sins of the world. This had to happen but each person made their own choice. They let themselves get caught up with the rabid mob and they chose murder.

Pilate handed Yeshua over to the Roman soldiers.

[255] https://translate.google.com/?sl=la&tl=en&text=exactor%20mortis&op=translate&hl=en, http://www.muncherian.com/s-mk15v16.html

Then the governor's soldiers took Jesus into the Praetorium and gathered the whole company of soldiers around him. They stripped him and put a scarlet robe on him, and then twisted together a crown of thorns and set it on his head. They put a staff in his right hand. Then they knelt in front of him and mocked him. "Hail, king of the Jews!" they said. They spit on him and took the staff and struck him on the head again and again. After they had mocked him, they took off the robe and put his own clothes on him.

Then they led him away to crucify him.

As they were going out, they met a man from Cyrene, named Simon, and they forced him to carry the cross. They came to a place called Golgotha (which means "the place of the skull").[256] *(Matthew 27:27-33, NIV)*

More to the Story

These Roman soldiers were professionals. They knew how to torture a man. They knew how to crucify a man.

---

[256] Matt. 27:27–33 (New International Version).

Many Roman tasks were broken down and assigned to squads of four men known as a quaternion.[257] Guard duty was often broken into four shifts through the night. A professional scourge crew, like the one assigned to Yeshua, consisted of four men.

The commander overall responsible for torture and executions was often a centurion. In scourging and crucifixions, this Roman Centurion was called the Exactor Mortis. He was there to ensure that terrible damage was inflicted but that the condemned did not die from the torture. The condemned man was expected to reach "half death," but no more. The execution was supposed to conclude on the cross, not under the whip.[258]

---

[257] "American Tract Society Bible Dictionary: Quaternion of Soldiers," Bible Dictionaries, StudyLight.org, accessed March 22, 2023, https://www.studylight.org/dictionaries/eng/ats/q/quaternion-of-soldiers.html.

[258]

https://www.researchgate.net/publication/19648788_On_the_Physical_Death_of_Jesus_Christ, https://catholicinsight.com/the-physical-effects-of-the-scourging-and-crucifixion-of-jesus/, https://digitalcommons.gardner-webb.edu/cgi/viewcontent.cgi?article=1646&context=gardner-webb-newscenter-archive, https://www.practicalhomicide.com/Research/042009.htm

Two of the soldiers were responsible for securely tying down the victim. The victim's clothes would be stripped off, and he would be stretched out over a pillar or a boulder, so his shoulders, back, buttocks, and upper thighs were bare and vulnerable. His hands were tied or shackled on either side of the pillar, tautly so he could not squirm. His head would be bent forward, safely out of the line of impact, and lessening the chance he would die during the torture. The soldiers avoided vital areas and usually had no limit on the number of strikes they could inflict. Once enough flesh and muscle were torn away, the Exactor Mortis would make the call when the punishment would end.

Two of the soldiers were the designated scourgers. They were usually powerful men, cold, calculating, and masters of their craft. They were experts in many tools of torture.

For Yeshua, they used the flagrum.[259] The flagrum had a short, rigid handle about eight inches long. Several straps of about a foot in length were attached to this handle. Each strap held a number of weights consisting of lead balls, pieces of bronze, jagged

---

[259] Ibid.

bones, rocks, sharp stones, or glass, tied and woven into the braided rawhide straps. The lead balls and rocks were designed to soften up the skin and tissue while the sharp stones, metal, and glass were designed to shred the skin and tear it apart. The goal was to reach the muscles under the skin to pulverize and pierce them without breaking bones.

The two scourgers would stand on opposite sides of the condemned man and take turns striking him across his shoulders, back, buttocks and legs. They worked as a team, one of them softening the flesh with a few blows and then the other one digging deep into the flesh, pulling pieces out, tearing blood vessels, serrating nerves, bruising lungs, causing severe internal bleeding.

This was not a whipping like we usually imagine. This was pure unadulterated torture.

Yeshua was not hanging vertically with the soldiers swinging in weird angles. He was laid over something, horizontal to the ground, so the scourgers could use their full force, arcing the flagrum high over their heads and coming down on his naked body with as much force as they could generate.

The true art of this atrocious act was not the sheer power and force of the strikes, but the nuance that each scourger would find to tear the flesh. The straps of the flagrum could be lightly laid across the back; the pulling away was what would do the damage. Victims of this torture were known to vomit, experience seizures, faint, and of course shriek with pain.

We don't know how Yeshua reacted to this torment. I believe that considering his stoic attitude during the trial and what we will soon see with his crucifixion, he likely bore this torture in silence. Undoubtedly, he prayed for the return of the angels to comfort him.

Bruised ribs and shredded intercostal muscles would make it difficult to breathe, and depending on the attention of the Exactor Mortis, internal organs could certainly be perforated.[260]

The crown of thorns still clung to his head, continuing to dig into his skull, poking the nerves that enervated his eyes, ears, and mouth. Stabbing

---

[260] Ibid.

pain like electric shocks would have radiated through his eyes, ears, face, and neck, causing him to spasm, compounding and complicating the timing of each strike of the whip.[261]

Once the condemned was beaten, bloodied, and "half dead," the Exactor Mortis would have been satisfied. At this point, another quaternion would take over—the execution squad.[262]

In the Roman tradition, the condemned man would be responsible for carrying the cross beam of their cross to the execution site.[263] This allowed the public to witness the event in a more personal way as the prisoner was paraded through the city streets. It was another level of humiliation heaped onto the criminal, and his charges were put on full display so that observers knew specifically why this man was going to be hanged on a cross.

This level of barbarism was intended to be a deterrent to the rest of the populace.

---

[261] Ibid.
[262] Ibid.
[263] Ibid.

With the cross fastened to his back, Yeshua departed the Praetorium and began his forced march to the hill where he knew he would die.

There is an old tradition, dating back over a thousand years, that commemorates Yeshua's final steps. It is called the Via Dolorosa in Latin, the Way of Suffering.[264] Many pilgrims solemnly walk this route in remembrance and honor of Yeshua's final moments. Most of the stations (there are fourteen in total), are purely symbolic and commemorative, but a few of them are grounded in archaeological discoveries and facts.

The precise location of the events commemorated on this route are of little importance compared to the intent of this solemn experience. At each station, pilgrims from around the world pray, ponder, and reflect on these brutal events that happened so long ago.

Station 1 is where the events we have been discussing began. It is where Pilate offered the final condemnation of Yeshua.

---

[264] https://en.wikipedia.org/wiki/Via_Dolorosa

Station 2 is where Yeshua was given his cross to carry. Because crucifixion was a common form of Roman execution, there was a systematic and intentional process to everything. The upright portion of the cross stanchions was called the stipes and the cross bar was called the patibulum. The patibulum weighed between 75-125 pounds.

Most people believe that Yeshua carried only the patibulum crossbar to Golgotha. This piece of wood was often placed on the convict's shoulders. His wrists were tied to it so it would not be repeatedly dropped but it was inevitable that men would stumble under its weight.

Station 3 is where we acknowledge the first time that Yeshua collapsed under the weight of his cross.

Try to imagine the pain of it all. The abuse of the previous night weighed heavily, and the early morning physical punishment was still settling in. A slip or fall with hands tied to a crossbeam would have been unspeakably painful.

Barefoot. Bloody. Exhausted.

The toll of it all was crushing him.

Station 4 is where we honor Mary, Yeshua's mother, as she watched her son pass by, potentially on his knees crawling, unable to stand under the weight of the cross beam.

Station 5 is where we recognize Simon of Cyrene who was forced by the Roman soldiers to help Yeshua carry his cross.[265] We don't know much about him. We don't know if Yeshua said anything to him. We don't know if Yeshua even had the energy to lift his eyes and connect with Simon.

Either way, it was one of the last acts of kindness shown to Yeshua before his death. Simon lifted some of the burden that our savior could no longer carry.

This man, this passerby, was one of the last people to offer some relief to Yeshua. He carried his cross for him, if only for a short time.

Station 6 is where tradition holds that a woman named Veronica wiped Yeshua's face with a cloth.

---

[265] Cyrene was a coastal town in Libya. Simon, along with his sons, are specifically named in Mark 15:1.

This may have been the woman Yeshua healed when she touched the tallit of his robe. We simply don't know enough of the details of the story, but there is a chance that this is the very same Veronica. Legend holds that Veronica returned to wipe the blood from Yeshua's face. She offered him just some slight relief, if only for a short time.

A small act of kindness.

As we continue to Station 7, we commemorate a place where Yeshua fell a second time. His condition was deteriorating, despite the small acts of kindness that were intermixed with the exhortations, berating, and beatings of the Roman detail.

Station 8 is where we stop to reflect on the interaction between Yeshua and the weeping, mourning women of Jerusalem.

At Station 9 he stumbled a third time and was dragged the final few meters to the place where he was prepared for crucifixion and nailed to the cross.

The final stations of the Via Dolorosa are all inside the present-day Church of the Holy Sepulchre.[266] They are solemn places to meditate, pray, and focus on the final moments of Yeshua's painful death and hasty burial.

Yeshua was stripped of any clothes that remained on his beaten body. Simon of Cyrene was allowed to drop the cross beam and was relieved of his duties. We don't know if he hustled away from the scene or simply slipped into the crowd to watch the Roman executioners continue their task.

The rocky soil in Israel makes it difficult to dig holes. The scarcity of straight wood also makes it likely that the crucifixion parts would have been saved and reused. This includes the nails, ropes, stipes, and the patibulum crossbars.

We don't know if the stipes, the vertical part of the cross, would be permanently fixed in place or not. What we can be sure about is that the holes were pre-dug, and everything was inventoried before and after use.[267]

---

[266] https://en.wikipedia.org/wiki/Church_of_the_Holy_Sepulchre
[267] Edwards, "On the Physical Death of Jesus Christ"; Terry McDermott, "The Physical Effects of the Scourging and Crucifixion

Good soldiers inventory everything.
The patibulum was pre-drilled with holes for each nail. The nails, used over and over, were blunt and worn, rusty and crooked.

The convicts were forced to lie down on their backs with the patibulum underneath them. Their first hand was stretched out so their wrist was directly over the pre-drilled hole. The spike was then pounded through their wrist until it protruded through the back of the hole where it was then pounded and bent around the back of the beam to secure it in place.

A rope was then fastened around the convict's other arm. The Roman guards would pull it, stretch it, and hold it in place until the second nail could be

of Jesus," *Catholic Insight*, March 13, 2020, https://catholicinsight.com/the-physical-effects-of-the-scourging-and-crucifixion-of-jesus/; Office of University Communications, "GWU Forensics Expert Discusses the Physical Death of Jesus from Medical Examiner's Perspective," *Gardner-Webb NewsCenter Archive*, April 7, 2017, https://digitalcommons.gardner-webb.edu/cgi/viewcontent.cgi?article=1646&context=gardner-webb-newscenter-archive; Vernon J. Geberth, "State Sponsored Torture in Rome: A Forensic Inquiry and Medicolegal Analysis of the Crucifixion of Jesus Christ," American Academy of Forensic Sciences, 2008, https://www.aafs.org/research/state-sponsored-torture-rome-forensic-inquiry-and-medicolegal-analysis-crucifixion-jesus.

hammered through the other wrist, lined up with the pre-drilled hole. If a man's arms were too short to reach, the guards would yank on the rope, dislocating the arm until it could be stretched enough to line everything up as needed.

The Roman execution squad needed to line up the predrilled holes even if this meant dislocating shoulders and elbows.

Two thieves were also sentenced to be crucified that day. They continued to curse their fate and struggle against the Romans, but I envision Yeshua laying himself down on the ground and willfully extending his arms.

I can see him lying flat on his back, arms spread out, staring up at heaven.

Heaven was close and getting closer, but it still must have seemed a long way off to him. Tears may have filled his eyes, but resolve, courage, and forgiveness were surely in his heart.

As the nail was driven through his right wrist, Yeshua extended his left, so that it was directly over the hole, and waited for the hammer. In Yeshua's battered state, he had few opportunities left to demonstrate his willingness to undergo this torment. Yet waiting is often worse than the pain itself.

Perhaps the soldiers fumbled around for the next nail until one of them pressed it against Yeshua's wrist.

Those in observance would have clearly seen that despite his suffering, he was allowing it all to happen. He would have been cooperating with his executioners, extending grace to them as they continued their torturous duties.

Then the second nail was hammered through his wrist. The nails were usually five to six inches long and about a third of an inch in width, with a slight taper to the blunt and bent end.

The nails would have severed the median nerve and the pain would have felt like an electric shock or red-hot poker shooting from the wrist, through the elbow, to the shoulder. The fingers on each hand would seize and be twisted and curled in a macabre clench that would be difficult to unlock.[268]

---

[268] Ibid.

Not yet fastened securely, seizing in pain, Yeshua awaited the next step.

He needed to be flipped over, face in the dirt, so the soldiers could bend the nails on the back side of the beam. Then he was lifted up so the cross could be pieced together. Once the patibulum was affixed to the stipe, his feet were nailed in place.

There are archeological remains of a crucifixion victim who had had the nails pounded through his heels and fastened to the vertical pole with one foot on each side, straddling the stipe. You can see the heel bone with the macabre rusted spike that is stuck there forever.[269] It must have been too difficult for the soldiers to remove, so they left the nail in place. In other cases, for ease of removal, they would hammer nails through the top of each foot instead.

This is how it must have been for Yeshua. The Bible makes a significant point to highlight that

---

[269] Livia Gershon, "Rare Physical Evidence of Roman Crucifixion Found in Britain," *Smithsonian Magazine*, December 10, 2021, https://www.smithsonianmag.com/smart-news/first-physical-evidence-of-roman-crucifixion-found-in-britain-180979190/.

Yeshua's bones were never broken, fulfilling an old prophecy.[270] Hence we can safely conclude that his feet were nailed through the metatarsals to a platform called the suppedaneum.

Roman crosses were historically about seven to seven and a half feet tall. A suppedaneum was a small platform affixed to the stipe that the crucified would use as a brace to push off from, so the condemned didn't suffocate too soon. Crucifixion was designed to be a long, excruciating, and terrifying death. If death happened too quickly, the Roman detail would be chastised.

During the crucifixion, the weight of the body hanging off the extended wrists would force the rib cage to expand, spasming the diaphragm and making breathing extremely difficult.[271] Crucifixion is a form of drowning. On top of all the pain, the convicted man slowly drowns in his own bodily fluids.

---

[270] Ps. 34:20.
[271] Edwards, "On the Physical Death of Jesus Christ"; McDermott, "The Physical Effects"; Office of University Communications, "GWU Forensics Expert"; Geberth, "State Sponsored Torture."

All of this, compounded by any previous torture, could kill a man in minutes. The suppedaneum was designed to prolong the suffering. Another purpose was to prevent the body from falling off the cross if the limbs tore away or the nails tore through the wrists.

The victims would bend at the knees and their feet would be pressed flat to the suppedaneum. A nail, like the ones used for the hands, would be hammered through the top of each foot, severing the plantar nerves. The pain would have been similar to piercing the median nerve, with electric shock or red-hot poker pain shooting through the legs. The victim would continually have to push off the nail, arch his back, and gasp for air.[272]

In most cases, crucified victims suffocated to death.[273] They would eventually lose the ability to raise themselves up to take a breath and simply suffocate. If a quick death was desired, the crucifixion squad would break the victims' legs so

---

[272] Edwards, "On the Physical Death of Jesus Christ"; McDermott, "The Physical Effects"; Office of University Communications, "GWU Forensics Expert"; Geberth, "State Sponsored Torture."
[273] https://en.wikipedia.org/wiki/Crucifixion_of_Jesus

they could not push off, and this would hasten the asphyxiation.

Yeshua was suffocating slowly. He was drowning in his own bodily fluids.

II. No Room for Hate

I could see that the high ranking two star officer was visibly upset.
I called the Sergeant Major and Kenny and told them to jump to another predesignated frequency to have a private conversation.

Once all three of us got to the alternate channel, I asked Kenny, "Whatcha got?"

"These dudes aren't getting it. Every time I drop one guy, another guy tries to pick up the RPG. I've got a stack going."

"Copy. We are about to exfil. I need you to stop killing people." I couldn't believe the words coming out of my mouth.

"What do you mean?" Kenny asked.

I used the high ranking officer's call sign and explained that he is getting upset.

"I don't give a fuck, these dudes need to die," Kenny said.

"Look man, I get it, but something just isn't right with the boss. Please stop killing dudes and come on back down. We're heading out in three minutes."

"Roger," was all Kenny said.

I felt like an idiot.

Everyone pulled off the objective and they were moving toward me and the high ranking officer for exfil. We quietly fell into PZ posture and called in the birds.

A loud explosion erupted from the target compound.

"What was that?" asked the two star officer.

"That's the moto getting destroyed."

"Was that absolutely necessary?" he asked.

"Yes sir."

I didn't understand him and he didn't understand me.

The Taliban still whip people and crucify people. They didn't deserve our mercy.

I didn't hate them but I had no mercy for them, either.

Maybe the high ranking two star officer had spent too much time in a climate-controlled marble building talking about how to end this war.

Maybe I had spent too much time in combat, physically fighting to end this war.

He was the commander of a multinational combined arms task force consisting of multiple countries with several layers of command and control to consider.

I was only an Assault Force Commander.

I have seen people die. In peace and in war. There really are only two ways to go in the end:

You suffocate. Your brain is starved of oxygen and your mechanical body begins to shut down.

Or you drown. Fluids leak out or seep into places where they don't belong, and your mechanical body begins to shut down.

This I understood very clearly.
I'm not sure he did.

He wore two stars on his uniform. My uniform had no insignia and was stained with blood. Maybe I didn't fully appreciate his job or even the heavy responsibilities that he had to carry.

But I am sure he did not appreciate my job or the heavy responsibilities that I had to carry.

He was a high ranking two star officer in charge of thousands.

I was the Exactor Mortis.

EMBRACE THE PAIN

TETÉLESTAI:
IT IS FINISHED

CHAPTER 26

I. Embrace the Pain

"Uh oh," I thought, "That doesn't look right."
My parachute was not fully open.
I grabbed both of the risers and jerked them.
Something wasn't right with my chute. It was dark
and I couldn't see it well, but it was not inflated like
it should be. I compared my drop rate with the
other chutes I could see and I was plummeting fast.
I looked down at the ground, back up at my canopy,
and grabbed the handle of my reserve parachute. I
hesitated. I wasn't sure if the reserve would make
things better or worse. I was falling fast but my
chute was open.
I decided to ride it in.

I put my feet and knees together and braced for impact.

This was gonna hurt.

Tetelestai: It is Finished

At nine o'clock in the morning (the third hour), the Roman crucifixion team hung Yeshua on the cross atop Golgotha.

At this same time, the Temple Priests placed the first lamb of the day upon the altar for the Passover sacrifice.

For three hours Yeshua hung on the cross, his lifeblood slowly draining away, and the breath in his lungs becoming shallow and mixed with fluid. He was slowly, inexorably dying.

Twelve o'clock noon would signal the end of the first daily sacrifice in the temple.

> *From noon to three, the whole earth was dark. Around mid-afternoon Jesus groaned out of the depths, crying loudly, "Eli, Eli, lama sabachthani?" which means, "My God, my*

God, why have you abandoned me?"[274]
(Matthew 27: 45-46, MSG)

What was he feeling?

At three o'clock in the afternoon (the ninth hour), the second lamb was sacrificed. Yeshua hung on the cross in agony, abandoned and alone except for his mother, a few of her friends, and the disciple named John.

> *Near the cross of Jesus stood his mother, his mother's sister, Mary the wife of Clopas, and Mary Magdalene. When Jesus saw his mother there, and the disciple whom he loved standing nearby, he said to her, "Woman, here is your son," and to the disciple, "Here is your mother." From that time on, this disciple took her into his home.*
>
> *Later, knowing that everything had now been finished, and so that Scripture*[275] *would be fulfilled, Jesus said, "I am thirsty." A jar of*

---

[274] Matt. 27:45–46 (The Message).
[275] Ps. 69:21; Adam Hamilton, "'I Thirst': More Here than Meets the Eye," *Adam Hamilton* (blog), March 24, 2015, https://www.adamhamilton.com/blog/i-thirst-more-here-than-meets-the-eye/#.YkDi5TfMK3I

wine vinegar was there, so they soaked a sponge in it, put the sponge on a stalk of the hyssop plant, and lifted it to Jesus' lips. When he had received the drink, Jesus said, "It is finished."[276] *(John 19: 25-30, NIV)*

More to the Story

"It is finished" is a simple Greek word: tetelestai.[277] This word has a couple of different meanings. "Tetelestai" also means "the sacrifice is complete." Every Jewish person watching Yeshua suffer would have instantly recognized this word as the equivalent of a Hebrew phrase that was used by the high priest. On the Jewish holiday called The Day of Atonement, the high priest would enter the temple and make a special sacrifice for the sins of the people of Israel and place that sin on the scapegoat.[278] As soon as the scapegoat was sacrificed, the high priest would declare to those gathered, "It is finished," in Hebrew.

Tetelestai.

---

[276] John 19:25–30 (New International Version).

[277]

https://en.wikipedia.org/wiki/Sayings_of_Jesus_on_the_cross#John_19:30

[278] https://en.wikipedia.org/wiki/Scapegoat

By saying "It is finished," Yeshua was announcing to all that there was no more need for sacrifices or temples because his work brought ultimate fulfillment to what their sacrificial system foreshadowed. He is the scapegoat for the whole world.

Tetelestai also means "the work is complete."

In Yeshua's time, when a builder or carpenter had completed a day's work or finished a project, he would announce, "Tetelestai." This was to indicate that whatever it was that he was assigned to do was now completed. Artists would do the same thing. When they completed their work, they would have a moment of unveiling during which they would declare, "Tetelestai." This, too, was to signal that their masterpiece was complete.

Yeshua the builder had completed what he was tasked to do.

Yeshua the artist had completed his masterpiece.

The task of earning the salvation of the world was completed in his work on the cross. No more additions or adjustments were necessary. Salvation was complete.

Tetelestai.

Tetelestai also means "the debt is paid in full."

Back then, when a person finally paid off a loan, they were issued a receipt that was stamped with the word "tetelestai." This was verification that they were no longer responsible for any debt—that everything they owed was completely and permanently paid for.
Yeshua paid off our debt.

The debt all mankind incurred through Adam was now erased.

Tetelestai.

II. Embrace the Pain

I crashed into the earth and felt my pelvis crack. It felt like my pelvis exploded. I did my best Parachute Landing Fall (PLF) but I landed with my left foot

on a tree stump and my right foot off of it. This
certainly didn't help things.

The pain was searing and white. It blinded me for a
minute and I was confused because of the contrast
with the dark night. The ball joint of my left hip
was protruding out of its socket. I could see the
bulge and I felt the round bone through my BDUs.
The ball joint had slid just past the leg strap and was
clearly sticking out.
"This can't be good," I thought.

I took both of my hands and pressed against the
protruding bone but it would not budge.
"Oh man, this is bad."
As I was releasing the clips for the leg straps, the
bone began to move by itself. It slowly slipped back
into position and then popped back into the socket.
The pain was excruciating. I think I may have
passed out for a second. I really am not sure. Either
way, it looked better and felt a little better.

I wiggled my way out of the rest of my parachute,
broke a red chemlite, and stuffed the chute into its
kit bag. I piled all of my gear on top of the kit bag,
popped a second red chemlite and began dragging
myself toward the assembly area. I couldn't really

move my legs so I dragged myself along with my hands. I could feel the bones in my pelvis grinding like broken glass.

This *really* wasn't good.

To be a solid Special Forces soldier, you need to figure out how to deal with pain. You must be able to endure a significant amount of physical and emotional pain, finding ways to cope with it.

For the inevitable sharp pain, you must embrace it. You confront the pain. You challenge it. You feel it and do not run from it. You face it head-on. You reach into it and take its power away. You find a way to appreciate it for what it is. You respect it. It is pain.

Deep, dull, enduring pain is different. It can be difficult confronting that kind of pain; it will wear you down and win in the end. You have to find ways to coexist with it. I would sometimes create my own mantra to manage it. I had a short saying that I would repeat sometimes in my head and sometimes aloud. I used it as I crawled in pain after that botched parachute jump and throughout recovery and rehabilitation. I used it all throughout selection, especially at the end of the final trek.

As the pain became more and more difficult to bear,
I would say,
"Blessed be the name of the Lord." With every step,
I would repeat it.
Blessed be the name of the Lord. Step.
Blessed be the name of the Lord. Step.

I would repeat this for hours until I made it to the
finish line. Until I completed the task assigned to
me—tetelestai.

I can envision Yeshua exhausted and bleeding,
meeting the pain of the whip. Facing the pain from
the nails being driven into his feet and hands.
Hanging on the cross, his limbs becoming numb
and his body slowly shutting down the parts
unnecessary to stay alive.

I can imagine Yeshua repeating a prayer, a mantra to
diffuse the pain.

His last words hearken back to David in Psalm 31,

> In you, Lord, I have taken refuge; let me never
> be put to shame; deliver me in your
> righteousness.

Turn your ear to me, come quickly to my rescue; be my rock of refuge, a strong fortress to save me.

Since you are my rock and my fortress, for the sake of your name lead and guide me.

Keep me free from the trap that is set for me, for you are my refuge.

Into your hands I commit my spirit; deliver me, Lord, my faithful God.

These words would have been in Yeshua's mind, since he likely first uttered them in Gethsemane as he sweated blood. They would have been a source of strength for him.

Perhaps part of Psalm 31 was on a repeat loop in Yeshua's mind, an inner voice strengthening him as he suffered. As the end drew near, his strength was running out.

"Into your hands I commit my spirit; deliver me, Lord, my faithful God."

Dealing with the dull pain.

> *"Into your hands I commit my spirit; deliver me, Lord, my faithful God."*

Confronting the excruciating pain.

> *"Into your hands I commit my spirit; deliver me, Lord."*

One last look at his mother.

> *"Into your hands I commit my spirit; deliver me."*

The pain began to grow distant.

> *"Into your hands I commit my spirit…"*

And then he breathed his last.

Yahweh. YHWH.

My body is broken, but I am not finished. My work is not complete. I still feel like a soldier committed to Freeing the Oppressed.

I am no longer the Exactor Mortis. I have a new role now. But my journey as a protector is not complete.

This book is another step in exorcizing my personal demons while sharing how my King, Yeshua, inspires me.

I find my story throughout the Bible.

I find myself in David's story.

I find myself in Mary's story.

I find myself in Joseph's story.

I find myself in Peter's story.

I find myself in Judas' story.

I find myself in Pilate's story.

I find myself in His story.

I want to help you find your story.

I want to help you rediscover some old heroes and meet some new ones.

And finish strong.

ABANDONED BUT NOT DEFEATED

DEATH:
A LAST BREATH

CHAPTER 27

I. Abandoned but Not Defeated

Then I saw Heaven open wide—and oh! a white horse and its Rider. The Rider, named Faithful and True, judges and makes war in pure righteousness. His eyes are a blaze of fire, on his head many crowns. He has a Name inscribed that's known only to himself. He is dressed in a robe soaked with blood, and he is addressed as "Word of God." The armies of Heaven, mounted on white horses and dressed in dazzling white linen, follow him. A sharp sword comes out of his mouth so he can subdue the nations, then rule them with a rod of iron. He treads the winepress of the raging wrath of God, the Sovereign-

Strong. On his robe and thigh is written, King of kings, Lord of lords. (Revelation 19: 11-16, MSG)

"Jeff, I don't know how else to say this." The Colonel on the other end of the phone hesitated a moment. "My guys are accusing you and your team of cowardice. They say that you got them into something they weren't ready for and then you abandoned them in the middle of the fight."

"Sir, are you being serious right now?" I asked.

"Yes, I'm sorry but I need to follow protocol. I need to put a JAG on the phone to read you your rights and then you and everyone from your team needs to write up a sworn statement."

I couldn't believe it. *His guys* had abandoned *us*. "Roger sir. Before we do that, I need to tell you something. I'd like to send you the ISR footage from the raid. It's all on tape. I wasn't going to bring this up to you today–I was going to wait after so many of your boys got wounded, but the opposite occurred. Your guys completely abandoned us. They left us alone on the target. They literally ran away. All the way back to the trucks at the VDO. It was unbelievable."

There was a slight pause on the line, then the Colonel said, "These were my best guys. I sent you my best guys."

"I don't know what to say. They weren't ready."

"Ok, send me the footage. How quickly can you get it here?" he asked.

"As soon as the flight crew's mandatory rest is over, I'll fly the CD to you."

"OK, thanks. Here's the JAG."

"Major Jeffrey Tiegs? This is Captain Smith from the Judge Advocate General's office."

"This is Major Tiegs."

"Sir, Article 31 of Uniform Code of Military Justice (10 U.S.C. § 831) protects service members against compulsory self-incrimination and requires that they be informed of the alleged offense before being questioned.

Article 31(b) states that "no person subject to this chapter may interrogate, or request any statement from, an accused or a person suspected of an offense without first informing him of the nature of the accusation and advising him that he does not have to make any statement regarding the offense of which he is accused or suspected and that any statement made by him may be used as evidence against him in a trial by court-martial."

In short, neither your commanding officer nor anyone else in your command can force you to answer their questions if they suspect you of criminal behavior; you have the absolute right to remain silent.

Furthermore, service members suspected of a crime have the absolute right to speak with a lawyer. It is essential to note that exercising these rights can never be used against you later in a trial.[279]

"Do you understand your Article 31 Rights?"

"I do," I answered. "This ain't the first time I've been read my rights trying to win this damn war."

Death: A Last Breath

While Yeshua was suffering and suffocating on the cross, his mother Mary was there on the hill called Golgotha, observing all of it.

When he finally died, as Mary watched his last breath leave his broken and battered body, her heart must have been torn apart.

---

[279] "Article 31(b) Rights," Military Justice Attorneys, accessed March 22, 2023, https://www.militaryjusticeattorneys.com/military-justice-center/article-31b-rights/#:~:text=In%20short%2C%20neither%20your%20commanding,to%20speak%20with%20a%20lawyer.

With Yeshua's final words, an earthquake shook the ground and Golgotha was cleaved in two. At that same moment, the temple veil that separated people from the inner sanctum of God's presence, His shekinah, tore in half.

Straight down the middle. From top to bottom.

Mark describes it this way:

> *But Jesus, with a loud cry, gave his last breath. At that moment the Temple curtain ripped right down the middle.*[280] *(Mark 15: 37-39, NIV)*

More to the Story

What Mary felt in her heart was felt by God Himself. At that moment, the sacrifice was complete and the separation between God and us was no more.

Tetelestai.

---

[280] Mark 15:37–39 (New International Version).

There are many stories, traditions, and legends about what happened the moment that Yeshua died.

What must be acknowledged is something impactful happened, but to what extent we cannot be certain. While some men, like Joseph of Arimathea, were emboldened to publicly side with Yeshua, others, like the disciples, hid in fear. It was not until after the resurrection, ascension, and anointing by the Holy Spirit that the disciples gained the courage to pronounce His message and make sure the fulfillment of the Old Covenant on Golgotha was known throughout the world.

Golgotha means "The Place of the Skull."[281] Legend has it that Golgotha was the place where the First Man's (Adam's) bones had been buried.[282] If you look at old medieval paintings, you will often see a skull and crossbones at the foot of the cross.[283]

---

[281] https://en.wikipedia.org/wiki/Calvary
[282] Chad Bird, "Golgotha: The Place of Adam's Skull," 1517, March 24, 2016, https://www.1517.org/articles/golgotha-the-place-of-adams-skull.
[283] Marina Montesano, "Adam's Skull," in *Disembodied Heads in Medieval and Early Modern Culture*, eds. Barbara Baert, Anita Traninger, and Catrien Santing (Leiden, Netherlands: Brill, 2013), 15–30,

The Romans deliberately used Golgotha as a place to crucify and punish Jewish criminals, rebels, and zealots.

The Romans could not stand the Jews. To the Romans, the Jews were a peculiar, backward, insufferable, and rebellious group. Any opportunity during which they could leverage their control and get away with debasing their Jewish beliefs, they would capitalize on it.

Because for many years the site of Golgotha was revered as the final resting place of Adam's bones, the rich and the influential, including the priests and members of the Sanhedrin, would secure tombs as close as possible to Adam's bones.[284] This was a place of honor.

Those Jews who believed in resurrection were looking forward to the day when they themselves would be resurrected, and the first person they

---

https://brill.com/display/book/edcoll/9789004253551/B9789004253
551_003.xml.
[284] "Adam's Skull," *Golgotha* (blog), accessed March 22, 2023,
https://marahdulce.com/adams-skull/.

would see would be Adam, the first man, and their Messiah, the second man.

To cordon off the crucifixion site on Golgotha, the Jewish leaders built a wall that obscured the view in and out of the site, and built lavish gardens to adorn it.[285]

When you visit Jerusalem today, it is very difficult to imagine the terrain of Yeshua's day. The first time I visited the Holy Sepulcher, I couldn't help but feel skeptical. The proximity of the tomb to the cross seemed much too convenient for tourism. But with research, you will find that it is accurate. There is irrefutable evidence that this is where Yeshua was crucified and buried.

When the Romans finally crushed the Jewish insurgency, they utterly destroyed Jerusalem. Their goal was to erase all evidence of Jewish independence. They razed everything that held any significance to the Jews. This occurred in 70 A.D.,

---

[285] Anne Catherine Emmerich, *The Dolorous Passion of Our Lord Jesus Christ: From the Visions of Anne Catherine Emmerich* (Charlotte, NC: TAN Books, 1983).

a couple of decades after Yeshua's death and resurrection.[286]

A few decades after that, in similar vehemence, Hadrian built Roman monuments over any of the sites he wanted to subjugate further. By this time, this included the sites that the upstart Christians were venerating. It was a fatal mistake.

In their haste to rewrite history and "Romanize" their empire, the Romans actually marked the sites for future generations to discover and validate through archeological efforts.

Hadrian built a temple to Aphrodite directly over the site of Golgotha around 130 A.D. When archaeological efforts were made to explore the site, the remains of the temple to Aphrodite were unearthed. You can still see them today on display at the Holy Sepulcher.

You can also descend into the cistern used to water the garden. You can stand in the old cistern, directly below the site of the cross, and touch the

---

[286] https://en.wikipedia.org/wiki/Church_of_the_Holy_Sepulchre

scar on the rock where the earthquake split it in two.

Yeshua's death left a scar on the earth.

I don't blame people for doubting the location and accuracy of a lot of the current tourist sites in Israel. Some of them are merely symbolic, but some of them are undoubtedly accurate and precise. If you really want to discern the authenticity of a location, you have to study and pray.
Let the Spirit guide you.

Visiting the Holy Sepulcher when it is busy is far from a religious experience. People are rude, selfish, combative, and far from inviting the mood you would want when visiting this sacred spot. Whenever I bring people to visit the Holy Sepulcher, we go at least twice. One time is with the crowds, when you have an opportunity to enter the Edicule, the precise location where Yehsua's body lay in a grave for three days.[287]

This community of believers, while it can be overwhelming, obnoxious, and rude, can also be a

---

[287] Ibid

moving and awe-inspiring experience of multiple cultures coming together to honor this site and what happened here.

You can see people from all over the world in awe of our Savior. Their devotion is moving, a tradition of deep reverence practiced for over two thousand years.

This experience can be moving, but it is better at 4:00 a.m. when you can be alone. Early in the morning, the rooms are not heavy with humanity, but light and thin with a spirit that is indescribable. You have to feel it for yourself.

Dating back to an agreement between Saladin and Richard the Lionheart, the custody of the door and the key to the Church of the Holy Sepulcher is entrusted to two Muslim families named Nusseibeh and Joudeh. Each morning at around 4:00, a member of one of these Muslim families will quietly unlock the doors to the church, and the ritualistic day begins.[288]

---

[288] Yousef Khanfar, "The Keys to the Church of the Holy Sepulchre," *World Literature Today*, Summer 2021, https://www.worldliteraturetoday.org/2021/summer/keys-church-holy-sepulchre-yousef-khanfar.

The Holy Sepulcher is one of the thinnest places I've ever been to. The space between Heaven and Earth here is razor-thin.

If you want to feel the thinness in this place, be waiting in the courtyard at 4:00 a.m. and enter quietly. Regardless of your faith tradition, the history, emotion, and reverence of this site are palpable.

I have experienced thinness at the Alamo, Arlington Cemetery, Normandy, and other places. For me, it usually involves an event that shifted the course of history. Sometimes you can experience this thinness in nature, or at events like weddings, baptisms, and funerals.

If you want to experience it, you must look for it. You must be quiet, be still, and allow the thinness to be felt.

You can't see it. You can't hear it. But you can feel it.

I imagine that Mary and the disciples were reeling after the events of Yeshua's death. It seemed to happen so quickly. One weekend he was being hailed as a king and the next weekend he was nailed to a cross with his "kingship" affixed in a sarcastic sign above his blood-soaked face.

The disciples scattered, hiding in places in and around Jerusalem, wondering if they were next.

As they sat in silence, trying to make sense of the past forty-eight hours, they would have searched the scriptures. They would have tried to recall all the things that Yeshua had told them.

Is this what he meant when he talked about his suffering and dying?
How could this be the end?
What do we do now?

These must have been the questions dominating the disciples' discussions. Confidently awaiting his resurrection would have been the last thing they were doing.

Except maybe Mary.

Mary was special. She often lived in the thin spaces, and she recognized them easily. She took all these things and pondered them in her heart. She, too, would have sought answers in the scriptures.

She was waiting for Yeshua to speak to her. She wasn't exactly sure what was happening or where her son was, but she knew where he was *not*. He was not in the darkness and the powerful wind that covered Israel. He was not in the earthquake that shook the land, tumbled buildings, and tore the temple curtain in two. He was not in the fire that followed the earthquake.

She waited for him in the same gentle whisper that gave Elijah his directions. Perhaps it came on that Sunday morning, telling her to go down to the tomb.

Friday afternoon, the first day, Yeshua experienced death. The disciples scattered, denying him, fearing for their own lives.

But the women seemed to understand it all better. They waited.

Friday evening into Saturday, the Sabbath, the
second day, Yeshua's body remained in the grave,
where he lay in repose behind the heavy stone.
Confusion and fear grew within the disciples.

The women continued to wait.

Saturday evening into Sunday, the third day, was
the day that rocked all human history.

Yeshua's spirit returned to his body, and he rose
from death. Either he or the angel neatly folded his
burial garments and rolled away the stone.

This Sunday was the seventeenth of Nisan. This
Sunday, the first day after the Sabbath of Passover
week, was The Feast of First Fruits. According to
Jewish Law, this feast celebrates the beginning of
the harvest, when the people present their first
fruits of the barley harvest at the Temple.[289]

We don't know where Yeshua was between his
resurrection and his first recorded appearance to
the women who visited his empty tomb in the
garden. But, I think we can make the educated

---

[289] Lev. 23.

guess that he visited the temple as the first fruits offering for all of mankind, fulfilling this Old Covenant once and for all.

Tetelestai.

It was required that the barley omer be presented at the temple to honor the faithfulness of Yahweh and indicate trust in the harvest to come.
Other significant events occurred on this day, the seventeenth of Nisan, throughout the Old Covenant.[290] This was the day, exactly five months from the time the flood began, that Noah's ark rested on the mountains of Ararat. God's judgment was complete.

On this date, Moses led the Israelites through the parted Red Sea. Deliverance was complete.

Also on this day, the Israelites no longer received manna from heaven. They ate the first fruits from the Promised Land. From here on out, they were on their own, required to reap the harvest that they would sow.

---

[290] Richard A., "First Fruits and Nisan 17th," Servant of Messiah Ministries, June 17, 2017, https://servantofmessiah.org/nissan-17th/.

Yeshua prepared his disciples. It was up to them now.

We are his disciples. It is up to us now. With Yeshua's resurrection, we no longer need an intercessor. The temple curtain was torn.

Our High Priest presented himself as the final sacrifice. The scapegoat. He carried it all for us. The sacrifice is complete.

Tetelestai.

From here on out, we are atoned through Yeshua HaMashiach. It is our responsibility to prepare the rest of the harvest.

This story is far from over.

II. Abandoned but Not Defeated

In the middle of a gunfight, our team was abandoned—not by our Iraqi partners, but by the American force we were supporting.

The thought of this event still bothers me. Soldiers need to protect each other. No man should overestimate his abilities or his courage, especially a soldier. A soldier needs to know before going to war that he (or she) is ready for whatever may come. A soldier needs to know what he is fighting for.

The operation did not go as planned, and surviving it required some heroics.

Later that day, I sent the Colonel the drone footage. He called me and apologized. He apologized on behalf of his men.

He apologized for himself.

He apologized that his men had fled.

He apologized for leaving us alone when we needed help.

I told him that it was ok.

We were ok.

We were alive and would live to fight another day.

I have never feared death. I do not fear it now.

I am a soldier. My King is in heaven imploring us to do our work here on Earth. And then he will return, not as a lamb but as a warrior.

I don't fear death because I will be there with him.
Mounted on a white horse and dressed in dazzling
white linen. I am a soldier in His army.
And we still have some killing to do.

28

JUST BREATHE

YHWH:
THE BREATH OF LIFE

CHAPTER 28

I. Just Breathe

This is my name forever, the name you shall call me from generation to generation. (Exodus 3:15, NIV)

The baby boy gulped for air and began to wail.

I started to cry.

He was alive. This was my son.

I have traveled the world, seen many atrocities, many acts of bravery, and many beautiful places. But the most amazing things I've ever witnessed are the births of my two sons.

I've seen men completely engulfed by fire still try to fight, running at us as if to take one last American down with him. I've seen men with half of their heads blown off, brain exposed, one arm missing, emerge from a tunnel with his other hand up to surrender, confused about where he was.

I've heard plenty of men breathe their last.

But, it's not death that is lasting in my mind— it's life. It's not a man's last breath but the sound of my sons' first breaths that are solidified in my memory.

Watching my wife struggle, writhe in pain, and birth our sons is the single most incredible thing I've ever witnessed.

Heroic.

YHWH: The Breath of Life

As we discussed earlier, during Yeshua's interrogation, he stood before the Sanhedrin and said to them "*I am*," declaring himself YHWH.

Yeshua was telling them, "I am not simply the Son of God, but I am the omnipresent, almighty creator that you have worshiped all of your life."

YHWH is the sacred, unspeakable name of God. It is the name He revealed to Moses at the burning bush on Mt Sinai.[291]

YHWH explains, *"This is my name forever, the name you shall call me from generation to generation."*

More to the Story

Y-H-W-H are four consonants in the Hebrew language. This mysterious name is known as the tetragrammaton.[292] It is unpronounceable.

There is a fascinating tradition behind this word. As time has gone on, Y-H-W-H has been translated, transliterated, and morphed into Yahweh, Jehovah, Lord, Adonai, and other words trying to capture the depth of those four consonants.

None of these names are wrong, but none of them are right, either.

---

[291] Exod. 3:5–15.

[292] https://en.wikipedia.org/wiki/Tetragrammaton

YHWH is simpler, and yet more complicated, than any single name can express.

Here is why: YHWH is not a word, nor is it simply a name. It is a sound that transcends all languages.

I want you to take a moment and sit still. Take a deep breath. Inhale. Exhale.

Do it again, please, deeper this time.

Not through your nose, but in and out of your mouth. Inhale deeply. Exhale slowly.

Do you notice anything? Do you recognize anything?

Do you hear His name? Can you feel His name?

Do it one more time, but this time say His name.

When you inhale, say Y-H.
When you exhale, say W-H.
YH...WH.
YH...WH.

As you breathe in and out, you are saying the holy name of our creator.[293] The creator of all things does not have a name bound by language. His name is built into the very thing that keeps us alive. His name is built into the very thing that keeps every creature alive. Every living creature repeats His name with every breath.

Every creature breathes His name and the trees and the plants take our exhaled breath, purify it, and return it to us to inhale during the continuous and incredible cycle of life.

Hard to believe? It shouldn't be. It makes perfect sense. It makes sense that the actual name of God is not a word bound by a specific language. YHWH transcends all languages: Hebrew, Aramaic, Italian, Greek, Hindi, Pashtun, Arabic, English, it doesn't matter.

His name is not bound by any language.
His name is found in every language.

If you believe in a Divine Creator, how could his name be bound in a language? How could his name be solely

---

[293] https://yrm.org/breathing-the-name-yahweh/

for humans? All of creation repeats the name of its creator in constant praise and recognition of His connection to it all.

The first word any human, of any race, gender, nationality, or religion will utter is the name YHWH as they take their first breath of life after entering this world.

The last word any human, of any race, gender, nationality, or religion will utter is the name YHWH as they take their last breath of life before leaving this world.

So, when Yeshua, standing before the Sanhedrin, was asked if he was the Messiah, he went much further and declared that He was YHWH.

His statement was a threat, loaded with meaning and imagery. That is why their reaction seemed so disproportionate to Yeshua's reply. Yeshua stood there humbly, silently, and then when he finally spoke, he invoked a judgment that struck fear into all of the accusers assembled there that night.

He claimed to be YHWH.

And if this was true, they were in deep trouble.

YHWH was the name on David's lips when he slew Goliath.

YHWH was the name Mary used as a mantra to manage the pain of childbirth as she brought Yeshua into the world.

YHWH is the name we exclaim as we arise from a fully submerged baptism.

YHWH was the name John the Baptist whispered as he sat in a cell, waiting for his end.

Judas held his breath as he kissed Yeshua in the garden, unable to utter YHWH as he betrayed the Son of God.

YHWH was the name Peter cried out as he wept bitterly after he betrayed his friend.

YHWH was the name Yeshua breathed with each whiplash, as he stumbled on his way to Golgotha, and as he was nailed to the cross.

YHWH was the name on Yeshua's lips as he breathed his last and surrendered his spirit.

For three days, Yeshua was dead in the grave. Silent.

And then Life returned to him and he once again praised his father YHWH with his first breath.

II. Just Breathe

Whenever I speak in public, and especially at a church, I try my best to hear if the Spirit draws me toward something or not. Sometimes I stick with my prepared remarks and other times I follow the faint tug from the Spirit.

Getting ready to speak at an event that honored fallen soldiers, I felt a tug from the Spirit to share this story about YHWH as the name of our Creator, the Breath of All Life.

I balked. This was a secular event. I was not supposed to give a sermon. I got nervous. I didn't want to do it. I felt foolish.

When I took the stage, I surrendered my pride and explained to everyone that I knew the story would be weird to some, but that I felt inclined to share it.

So, I shared about YHWH.

The crowd didn't seem very impressed.

There was polite clapping after I exited the stage, but I felt a little embarrassed. Other speakers went up and were much better received than I was. The last speaker was incredible. She really brought it home.

As the event ended, and people began to shuffle away from their tables, I stood on the side and listened to the other speakers receive their accolades.

Then it happened.

A couple approached me, the woman in tears, and thanked me for what I said. They were the parents of a fallen soldier. They didn't have many details about his death and just couldn't find closure. They lost their son years ago.

The father thanked me again and explained that they finally felt a sense of closure.

They didn't know if their son died quickly or suffered. The lack of details haunted them. But now they understood that regardless of the situation, their son, a follower of Yeshua, breathed his last with the words of our Eternal Father on his lips.

It didn't matter if their son's last breath was a painful cry or a peaceful whisper.

Whatever it was, it was the name of God—the unpronounceable name of God. Loud or soft, God heard it. This thought comforted this mother and father. I wept with them.

I am weeping as I write this, partly because of this memory, but also because of Ferg. The same thing happened with him. The last word he breathed was YHWH. I heard it clearly.

I wrote this book because I felt called to do it. I still feel a little foolish. Who am I to write a book about YHWH and Yeshua?

I pray that this book sparks something in you, and causes you to reconsider some things. I pray this book brings closure for some and hope to others. If you listen intently, you will hear the Spirit speak to you.

And sometimes, you just need to breathe.

No more, no less.

He will hear you.

I felt helpless as my wife struggled to give birth to our boys. All I could do was hold her hand and help her focus on her breathing.

My wife doesn't get a medal for her bravery but she doesn't want one. Our sons don't get recognized for their sacrifice as their dad left them for half of their childhood to go to war. They don't get medals for being sons of a soldier but they don't want one, either. They are, however, heroes in their own right.

My wife is my hero.

My boys are my heroes.

And they have their own stories to write.

CONCLUSION

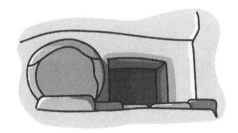

THE STORY IS NOT OVER

Conclusion

This story is not over.
Your story is not over.

There is, inevitably, much more to learn.

The Bible, like life, is filled with wisdom, intrigue, treachery, beauty, warfare, friendship, and anything else that you can imagine. The characters are nearly endless. The plotlines crisscross over millennia.

Sometimes the story is simple and straightforward, and other times it is really complex and difficult to comprehend.

I want to invite you to dig into the Bible and find other stories that interest you, confuse you, or inspire you. It is my wholehearted intent to chronicle more stories in the future. I will continue my search in the Bible, the legends and traditions, hunting for more.
Searching for more heroes.

I want to offer you the Chavruta Complement as a way to experience these stories in community. Be bold. Share. Go deeper. Experience more.

I want to encourage you to take a pilgrimage to Israel and visit these lands that are the setting for this book, not as a mere visitor, but as a seeker. See what you can find.
Explore the books that inspired me and the teachers and writers who were guideposts for me along the way. You will not be disappointed. Be the main character in your own story. Be part of the supporting cast in other stories. Find your adventure. Accept your mission.

Be your own hero.

There's always more story to write.

Tetelestai.

Where Have All the Heroes Gone?

Chavruta Complement

> *When two of you get together on anything at all on earth and make a prayer of it, my Father in heaven goes into action. And when two or three of you are together because of me, you can be sure that I'll be there. (Matthew 18: 19-20) MSG*

For those of you who want to continue on this journey, I want to offer you this Chavruta Complement. It will help you find even deeper meaning in these ancient texts as you examine your own life experiences.

Chavruta, also spelled chavrusa or havruta, is an Aramaic word that means "friendship" or "companionship." It is a traditional Jewish approach to studying where a small group of students (usually two to five) analyze, discuss, and debate a shared text. Chavruta companions analyze the text, organize thoughts into logical arguments, and share their ideas with each other. This process helps sharpen each other's ideas and arrive at entirely new insights that are otherwise overlooked.[294]

How to Practice Chavruta

Look at each chapter and experience each section in a new way.

Sit where everyone is facing each other.

One person reads aloud while the others listen. One person can read an entire chapter, or you can break the chapters into parts.

The key is to listen.

Really listen.

You can read sections more than once.

---

[294] https://en.wikipedia.org/wiki/Chavrusa

Take turns discussing the ideas.

Take turns highlighting the details.

Challenge each other to think more deeply.

Encourage each other to be vulnerable.

Share how any of it makes you feel.

Create new ideas.

Ponder it together.

Pray about it.

Let your sense of wonder flow.

Support each other.

You may all come away with something different.

You may all arrive at a new insight. (If you do, please share it with me.)

Build off each other's ideas.

Don't be afraid to disagree.

This is not an exercise to find out who's right or wrong.

We are looking for more to the story.

We are looking for heroes.

Getting Started

"What has been will be again, what has been done will be done again;

there is nothing new under the sun.

Is there anything of which one can say, "Look! This is something new"?

It was here already, long ago; it was here before our time.

No one remembers the former generations,

and even those yet to come will not be remembered by those who follow them."

(Ecclesiastes 1)

Before you get deep into the Chavruta learning, I'll get you started on the first one. We call it a confidence target. Run through the seven points below that conclude with a personal statement. This will help set the tone for a deeper experience with your group. It'll build your confidence.

1. What type of story do you think you are in right now?

   An adventure?

   A rom-com?

A tragedy?

Share your thoughts.

2. What type of story do you want to be in?
    a. How can you begin to create the story you want to be in?

3. At my core, I am a soldier. What are you at your core?

4. I didn't set out to write a story about Love. As we whittled away at the book, a story of Love simply rose to the top. Can you find Love and Grace in your day to day?

5. Do you ever experience doubts about your faith tradition?
    a. Do you face those doubts?
    b. Would you like to face them now?

Practical Exercise

Write a statement of personal belief. I understand how challenging this is—it requires an intimacy that we don't usually invite. To guide you through this process, I offer these suggestions:

Tell a story about you: be specific. Take your belief and ground it in the events of your life. Consider moments when belief was formed or tested or changed. Think of your own experience, work, and family, and tell of the things you know that no one else does. Your story need not be heart-warming or gut-wrenching—it can even be funny, but it should be real. Make sure your story ties to the essence of your daily life philosophy and the shaping of your beliefs.

Be brief. Your statement should be between 500 and 600 words. That's about three minutes when read aloud at your natural pace.

Name your belief. If you can't name it in a sentence or two, your essay might not be about belief. Also, rather than writing a list, consider focusing on one core belief because three minutes is a very short time.

Be positive. Please avoid preaching or editorializing. Tell us what you do believe, not what you don't believe. Avoid speaking in the editorial "we." Make your essay about you; speak in the first person.

Be personal. Write in words and phrases that are comfortable for you to speak. We recommend you read your essay aloud to yourself several times, and each time edit it and simplify it until you find the words, tone, and story that truly echo your belief and the way you speak.

We are guided by the original *This I Believe* radio series and the producers' invitation to those who wrote essays in the 1950s.[295] Their advice holds up well and we are sticking to it. Please consider it carefully in writing your piece.

Introducing the original series, host Edward R. Murrow said,

"Never has the need for personal philosophies of this kind been so urgent."[296]

Set a date to share your story with your chavurah.

---

[295] https://en.wikipedia.org/wiki/This_I_Believe
[296] Special thanks to Preston Cline that introduced me to this idea.

Tetelestai

Acknowledgements

I want to thank all of the pastors, teachers, and coaches who first guided me on this pilgrimage to find heroes wherever they may hide. I also want to thank the men and women who smoked me, hazed me, trained me, and taught me how to be a soldier. Without your dedication to duty, I am not sure I would have made it out alive.

I want to thank my parents for introducing the Bible stories to me before I could even talk. As I've traveled the world and sought deeper truths, I keep arriving back at the same place you first showed me. I also want to thank you for the unconditional love you've always offered and your selfless perseverance as I lived the life of a soldier at war.

I want to thank my brother and sister for continuing to support me and my family even when distance and war were constant obstacles. Knowing you are both living near mom and dad, and are able to look after them as we all grow older, is an immeasurable comfort to me.

I want to thank Jules' family for stepping in to take care of her and the boys whenever we needed it. We would not be here without you.

I want to thank the men and women who trusted me to lead them into and back out of the fray. We never backed down from a good fight and we never lost one, either.

And when it comes to writing this book, I want to thank Randy for literally standing next to me, helping me write and edit. I also want to thank Linda and Laura for the initial editing work. I want to thank Michal, Chaz, Michael, Keni, Tucker, and a few others who acted as early readers and encouraged me to continue and get this book to be the best one I can write.

And finally, just like in the dedication, I want to thank my wife and sons for always being there for me.

Works Cited and Stories that Inspired this Book

There are many people to acknowledge and honor for the ideas in this book. Some of the ideas were drawn directly from other works and discussions, while other people provided the inspiration to search for heroes.

Books and authors that I drew directly from include:

- Bargil Pixner- *With Jesus Through Galilee According to the Fifth Gospel*
- Bargil Pixner- *With Jesus in Jerusalem*
- Anne Catherine Emmerich- *The Dolorous Passion of Our Lord Jesus Christ*

- Anne Catherine Emmerich- *The Complete Visions of Anne Catherine Emmerich*
- Lois Tverberg- *Walking in the Dust of Rabbi Jesus: How the Jewish Words of Jesus Can Change Your Life*
- Ann Spangler and Lois Tverburg- *Sitting at the Feet of Rabbi Jesus: How the Jewishness of Jesus Can Change Your Faith*
- Roger D. Joslin- *Running the Spiritual Path: A Runner's Guide to Breathing, Meditating, and Exploring the Prayerful Dimension of the Sport*
- George Rawlinson- *The Kings of Israel and Judah*
- Louis Ginzberg- *The Legends of the Jews*
- Frederic William Farrar- *The Life of Christ*
- Lawrence Kushner- *God Was in This Place and I Did Not Know: Finding Self, Spirituality, and Ultimate Meaning*
- David Limbaugh- *Jesus on Trial*
- David Limbaugh- *Finding Jesus in the Old Testament*
- David Rudolph and Joel Willitts- *Introduction to Messianic Judaism*
- Ron Cantor- *Identity Theft: How Jesus was Robbed of His Jewishness*
- Gene Edwards- *The Day I was Crucified*

- Jodi Magness- *The Archaeology of the Holy Land*
- Bill O'Reilly and Martin Dugard- *Killing Jesus*
- *The Lost Books of the Bible and The Forgotten Books of Eden*- Translated by J.B. Lightfoot and R.H. Charles
- William Wake- *Forbidden Books of the Original New Testament*
- Josephus Flavius- *Complete Works*
- Josephus Flavius- *The Wars of the Jews*
- Stephen Mansfield- *Killing Jesus: The Unknown Conspiracy Behind the World's Most Famous Execution*
- Phillip Yancey- *The Jesus I Never Knew*
- Marvin R. Wilson- *Our Father Abraham: Jewish Roots of the Christian Faith*
- Alfred Edersheim- *Life and Times of Jesus the Messiah*
- Alfred Edersheim- *Sketches of Jewish Life in the Days of Christ*
- Roger D. Joslin- *Running the Spiritual Path*

Inspired by:

- C.S. Lewis
- Richard Rohr

- Rob Bell
- Malcolm Gladwell
- Donald Miller
- Francis Schaeffer
- Dennis Prager
- Steven Pressfield
- Michael S. Heiser
- F.B. (Frederick Brotherton) Meyer
- Anne Rice
- Dinesh D'Souza
- Moshe, Yesha'yahu, Dawid, Shimon, Paulos, Yohanan, Lukas, Marcus, Mattityahu

About the Author

LTC (Ret.) Jeff Tiegs is a Counter Terrorism and Counter Insurgency Expert with over 25 years of service in US Army Special Operations. He has commanded units during combat operations around the globe including Panama, Iraq, and Afghanistan. He was first introduced to the heroes of the Bible as a child and has revered them ever since.

Jeff entered the United States Army as a Private in 1987, first serving in the 1st Ranger Battalion and culminating his career as a Lieutenant Colonel in Delta Force, retiring in 2015.

He has a Master's Degree from the Naval War College in Newport, Rhode Island and has earned numerous military decorations including the Ranger and Special Forces Tabs, Special Forces Combat Diver Badge, and the Military Freefall Badge. He has received numerous awards, including five bronze stars for distinguished service during combat in Iraq and Afghanistan and a silver star awarded for valor during combat in Iraq. He has been married to his high school sweetheart for the past 34 years. They have two boys who have turned out to be incredible young men.

He is taking those hard-earned skills to free the oppressed around the globe, combat sex traffickers and the exploitation of women and children, and build leaders to protect the vulnerable. As the President of Skull Games Inc. he leads a team of dedicated professionals to shed light in the darkness, wherever it may try to hide.

The Creeds

These are the creeds that I've lived by throughout my life. I hope you can find some inspiration in them.

The Ranger Creed

Recognizing that I volunteered as a Ranger, fully knowing the hazards of my chosen profession, I will always endeavor to uphold the prestige, honor, and high esprit de corps of my Ranger Regiment.

Acknowledging the fact that a Ranger is a more elite Soldier who arrives at the cutting edge of battle by land, sea, or air, I accept the fact that as a Ranger my country expects me to move further, faster and fight harder than any other Soldier.

Never shall I fail my comrades. I will always keep myself mentally alert, physically strong, and morally straight and I will shoulder more than my share of the task whatever it may be, one hundred percent and then some.

Gallantly will I show the world that I am a specially selected and well-trained Soldier. My courtesy to superior officers, neatness of dress and care of equipment shall set the example for others to follow.

Energetically will I meet the enemies of my country. I shall defeat them on the field of battle for I am better trained and will fight with all my might. Surrender is not a Ranger word. I will never leave a fallen comrade to fall into the hands of the enemy and under no circumstances will I ever embarrass my country.

Readily will I display the intestinal fortitude required to fight on to the Ranger objective and complete the mission though I be the lone survivor.

Rangers lead the way.[297]

---

[297] "Ranger Creed," U.S. Army, accessed March 22, 2023, . https://en.wikipedia.org/wiki/Ranger_Creed

The Apostle's Creed

I believe in God, the Father almighty, creator of heaven and earth.

I believe in Jesus Christ, his only Son, our Lord, who was conceived by the Holy Spirit and born of the virgin Mary.

He suffered under Pontius Pilate, was crucified, died, and was buried; he descended to hell.

The third day he rose again from the dead.

He ascended to heaven and is seated at the right hand of God the Father almighty.

From there he will come to judge the living and the dead.

I believe in the Holy Spirit, the holy catholic church, the communion of saints, the forgiveness of sins, the resurrection of the body, and the life everlasting. Amen.[298]

The Infantryman's Creed

I am the Infantry.

---

[298] "Apostles' Creed," Christian Reformed Church, accessed March 22, 2023, . https://en.wikipedia.org/wiki/Apostles%27_Creed

I am my country's strength in war, her deterrent in peace.

I am the heart of the fight… wherever, whenever.

I carry America's faith and honor against her enemies.

I am the Queen of Battle.

I am what my country expects me to be, the best-trained Soldier in the world.

In the race for victory, I am swift, determined, and courageous, armed with a fierce will to win.

Never will I fail my country's trust.

Always I fight on…through the foe, to the objective, to triumph over all.

If necessary, I will fight to my death.

By my steadfast courage, I have won more than 200 years of freedom.

I yield not to weakness, to hunger, to cowardice, to fatigue, to superior odds,

For I am mentally tough, physically strong, and morally straight.

I forsake not my country, my mission, my comrades, my sacred duty.

I am relentless.

I am always there, now and forever.

I AM THE INFANTRY!

FOLLOW ME![299]

The Airborne Creed

I am an Airborne trooper! I jump by parachute from any plane in flight. I volunteered to do it, knowing full well the hazards of my choice.

I serve in a mighty Airborne Force – famed for deeds in War – renowned for readiness in peace. It is my pledge to uphold its honor and prestige in all that I am – in all I do.

I am an elite trooper – a sky trooper – a spearhead trooper.

I blaze the way to far-flung goals – behind, before, above my country's enemy's front lines.

---

[299] "The Infantryman's Creed," Fort Benning, U.S. Army, accessed March 22, 2023, .
https://en.wikipedia.org/wiki/Infantry_Branch_(United_States)

I know that someday I may have to fight without support for days on end. Therefore, I keep my mind and body always fit to do my part in any Airborne mission. I am self-reliant and unafraid. I shoot true, and march fast and far. I fight hard and will excel in everything I do just in case of war.

I will never fail a fellow paratrooper. I cherish the sacred trust and the lives of men with whom I serve. Leaders have my fullest loyalty, and those who I lead will never, never find me lacking.

I have pride in being Airborne! I will never let it down! In peace, I do not shrink from the dullest duty nor protest the toughest training. My weapon and equipment will always be combat-ready. I will be neatly dressed, show courtesy and watch my behavior in a proper Airborne military manner.

In battle, I fear no enemy's ability, nor underestimate his ability, power or threats. I will fight him with all my might and skills – staying alert to avoid traps and try to escape if I should ever be captured. I will never surrender while I still have the means to fight, though I may be the last paratrooper.

My goal in peace and war is to succeed in any mission of the day or night, even though I may die doing so. For I belong to a proud and glorious team…

The AIRBORNE, the ARMY, my Country – the UNITED STATES OF AMERICA. I am its chosen few, I volunteer to fight where others may not want to go or serve.

I am a trooper of the sky! I am my Nation's best! In peace and war I will never fail, Anytime, Anyplace, Anywhere…I am Airborne!

I volunteered as a parachutist, fully realizing the hazard of my chosen service and by my thoughts and actions will always uphold the prestige, honor and high esprit-de-corps of parachute troops.

I realize that a parachutist is not merely a Soldier who arrives by parachute to fight, but is an elite shock trooper and that his country expects him to march farther and faster, to fight harder, and to be more self-reliant than any other Soldier. Parachutists of all allied armies belong to this great brotherhood.

I shall never fail my fellow comrades by shirking any duty or training, but will always keep myself mentally and physically fit and shoulder my full share of the task, whatever it may be.

I shall always accord my superiors fullest loyalty and I will always bear in mind the sacred trust I have in the lives of the men I will accompany into battle.

I shall show other Soldiers by my military courtesy, neatness of dress and care of my weapons and equipment that I am a picked and well-trained Soldier.

I shall endeavor always to reflect the high standards of training and morale of parachute troops.

I shall respect the abilities of my enemies, I will fight fairly and with all my might, surrender is not in my creed.

I shall display a high degree of initiative and will fight on to my objective and mission, though I be the lone survivor.

I shall prove my ability as a fighting man against the enemy on the field of battle, not by quarreling with my comrades in arms or by bragging about my deeds.

I shall always realize that battles are won by an army fighting as a team, that I fight first and blaze the path into battle for others to follow and to carry the battle on.

I belong to the finest unit in the world. By my actions and deeds alone, I speak for my fighting ability. I will strive to uphold the honor and prestige of my outfit, making my country proud of me and of the unit to which I belong.[300]

The Nicene Creed

I believe in one God, the Father almighty, maker of heaven and earth, of all things visible and invisible.

I believe in one Lord Jesus Christ, the Only Begotten Son of God, born of the Father before all ages. God from God, Light from Light, true God from true God, begotten, not made, consubstantial with the Father; through him all things were made. For us men and for our salvation he came down from heaven, and by the Holy Spirit was incarnate of the Virgin Mary and became man. For our sake he was crucified under Pontius Pilate, he suffered death and was buried, and rose again on the third day in accordance with the Scriptures. He ascended into heaven and is seated at the right hand of the Father. He will come again in glory to judge the

---

[300] "Airborne Creed," Association of the United States Army, accessed March 22, 2023, https://www.ausa.org/airborne-creed

living and the dead and his kingdom will have no end.

I believe in the Holy Spirit, the Lord, the giver of life, who proceeds from the Father and the Son, who with the Father and the Son is adored and glorified, who has spoken through the prophets.

I believe in one, holy, catholic and apostolic Church. I confess one Baptism for the forgiveness of sins and I look forward to the resurrection of the dead and the life of the world to come. Amen.[301]

The Special Forces Creed

I am an American Special Forces soldier. A professional! I will do all that my nation requires of me.

I am a volunteer, knowing well the hazards of my profession.

I serve with the memory of those who have gone before me: Roger's Rangers, Francis Marion, Mosby's Rangers, the first Special Service Forces and

---

[301] "The Nicene Creed," United States Conference of Catholic Bishops, accessed March 22, 2023, . https://en.wikipedia.org/wiki/Nicene_Creed

Ranger Battalions of World War II, The Airborne Ranger Companies of Korea. I pledge to uphold the honor and integrity of all I am - in all I do.

I am a professional soldier. I will teach and fight wherever my nation requires. I will strive always to excel in every art and artifice of war.

I know that I will be called upon to perform tasks in isolation, far from familiar faces and voices, with the help and guidance of my God.

I will keep my mind and body clean, alert and strong, for this is my debt to those who depend upon me.

I will not fail those with whom I serve. I will not bring shame upon myself for the forces.

I will maintain myself, my arms, and my equipment in an immaculate state as befits a Special Forces soldier.

I will never surrender though I be the last. If I am taken, I pray that I may have the strength to spit upon my enemy.

My goal is to succeed in any mission - and live to succeed again.

I am a member of my nation's chosen soldiery. God grant that I may not be found wanting, that I will not fail this sacred trust.[302]

Aaronic Blessing

The Lord bless you and keep you;

The Lord make his face shine on you and be gracious to you;

The Lord turn his face toward you and give you peace.[303] (Numbers 6:24-26, NIV)

---

[302] "Special Forces Creed," Chapter LX Special Forces Association, accessed March 22, 2023, .
https://www.soc.mil/USASFC/SFcreed.html
[303] Num. 6:24–26 (New International Version).

Visiting Israel

A Pilgrimage In Search of More Heroes

I want to encourage you to visit Israel. If you go there with an open mind and an intentional spirit, you will be changed. There are many ways to experience Israel but the list below are my must-see locations. It will take you over a month to see all of these sites but you can pick and choose a bunch of them for a fast-paced seven to ten days of adventure.

Jerusalem

- Via Dolorosa (Holy Sepulcher, Golgotha)
- Ecco Homo Convent
- Prison
- Ramparts Walk (two parts)
- Temple Mount (underground tour)
- City of David (Hezekiah's tunnel)
- Archaeological Park
- Pools of Bethesda (St. Anne's Church)
- Western/Wailing Wall
- Mount Zion
- Last Supper Room
- Church of St. Peter Gallicantu (Caiaphas Palace)
- Dormition Abbey
- David's Tomb
- Mount of Olives
- Garden of Gethsemane/Rock of Agony (Church of All Nations)
- Gethsemane Grotto (Mary's Tomb)
- Dominus Flavit
- Pater Noster
- Church of Ascension
- Garden Tomb

- Zedekiah's Cave
- Israel Museum
- Rockefeller Museum
- Yad Va-Shem (Holocaust Museum)
- Gibeah
- Samuel's Tomb
- Mahane Yehuda Shuk
    - Bethany- Lazarus Tomb
    - Temple Mount Sifting Project
    - Ein Karem
    - Baptist Cave
    - Abu Ghosh (HUMMUS!)
    - Ramat Rachel/Kathisma

Bethlehem

- Church of the Nativity
- Shepherd's Field
- Herodian
- Haritun Cave
- Tombs of the Innocents

Day Trips from Jerusalem

- Valley Of Elah (David and Goliath)
- Azekah

- Bet Guvrien
- Bet Guvrien Dig for a Day
- Midras/Adullam
- Samson's Tomb
- Khirbet Qeiyafa
- LaChish

Tel Aviv (en route & coastal vicinity)

- Latrun (Emmaus)
- Jaffa (Jonah and the Whale)
- Ashkelon / Ashdod (Sampson)
- Gezer
- Megiddo (Armageddon)
- Akko
- Rosh Ha Nikra
- Caesarea Maritima
- Mount Carmel (Haifa)

Jericho and Dead Sea Area

- Ancient Jericho Ruins
- Hashim's Palace (Islamic Period)
- Mount of Temptation
- St George's Monastery
- Baptism Site on the Jordan River
- Wadi Qelt

- Qumran Settlement (Dead Sea Scrolls)
- Dead Sea
- En Gedi
- Masada
- En Bokek
- Flour Cave
- Salt/Sodom Cave

Galilee (& en route)

- Tabghe (Church of Bread and Fish)
- Church of Primacy of St. Peter
- Leper's Well
- Jesus Cave
- Mount of Beatitudes
- Capernaum
- Jesus era Boat
- Kursi
- Korazim
- Yardenit (Baptism Site)
- Yehudia Trail
- Gamla
- Susita/Hippos
- Bethsaida
- Bet Shean
- Bet She-arim

- Fort Belvoir
- Zippori

Golan

- Nimrod's Fortress
- Banyas (Caesarea Philipi)
- Alma Cave
- Tel Dan
- Hazor

Nazareth

- Church of the Annunciation
- Nazareth Village
- Cana
- Nain
- Mount Tabor

West Bank/Palestinian Authority

- Tomb of the Patriarchs (Hebron)
- Joseph's Tomb (Nablus)
- Jacob's Well (Nablus)
- Shechem

Tetelestai

If you want to go further on your own hero's journey, or stay up to date with Jeff on his adventures, please go to jefftiegsbooks.com or wherehavealltheheroesgone.com.